Geoffrey
HYPOTH

Geoffrey Robertson's
HYPOTHETICALS

Dramatisations of the moral dilemmas of the 80s

ANGUS
& ROBERTSON
PUBLISHERS

*in association with the
Australian Broadcasting Corporation*

ANGUS & ROBERTSON PUBLISHERS

Unit 4, Eden Park, 31 Waterloo Road,
North Ryde, NSW, Australia 2113, and
16 Golden Square, London W1R 4BN,
United Kingdom
in association with the Australian Broadcasting Corporation
145-153 Elizabeth Street, Sydney, NSW, Australia 2000

First published in Australia
by Angus & Robertson Publishers in association
with the Australian Broadcasting Corporation in 1986
Reprinted 1987

© *Copyright Geoffrey Robertson, 1986*

ISBN 0 207 15518 6

Typeset by Midland Typesetters
Printed in Australia by
The Book Printer, Maryborough, Victoria

CONTENTS

GEOFFREY ROBERTSON'S HYPOTHETICALS
Introduction

My discovery of the new world of the "hypothetical" happened in Boston one wintry afternoon in 1969. I was there to look up a friend from student politics, who had decided that a Harvard degree in Business Administration might be a useful first step towards the premiership of New South Wales. I found Nick Greiner—once the most indolent of pupils—in a lather of frenetic preparation for his class the following day. It would be no ordinary lecture, he explained in fearful tones, but a "case study" in which his hypothetical company could, unless he mastered the background material better than his student competitors, be taken over or liquidated or sent to the bottom of the harbour, whereupon he would be sent to the bottom of the class. This "case study" method of tuition, which drives students not merely to swot up their subject, but which goads and prods and stings them into making practical use of their book-learning by playing out imaginary but realistic scenarios, has been a hallmark of Harvard law and business teaching since the 1930s. Recalling its impact on the youthful Greiner, I introduced the technique into some tutorials I conducted at Warwick University in 1980.

That, coincidentally, was the time when Granada Television came looking for an English barrister to join a trio of Harvard Law Professors in moderating hypotheticals for television. The transition of the Socratic method from classroom to sitting room had come about in two stages, each presided over by a media genius. It was Fred Friendly of the Ford Foundation who organised a series of private conferences at which powerful men and women took the place of students grilled by Olympian professors, and it was Granada's Brian Lapping who, at the instigation of Sir Denis Foreman, adapted the idea for television. Under Brian's guidance, I learnt how to offer bribes to businessmen, despatch policemen into massage parlours to arrest High Court judges, encourage American generals to invade Caribbean islands, arrange deals between journalists and terrorists and become the world's first pregnant man. All in the service of imaginary stories which might—and sometimes did—come true before the program went to air.

For all its distinguished ancestry, the hypotheticals format is simple. You place about sixteen relevant persons around a horseshoe table, with cameras secreted strategically to capture the result as the moderator draws participants into an unfolding scenario. The parts allotted to the panellists must be those they have played, or might well play, in real life, and the imaginary story-lines are built up from careful research. My own approach is to swot up the subject quickly, as barristers must to cross-examine expert witnesses, and then to close the textbooks and dream up a tale which will pose in its course the most interesting of the practical and ethical dilemmas encountered in the literature. The difficulty is always to pare down complicated material to a level which can engage a general audience without fudging the real issues—in other words, to be simple without becoming simplistic. The true tyranny of the television format derives from the short span of audience attention (three minutes is the sociologically-certified maximum time an average viewer can follow an argument from a talking head) and to maintain viewer involvement over sixty to seventy-five minutes requires a story which generates some degree of amusement, tension or excitement. The real secret of such success as hypotheticals enjoy is that, unlike the stock studio discussion, they have a dimension familiar to television viewers: the acting out of roles. For this reason, I try to produce a program which viewers will perceive as a kind of drama—a movie, almost, in which the actors are playing themselves.

Unlike movies, however, hypotheticals are current affairs television without scripts or props. Participants are given no inkling beforehand of the questions they will be asked or the scenes they will be called upon to play, and the moderator has to fashion the story to their sometimes unpredictable responses. What this approach loses in *gravitas* and polish it gains in spontaneity and, I suspect, in honesty. There are other advantages of the format for eliciting uncomfortable truths from normally cagy or practised performers. The atmosphere conduces to candour, as the panellist is surrounded by experts who know how he or she has acted in similar situations. The libel-free zone of the hypothetical—so near and yet so far from actual events—enables truths to be told without the constraints of betraying confidences or embarrassing colleagues.

Another advantage of the format is that a participant cannot dodge a difficult decision by saying "I'd call my lawyer" or "I'd need to consult my advisers": the lawyer and the advisers are there to be called and consulted, after which the decision must still be taken. The viewer is invited to become a fly on the wall, a witness to scenes that television cameras normally cannot capture because they do not penetrate behind the closed doors of smoke-filled lobbies or lawyers' offices or doctors' surgeries. The object is to show something of the process by which important decisions are actually made, something more than can be revealed amid the pleasantries of a studio chat show or the predictable ritual of a press conference. The moderator must ask the simple question "Why?" often enough to push panellists into identifying and articulating a principle behind their decisions, a rationale both capable and worthy of consistent application.

Phillip Adams has made the point that hypotheticals are true to life because role-playing is precisely what public and professional people do much of the time, in living up (or down) to other people's expectations. But when the program makes unaccustomed demands—for a personal or a moral stance—there can be no hiding behind prepared responses. Some of the best moments come when participants are driven by the flow of the debate to step out of character, and to take a course fraught with political or professional difficulty, yet courageous and correct within the context of the case as it has developed. The hypothetical format is sufficiently flexible to confront future developments as if they were already in place, as well as permitting an occasional retrospective agony over what has gone before. Debates over genetic fingerprinting and male pregnancy are prophetical as well as hypothetical, while anxieties over the powers of Royal Commissions and the invasive role of the press stem from recent history. The "case study" is used as a springboard for important arguments over ethics and principles which would be dry and academic if unrelated to the behaviour of realistic, albeit imaginary, characters.

The Australian hypotheticals began, appropriately enough, over a game of tennis. This recreation had once won me the sort of Oxford scholarship which required an ability at "manly sports", and one pleasure of returning to Australia each Christmas was to play against old friends with similarly spreading waistlines, now ensconced in media-fashionable East Balmain. One of them, Peter Luck, was sufficiently enthused by the idea to send a proposal to the ABC, but answer came there none. When Peter became producer of Channel 9's *Sunday* program, however, he decided to give it a try. Thus it came about that one Sunday morning in early 1984 his viewers were exposed to ninety minutes of corporate chicanery, as Bob Ansett piloted a hypothetical helicopter company through the turbulence of take-over bids from Ron Brierley, strikes led by John Ducker, moral scruples emanating from Richard Walsh and government intervention from Nick Greiner, who had at last progressed to Premier, if only in my imagination. *Sunday* viewers at first jammed the switchboard in protest against being deprived of their normal program: at the end, they called in sufficient numbers to justify a series. Programs on medical ethics and foreign policy were screened by *Sunday* later in the year, and a hypothetical about the media was taped but regrettably not put to air. Commercial television in Australia has its taboos and its "no go" areas, which is just one reason why the national broadcaster is so important. Its then Chairman, Ken Myer, sent a telegram inviting me to do a series of hypotheticals for the ABC.

The six programs which make up this book were recorded by the ABC between August 1985 and April 1986. "The Angel's Advocate" was performed for the 23rd Australian Legal Convention, and looks at the tension between the protection of civil liberties and the effective prosecution of crime in the aftermath of the Costigan Royal Commission. "The Fast Track" surveys the relationships between politicians and public servants, while "We Name the Guilty Men" examines some of the issues of privacy and defamation which were the subject of the suppressed "media hypothetical". These three programs, together with a hypothetical conducted for Granada Television in Britain, made up the first ABC series. "Unto Us a Child is Born", which debates the legal and ethical problems of the revolution in bio-technology, was shown as a Christmas special. Film Australia invited me to devise a hypothetical on issues relevant to the International Year of Peace, and "Should You Tell the President?" is the result. Although the filming was financed by a government grant, a stringent condition of the ABC's participation was that I should have complete control over the story-line, the choice of panellists and the editing. We were subsequently to receive a grovelling apology from a backbench MP who falsely alleged that the government in some way "controlled the outcome" of this program. Finally, "Till Divorce Us Do Part" is a study of the operation of the Family Court, which was made to mark National Law Week 1986.

Each hypothetical lasts for about three hours, without any

breaks. It is a concentrated, adrenalin-pumping and bladder-stretching exercise for everyone, and one justification for a hypotheticals book is that much more of the proceedings can be published than television time-slots permit. We lose the vocal inflections and the pictures that may be worth a thousand words, but we gain, over many thousand words, a more detailed appreciation of the dilemmas and the way in which the participants resolve them. Each transcript has been edited for grammar, punctuation and flow of argument, but otherwise all dialogue is guaranteed verbatim.

On a personal note, a book permits more permanent expressions of thanks than can be captured on rolling captions. Firstly to all the panellists, who have donated their time and intelligence to making these exercises work, and to Richard Walsh, Norm Rowe and Jenny Rowe at Angus and Robertson who have helped to translate them into print. The loneliness of the long-winded barrister has been made bearable by a support system embracing Ken Chown, Pauline Thomas, Barbara Fryer, Sue Cram and Peter Ross—the ABC's "Hypotheticals Unit". Thanks are also due to my initial Granada mentors, Brian Lapping, Andy McLaughlin and Clarissa Haymen; to Peter Luck, Andrew Olle and Marion Thompson for the early thrills and spills of *Sunday*; to Tom Molomby, Paddy Conway and Richard Thomas at the ABC, and to Claire Davis, Jennifer Byrne, Robyn Burgess and Francis Pardell. Above all else has been the inspiration, criticism and support from my parents, and from Julian Disney and Tim Robertson.

THE ANGEL'S ADVOCATE

Whatever can be ailing the favourite for the Melbourne Cup? Can it have something to do with the disappearance of his trusty stablegirl, the arrest of his trainer, the marital problems of his jockey or the tax-avoidance schemes of his owner? There's a suspect on the run, a policeman on the case, a journalist on the phone and blood on the straw. In due course, somebody will doubtless be convicted of murder—but who?

Some of Australia's leading lawyers wrestle with their consciences, their professional ethics and each other, in a Victorian melodrama about the dilemmas of reconciling civil liberties with demands for more effective prosecution of criminals.

THE ANGEL'S ADVOCATE
Participants

WENDY BACON
  Journalist, *National Times*

DIANA BRYANT
  President, Family Law Practitioners, Western Australia

RON CASTAN Q.C.
  President, Australian Council for Civil Liberties

FRANK COSTIGAN Q.C.
  Royal Commissioner

MARK DAY
  Publisher

JULIAN DISNEY
  Solicitor and President, Australian Council of Social Service

GARETH EVANS Q.C.
  Labor Senator; former Attorney-General

FRANK GALBALLY
  Barrister and Solicitor

TOM HUGHES Q.C.
  Former Attorney-General

GORDON LEWIS
  Executive Director, Law Institute of Victoria

RACHELLE LEWITON
  Barrister

JOHN MARSDEN
  Solictor and President, New South Wales Council for Civil
  Liberties

DOUGLAS MEAGHER Q.C.
  Counsel assisting Costigan Commission

ALAN MISSEN
  Liberal Senator, Victoria

JUSTICE HOWARD NATHAN
  Supreme Court of Victoria

NOEL NEWNHAM
  Assistant Commissioner, Victorian Police Force

Recorded at the 23rd Australian Legal Convention,
Melbourne Concert Hall,
August 1985.

THE ANGEL'S ADVOCATE

MODERATOR

There's movement at the police station, ladies and gentlemen, for the word has passed around that the favourite for the Melbourne Cup has been nobbled. Victorian wonder horse Phar Out stands this morning in his stable, alone and palely loitering. The stable door is wide open; there's no sign of his trusty minder, young stablegirl Amanda Innocent. No sign, that is, of her body; her clothing, stained with blood, lies strewn around the straw. Only one other person had the key to the electronically locked stable: Phar Out's trainer, William Sykes—the man seen driving away from the scene of the crime at five o'clock this morning. Sykes is a man you would very much want to interrogate, isn't he Mr Newnham?

NOEL NEWNHAM

Certainly.

MODERATOR

But where is he? Right here, in the office of a solicitor, John Marsden. "I need your help. Can I trust you?"

JOHN MARSDEN

You certainly can.

MODERATOR

"The cops want to see me but I'm not ready to talk to them yet. I want to lie low for a couple of days to get my story straight—I mean, get my thoughts straightened out. Can I do that?"

MARSDEN

Certainly you can.

MODERATOR

"I can just go away and keep my head down?"

MARSDEN

It's their responsibility to find you.

MODERATOR

"You're not going to help them?"

MARSDEN

No.

MODERATOR

There's a missing girl, a queasy horse . . . Isn't it your duty to put Sykes in touch with the police?

MARSDEN

No.

MODERATOR

You put a bet on Phar Out yesterday. Aren't you interested in finding out the truth of the matter?

MARSDEN

No, my interest is only in my client. As I've accepted your instructions, you're my only interest.

MODERATOR

"If I killed that girl it would be murder, wouldn't it?"

MARSDEN

Not necessarily.

MODERATOR

"Suppose we were making love and I couldn't perform and she taunted me and I just went into a rage and killed her. Would that be murder?"

MARSDEN

Not necessarily. There could be an element of provocation involved.

MODERATOR

"Ah ha; so I wouldn't get life imprisonment. Suppose—just suppose—that we'd decided to elope, and that I had to go to the stable that morning to tell her that I decided to stay with my wife and kids. She got so angry she pulled a pistol on me, we grappled and it went off, accidental like. Would that be murder?"

MARSDEN

Certainly not.

MODERATOR

"I might get off entirely?"

MARSDEN

You certainly might get off . . . particularly if you instruct me as your solicitor. (laughter)

MODERATOR

What you are doing by answering these questions is helping Sykes to trim his evidence, to outsmart the police when they finally catch up with him?

MARSDEN

Not at all. You see, the situation is that the police are seeking to outsmart him. In this State I'd have to say to him that I couldn't trust the police. I have a feeling that they are basically a dishonest force. So it is important that he doesn't give them any information that may assist them to concoct evidence against him in seeking to get a conviction.

MODERATOR

But aren't you helping him, by your advice, to concoct a story that will get him off?

MARSDEN

No. He has told me a set of facts and basically on those facts he has a valid defence. Why give the police the opportunity to verbal him, as is their favourite habit?

MODERATOR

Let me ask your partner, Mr Disney. What's the justification for answering those questions from Sykes? Helping him work out a defence?

JULIAN DISNEY

Well, it's important that people who are in that situation do find out what their rights are. Certainly our firm has a long and honourable tradition of representing people whether we in fact know at the outset that they're guilty or not.

MODERATOR

Helping them concoct a defence to get them off before a jury?

DISNEY

No, not helping them to concoct, but providing them with their rights. There is a fine line between just providing answers and information in response to their questions, and helping them to fabricate a story. As yet we haven't got into the fabrication process and our approach would certainly be to avoid that.

MODERATOR

"One more thing Mr Marsden before I go. The wife and kids are going to be terribly cut up about this. When it's all over I'd like to take them for a holiday overseas; to some place with a sunny climate, interesting people and no—what would you call it—'extradition' treaty with the government. Will you advise me?"

MARSDEN

At this stage I wouldn't be prepared to advise you because I would want to know more about the facts before I got into that.

MODERATOR

"Here's a thousand dollars. This is so important to me I'd like counsel's opinion on it."

MARSDEN

I'm certainly not prepared to instruct any counsel on the basis of a thousand dollars . . .

MODERATOR

"Ten thousand?" (laughter)

MARSDEN

I would have a problem. As far as I'm concerned the oath I took when I was admitted as a solicitor is very important to me. I'm not prepared to be party to advising you how to get out of the jurisdiction.

MODERATOR

He just wants to take a holiday when the fuss has died down.

MARSDEN

Well then, we'll look at the situation when the fuss has died down.

MODERATOR

But he wants an opinion now.

MARSDEN

Well then it's not available to him.

MODERATOR

Will *you* instruct counsel, Mr Disney?

DISNEY

In that situation I think there would be a case for instructing counsel, if all he is looking for is information about his rights. Whether one would go any further than that one would have to decide in the light of the counsel's advice. But I see no problem at first in instructing counsel.

MODERATOR

"I think I would prefer to be represented by Mr Disney." (laughter) Which counsel are you going to instruct? You've got a choice—Tom Hughes, Frank Costigan, Ron Castan.

DISNEY

Ron Castan is an expert on extradition.

MODERATOR

Interesting books you've got on your shelves, Mr Castan . . . *Paraguay on Five Dollars a Day, Romantic Dublin Hotels*. (laughter) Would you give this advice?

RON CASTAN

Certainly. If someone briefs me to advise on the state of Australia's extradition treaties with various countries, I'll advise them on it.

MODERATOR

Your instructions are to advise Mr Sykes, whom you've heard on the radio this morning is being sought by the police for suspected murder.

CASTAN

If all I've heard on the radio is that someone is sought after by the police . . . well I don't place particularly great reliance on radio broadcasts. I would take instruction from my instructing solicitor, and I would give the legal advice.

MODERATOR

You would advise Sykes about which countries he could go to without fear of being extradited back to Australia?

CASTAN

I would find that out for any client who sought that information.

MODERATOR
  Mr Meagher, if that brief came to you, would you give that advice?

DOUGLAS MEAGHER
  I'd decline to give the advice.

MODERATOR
  You'd decline? Why?

MEAGHER
  I just don't see any part of my role to assist in that matter. I'd decline the brief.

MODERATOR
  But I thought a barrister was like a taxi on the rank — on hire to anyone?

MEAGHER
  Yes.

MODERATOR
  You're not?

MEAGHER
  Oh yes, but you're putting it in a context of man who's on the run, and it's that factor which leads to some inhibition on my part.

MODERATOR
  Tom Hughes?

TOM HUGHES
  Well if the brief came to me I think I'd say I'm not in the business of thumbing through extradition treaties, when to do so involves no difficult question of law, for the purpose of providing an answer which can be found quite mechanically by someone else. (laughter)

MODERATOR
  Attorney-General, I suppose we could short-circuit this process by ringing up your department and asking them which countries Australia *doesn't* have an extradition treaty with?

GARETH EVANS
  I don't think that information would be given.

MODERATOR

But it would be in someone's bottom drawer though, wouldn't it?

EVANS

We'd tell them that we would be capable of putting this treaty in place within twenty-four hours; as we did in the case of Ireland, last year.

MODERATOR

Do you think that lawyers like Mr Castan, who are prepared to give that advice, are doing the right thing?

EVANS

I'm inclined to agree with Mr Meagher, that if the context is screamingly obvious, where someone is trying to evade criminal responsibility, then it's appropriate for a lawyer to refuse to give that advice.

MODERATOR

Mr Sykes is well pleased with his time with you this morning, Mr Marsden. "I'm going away now. I'll lie low and I'll call you in a couple of days. I'm not going to stay at home, but here's a telephone number of a friend if you need to get in touch." Mr Newnham, you now get a call from a reliable source: "I've just seen Sykes. Ten minutes ago he left Mr Marsden's office." What do you do?

NEWNHAM

(to Marsden) Mr Marsden, we are interested in speaking with Mr Sykes. We have a case where a girl is missing and a substantial amount of blood, which my experts tell me is human blood, has been found at the location where she was last known to be. A Mr Sykes, who was also known to be in that vicinity, was seen about ten minutes ago leaving your office. What I'd like you to do, if you can, is tell me please where Mr Sykes is, and whether he has any connection with this missing girl?

MARSDEN

I appreciate your calling but you should know better than to come to a solicitor's office to ask those questions, and would you leave immediately. I wouldn't want any of my other clients to see a police officer in my waiting room. (laughter)

NEWNHAM

You're tempting me to apply for a search warrant.

MODERATOR

You have your warrant, Mr Newnham. How do you execute it on Mr Marsden?

NEWNHAM

By the sound of Mr Marsden's answer, with great difficulty. (laughter)

MODERATOR

Sergeant Doberman suggests you try the drink cabinet.

NEWNHAM

Well, that would be a good place to start.

MODERATOR

Solicitors normally open files on new clients, and lo and behold, just behind the whisky there's a file marked "Sykes". Do you take a look at it?

NEWNHAM

Yes.

MODERATOR

It relates to *Barry* Sykes, the prominent MP who has sought advice from Mr Marsden about a bottom of the harbour tax scheme that he was once involved in. The special prosecutors don't known about it yet. Do you take that file?

NEWNHAM

No, but you take sufficient notice of a file to ascertain whether or not it is what you are looking for.

MODERATOR

It's not what you are looking for, but it's evidence of another offence isn't it?

NEWNHAM

I read no further.

MODERATOR

But you have the information in your head, and you have a friend in the Special Prosecutor's office.

NEWNHAM
 Yes.

MODERATOR
 Will you ring him up and tell him?

NEWNHAM
 Yes.

MODERATOR
 Tell him that Barry Sykes MP is involved in a bottom of the harbour tax scheme?

NEWNHAM
 Tell him what I've learned, yes.

MODERATOR
 Even though that information is outside the warrant?

NEWNHAM
 Yes.

MODERATOR
 So in fact, once you are inside a solicitor's office, you could rifle through all his files, and pick up whatever intelligence you can about all of his clients?

NEWNHAM
 No.

MODERATOR
 But you've just picked up the intelligence on Barry Sykes.

NEWNHAM
 I have unavoidably obtained some information and I'm prepared to pass that on.

MODERATOR
 Several hours later you have unavoidably picked up a lot of information. (laughter) This will be a bonanza for Central Intelligence. There's nothing to stop you from passing on anything you find about Mr Marsden's clients?

NEWNHAM
 None at all.

MODERATOR
 Attorney-General, are you happy with the police having power to

go into a solicitor's office not just to look for an individual item but to gather information generally if they so find it?

EVANS

No, not happy at all. I think that the law is a little mysterious around the edges when it comes to the search warrant area, and I've been trying for years to reform the law in a way which will clarify this situation in the future.

MODERATOR

Mr Costigan, you are special prosecutor for tax evasion schemes. Mr Newnham has passed on the information he obtained about Barry Sykes while searching Mr Marsden's office. Would you act upon it?

FRANK COSTIGAN

I am disquietened about the information coming to me in that way, although I wouldn't attribute any malice to its acquisition. Nonetheless, if the information came to me I'd probably make use of it.

MODERATOR

Senator Missen, has Mr Costigan done the right thing in using the information that has come from that particular source?

ALAN MISSEN

I would probably raise an objection in the parliament to that use, and I would certainly have something to say about the misuse of information that was obtained by this method.

MODERATOR

So you would criticise Mr Newnham for handing that information on to the Special Prosecutor's office. Mr Newnham, how would you respond to that?

NEWNHAM

I think the community would criticise me if I turned a blind eye to evidence of criminal acts.

MODERATOR

The community would criticise you. Mr Day, will you write an editorial criticising Mr Newnham? Or criticising Senator Missen?

MARK DAY

No, I'm far too busy finding out about the secret love-life of the missing girl. (laughter)

MODERATOR

I should explain, Mr Day, that you are the editor and proprietor of *Strewth*, the well-known family newspaper. (laughter) The police are concerned about finding Amanda, and they give you a photograph to publish for your readers. It's a photograph taken at her first communion; head and shoulders, very clear. Will you publish that?

DAY

Certainly, if that's the only one we have.

MODERATOR

Ah, but you have another one. Amanda was Stablemate of the Year in 1984, and you do have a picture in your files of her receiving a victory kiss from Australia's top jockey, Lester Gallop. She's dressed in a very brief bikini.

DAY

Sure. That's a better one. But we would also go to the photographer who took that series of pictures of Stablemate of the Year, and see if we could get a topless one.

MODERATOR

What about her family's grief?

DAY

Well, you see, we've already been to see the mother and father and we've asked about boyfriends because we've had a nudge-nudge, wink-wink from the police that she was a bit of a goer . . .

MODERATOR

See if you can get a nudge or a wink from Mr Newnham.

DAY

(to Newnham) Can you help us with any details about the girl's private life, perhaps?

NEWNHAM

We're not prepared to tell you anything about her private sexual life, if that's what you're hinting at.

DAY

Difficult copper!

MODERATOR

Mr Day, you do have interesting information from your correspondent in New Zealand. Phar Out was racing in

Auckland last week. He won the ANZUS Handicap, and Sykes was over there with him, photographed in the enclosure with a man who was arrested yesterday on serious drug charges.

DAY
Yes, that's very interesting.

MODERATOR
You do a fair bit of work and you find that the man was previously convicted of drug offences, that Sykes was seen with him a lot in Auckland and that Sykes was in financial difficulties. Will you publish that?

DAY
Yes, given that Sykes hasn't been found.

MODERATOR
Sykes hasn't been found; he's on the run. What headline? "Drugs Link to Missing Trainer"?

DAY
Yes.

MODERATOR
What chance, Mr Castan, would Sykes have of getting a fair trial after that was displayed all over *Strewth*?

CASTAN
Very little.

DAY
Why? It's going to be six months before he comes up for trial. Everbody's forgotten.

CASTAN
I don't think jurors have such short memories.

DAY
Oh, of course they do.

CASTAN
That's highly prejudicial to him.

MODERATOR
Highly prejudicial?

HUGHES
Yes, but the problem about contempt of court in that situation

is that no charge has yet been made and there are no pending proceedings. To publish those allegations would not be a contempt of court because there are no pending proceedings. Sykes hasn't been arrested; there's no charge laid.

DAY

We've got a picture of Sykes, a man on the run, in company with a convicted drug trafficker a week ago in New Zealand. Now by publishing that picture you support a headline, "Drugs Link with Missing Trainer". There it is. Now what's wrong with that?

HUGHES

All I'm telling you is it's not a contempt of court because there are no pending proceedings. It is obviously highly defamatory and you are at risk of being sued by Mr Sykes for extensive damages.

MODERATOR

There's no way that Mr Sykes is going to come to court and sue you. He's on the run. So what your learned counsel is telling you is that there's no risk here of contempt. Do you publish?

DAY

Yes.

MODERATOR

Mr Castan, can you stop it?

CASTAN

No, I don't think we can stop it. I'm simply saying I don't think it should be done. It's part of the responsibility of the media not to act in ways that are obviously inflammatory and which may significantly affect the possibility of a fair trial.

MODERATOR

If you were Sykes' solicitor, Mr Lewis, would you try to prevail on Mr Day's better nature?

GORDON LEWIS

I think it'd be a waste of time. (laughter)

MODERATOR

But basically, if someone goes on the run, they forfeit their right to the fair trial protection of the law of contempt?

EVANS

Well, I'd take Mr Hughes' point that the law of contempt has no formal application at this stage. Unquestionably, were formal legal proceedings in train, this could be a proper case for the law of contempt and I'm sure that governments and law officers would act accordingly, because the right to fair trial is absolutely crucial. It's a nice balance between that and the freedom of the press, but in this context you're putting — if legal proceedings were in train — you'd have to act.

MODERATOR

You are not getting very far very fast with the search for Amanda, Mr Newnham, so you and Sergeant Doberman go back to the scene of the crime. Phar Out seems far from well, and he whinnies nervously as you approach. Then he does something that horses as well as humans sometimes have to do when they're frightened of policemen. You avert your eyes, but Sergeant Doberman was raised on a farm and he notices something odd. To use the words of your forensic report, "Amongst the horse's droppings was found a rubber prophylactic containing a white crystalline substance which proved on analysis to be cocaine." What does that suggest?

NEWNHAM

It suggests all sorts of possibilities.

MODERATOR

The horse was racing in New Zealand last week, it then spent four days in quarantine and your vet tells you it would take seven days for that condom to pass through the horse's intestines. New Zealand has become a staging post for the running of cocaine into Australia from South America. It's alimentary, my dear Inspector. (laughter)

NEWNHAM

Yes.

MODERATOR

What do you do?

NEWNHAM

I find out who has been handling the horse in Australia and I communicate the information to the New Zealand police for investigation at their end.

MODERATOR

Sergeant Doberman thinks you should take the horse into custody.

NEWNHAM

That has been done.

MODERATOR

Of course, with drugs in the picture, this now becomes a federal offence. You have additional powers, don't you Mr Meagher? You are advising this police investigation.

MEAGHER

With the federal police involved, they have the power to apply for a warrant to tap telephones.

MODERATOR

And it's becoming increasingly important to find the missing girl. A life is still at stake, and now there's a very inventive, very dangerous new scheme to import drugs.

MEAGHER

They are going to have to persuade a Federal Court judge that the tapping of that telephone is going to produce information that would relate to the drug investigation.

MODERATOR

Suppose, Mr Justice Nathan, that you were elevated to the Federal Court, and the police satisfy you that there is a reasonable suspicion that Mr Marsden and his client are involved in this method of importing cocaine. Would you make an order to tap Marsden's telephone?

HOWARD NATHAN

Yes. You would give power to tap.

MODERATOR

Are there any precautions you would take? Would you insist that it be for a limited period?

NATHAN

On the fact situation, yes; fourteen days.

MODERATOR
Mr Marsden has friends and clients who are politicians,
footballers, judges. Is there any way you can stop the recording
of conversations that he has with people other than Sykes?

NATHAN
No.

MODERATOR
So the police are going to hear every conversation he has?

NATHAN
Yes.

MODERATOR
The federal police will be transcribing them all and listening to
them all . . .

NEWNHAM
Not necessarily transcribing, but listening in one form or another
. . . yes.

MODERATOR
And any intelligence that the federal police pick up about
criminal activity relating to Mr Marsden's clients will be available
for general investigation purposes, Senator Evans?

EVANS
I think what that points to is the potentially huge overreach of
any telephone tapping exercise, far more so than with any
other search warrant, and the need accordingly to circumscribe
in great precision the dimensions of that warrant. There needs
to be a power for judges granting a telephone tap warrant to
limit very precisely the amount of information that can in fact
be recorded. The judge's role in this situation is to act as the
guardian and defender of the public interest in these
matters.

MODERATOR
Let's go on a little. Wendy Bacon, you work for *Strewth*, and
you receive a telephone call from Sykes. He says, "I'm on the
run. Before they catch me and lock me up and throw away the
key, there is something I want to tell you. I've got dynamite
information about corruption and tax avoidance in this town."
Do you want to talk to him?

WENDY BACON
Yes . . .

MODERATOR
There is a warrant out for his arrest. Do you want to talk to him?

BACON
Yes . . . yes . . . I do.

MODERATOR
He's been sleeping rough. Would you buy him a meal?

BACON
No. I would be very careful, but I would certainly like to hear what he had to say. We could go where he wants.

MODERATOR
The Regent Hotel?

BACON
I would have to discuss it with the editor of *Strewth*.

MODERATOR
Discuss it with the editor.

BACON
Well, I have just had a call from Sykes and it seems he's got a lot of information about bottom of the harbour, and judges, and police involved with drug trafficking, and it sounds like a terrific story . . . (laughter) There is a bit of a problem. It seems he is putting some sort of condition on it, that we have to put him up at the Regent Hotel. I said we wouldn't do that. I just wanted to check with you that you agreed.

DAY
Talk to him. Don't under any circumstances knowingly break the law. (laughter)

BACON
Right . . . (laughter)

MODERATOR
Don't knowingly break the law but talk to him . . . Would you ask your counsel Mr Hughes's advice on what amounts to breaking the law?

DAY
It all depends on what the advice was.

MODERATOR
You had better go and see your solicitor—Mr Lewis. You can't talk direct to counsel.

DAY
(to Lewis) I have this problem where this bloke is on the run but he has some dynamite stuff and obviously we don't want to get too close to him, but he is insisting that we do just that. Now, how far can we go? If we know where he is are we bound to tell the gendarmes?

LEWIS
Well clearly you should try and get the story without breaking the law.

MODERATOR
That's typical solicitor's advice. I think you probably need counsel's opinion.

DAY
Let's ask Castan . . . (to Castan) We have this opportunity to get the scoop story of the century. This fellow has got dynamite information about drug trafficking, doped horses, the winner of the Melbourne Cup, and a couple that have made love in front of the horse. We have the opportunity to get the story. We have an ace reporter. Our Miss Bacon is going to go out and see him. How far can we go to perhaps entertain him a little and spend a little time with him to induce him to give the full facts so that as usual our paper publishes the truth?

CASTAN
You can't do anything for him. You can go and talk to him, you can sit down with him, you can find out what he has got to say. But if you harbour him, if you assist him, if you help him . . .

DAY
I didn't say that . . . but I was just about to say that. (laughter)

CASTAN
Well, with a warrant out for him don't do anything to help him.

DAY

Does that mean that Wendy can make an appointment at the Regent's coffee shop and go meet him there as long as she doesn't harbour him?

CASTAN

I don't think you should go to the Regent coffee shop. I think that might be harbouring. I would advise you not to give him anything. Just go and get the story.

DAY

Sure. Easier said than done. What would happen if I told him to be at the Regent and I didn't offer him any lunch or anything like that, I just said "You be there" and he agreed to go there and I just happened to send Wendy to the Regent for a cup of coffee.

CASTAN

Just bump into him. That's the way I would do it, yes.

MODERATOR

Suddenly, there's a news flash. The police have Sykes surrounded in a house in Hawthorn. He's got an armalite rifle and he says that he won't come out quietly unless he has a chance to talk to his Q.C., Tom Hughes. Mr Newnham, are you going to invite Mr Hughes to talk to him?

NEWNHAM

If we are satisfied that is the only way we can resolve the situation without loss of life and we can facilitate that over a telephone.

MODERATOR

There is no telephone in the house, but you do have a loudhailer.

NEWNHAM

Well Mr Hughes, Sykes is in the house and he has an armalite rifle. The situation is dangerous to life, and we are satisfied that the only way to resolve this situation peacefully is for the time being to accede to his request that you be allowed to communicate. The method of communication is by loudhailer, and we would allow you to use that from a position of safety behind police lines. Are you prepared to cooperate in this exercise?

HUGHES
    I would say that I would view with disquiet and resistance any idea
    of counsel acting as an intermediary in a situation involving a
    fugitive. It's just not my business. Counsel has certain duties, and
    that is not one of them, or anywhere near one of them.

MODERATOR
    Would that be your reaction, Mr Galbally?

FRANK GALBALLY
    I would always act as an intermediary for the benefit of my client,
    and indeed have done so in the past.

MODERATOR
    You see no difficulty if the police asked you to act as an
    intermediary with your client in a house with a gun?

GALBALLY
    Certainly, if it was in the interest of my client, and I would believe
    it would be in this case.

MODERATOR
    Sykes sees Frank Galbally, gives himself up, and is taken away to Pentridge
    Prison. Let's move to another side of town. A side of town where the
    phrase "criminal lawyer" is regarded as tautology. (laughter) That's the
    view of some of the partners of Teague and Lewis, the prestigious
    commercial law firm and it's certainly the view of its wealthiest client,
    Mr J. B. Kleen—"Squeaky" Kleen to his friends at the Melbourne Cup.
    He's a businessman, racehorse owner, philanthropist, and he's in your
    office this morning wanting some tax advice. "You know that company
    of mine with a million dollars undistributed profits? I want to get them
    into my own hands without paying tax. There's been some trouble at
    the stables, Phar Out's had to be scratched from the Melbourne Cup,
    the girl is missing and my trainer arrested—nothing to do with me,
    no worries—but I keep getting telephone calls from this journalist called
    Bacon from *Strewth*. Says she's doing an 'in depth' report on me. 'In
    depth' reporting is libellous in this country, isn't it?"

LEWIS
    It depends on how it is handled.

MODERATOR
    "Anything Bacon writes is sure to be libellous. Isn't it the case
    that libel damages are tax free?"

LEWIS
Yes.

MODERATOR
"Libel damages are tax free. Suppose my company with the million dollars undistributed profits buys *Strewth*. Miss Bacon publishes her story, I sue the newspaper for libel, and we settle for an apology and a million bucks in damages, tax free. Isn't that a good way of getting my company's profits into my hands without paying any tax?"

LEWIS
I wouldn't touch the proposition with a barge pole.

MODERATOR
Why not?

LEWIS
Because I like practising law and I have no other skills. (laughter and applause)

MODERATOR
But it's just a little bit of "creative lawyering". That's exactly what he wants from his solicitor.

LEWIS
That would be regarded here in Victoria—I can't speak for New South Wales because they have lower standards there—as unprofessional conduct.

MODERATOR
"But I'm a great believer in the free press, especially when it's tax free. I mean, Miss Bacon publishes her story, I buy the newspaper, and then sue for libel . . ."

LEWIS
I see it as a ploy, a devious ploy to cheat the revenue-collecting authorities. I see it as a deception of the court and I see it as the end of my career.

MODERATOR
Miss Bryant, you're an associate at Teague and Lewis and you are the expert on the Treasurer's new capital gains tax. You've got a draft in front of you this morning and Mr Kleen wants some advice from you. You notice one loophole—Mr Kleen has

a very valuable art collection. If he were to transfer it to his family trust in Vanuatu, they could let him have it back on permanent loan for his life and then when he dies, it could be sold without incurring the capital gains tax. Would you advise him to do that?

DIANA BRYANT

Well, the government has been legislating a lot lately in respect of tax and tax avoidance and therefore I would consider that the legislation would allow for that and it was proper for me to advise him to do it.

MODERATOR

You would advise to go ahead?

BRYANT

Yes . . . and I would probably get counsel's advice as well.

MODERATOR

Mr Castan, if that came to you, and it seemed to be a loophole that the government had overlooked, would you advise him to go ahead?

CASTAN

Yes, I would advise him to go ahead, but I would also be concerned to make sure there was going to be full disclosure of all the elements that you have outlined, including the Vanuatu trust.

MODERATOR

Attorney-General, as leader of the legal profession, these lawyers are performing a valuable service for Mr Kleen?

EVANS

Hardly. But it has to be acknowledged that lawyers do have a capacity within their professional ethics, and it is probably their duty, to advise as to what the law is rather than what it might be, and it is just simply up to us in government to keep one step ahead.

MODERATOR

So it's a good thing for lawyers to advise their clients to take advantage of tax loopholes, because it keeps your parliamentary draftspersons on their toes.

EVANS

I wouldn't quite put it in those terms, but certainly it has to be acknowledged that it's a role for the profession, and it's up to us to keep one step ahead of them.

MODERATOR

The other matter that Mr Kleen wants advice on is the Treasurer's new service tax. One of his companies is the proprietor of Melbourne's leading licensed massage parlour-cum-brothel, the Sigh of Relief. It's a motto of the establishment that nothing gets passed on to customers, and he's very keen to avoid the new service tax. (laughter) You notice, Mr Lewis, that there's an exemption in the new service tax for "therapeutic health establishments". You and Mr Disney are asked to advise him.

LEWIS

I think we can look at the legislation and tell him of his legal rights.

DISNEY

Yes I would see no problem in that. Again it's the difference between whether or not one helps him concoct something or just provides him with advice about what his rights are.

MODERATOR

"Therapeutic health establishments"; how are you going to bring the Sigh of Relief within that exemption?

DISNEY

Well, I think they would have to clean up their act a bit. They will have to provide some additional services—perhaps a gymnasium for clients, or offering acupuncture as an additional service, that sort of thing.

MODERATOR

Mr Costigan, you are chairing a Royal Commission into crime in Australia, and counsel assisting you is Douglas Meagher Q.C. Mr Kleen comes to your attention from time to time. Nothing positive, but some of his employees have been arrested for drug offences, he seems to be living beyond his means, he's a very wealthy man but he lost five million at the racetrack last year . . . Would you consider targeting him?

MEAGHER

Yes, in a word.

MODERATOR

What is going to happen to Mr Kleen if he gets targeted?

MEAGHER

He's going to be made very uncomfortable indeed. Very
uncomfortable. We are going to start making inquiries into his
business associates. Inevitably the word's going to get around
amongst them that our Commission is inquiring into him, and
of course that's going to affect his reputation severely.

MODERATOR

So on what principle do you target somebody? What's your
test?

MEAGHER

Well, that's one of the most difficult questions to answer. One
can lay down certain basic requirements without too much
difficulty. You can require to be persuaded that there must be
good grounds for suspicion. But those words can be empty of
any meaning . . . and to be perfectly frank with you I can only
say it's a matter of judgement by people experienced in
investigation.

MODERATOR

"A matter of judgement by people experienced in investigation."
A matter of your instinct, your sense of smell?

MEAGHER

Yes, very much so.

MODERATOR

Do you trust Mr Meagher's sense of smell, Tom Hughes?

HUGHES

Not really. Of course a great deal depends on the judgement and
sense of propriety of the investigator. That's all I can say.

MODERATOR

Mr Costigan, it's your judgement and your propriety. Do you
go along with Mr Meagher's sense of smell?

COSTIGAN

Yes I do, but I think the sense of smell includes a whole range
of experience and evidence. You don't smell in a vacuum. I
would have to have information and advice from other people in
my Commission, and consider myself as to whether there was
sufficient evidence to produce a reasonable suspicion; that there
was something of importance.

MODERATOR

Do you think your background and experience as a barrister really qualifies you for making that instinctive decision on whom to target, given the dramatic consequences that targeting can have?

COSTIGAN

Yes, I think it's probably as good a background as you can get. There is no such thing as a perfect background, and after all I have been doing this investigation for a long time and I have developed a bit of experience and smell.

MODERATOR

Do you feel that, Mr Hughes?

HUGHES

My problem in this area is that once these inquiries start they become self-perpetuating, and the people who are conducting them tend to assume the mantle of omniscience and ultimate wisdom.

MODERATOR

Attorney-General, are you happy to leave the mantle of omniscience on Mr Costigan?

EVANS

I am never happy with open-ended Royal Commissions, but one does depend enormously on the judgement, commonsense and sensitivity of the people concerned.

MODERATOR

Judgements that lawyers can make, Mr Castan?

CASTAN

A judgement I don't think they are very good at making. What Meagher says illustrates the whole danger of the process he is talking about. The problem is that there is no logical basis on which the decision is made. It can have extremely harmful effects and most notably he said nothing about what he'll do when he finds out that there is nothing to the investigation, and the target is clean—truly clean.

MODERATOR

What can you do, Mr Costigan, to clear the name of someone whom you've maligned?

COSTIGAN

There is a very serious problem of course in relation to his associates, the destruction of his business and so on. Even if that's not a matter of public record, in the sense of *Strewth* or other newspapers, it's very difficult to cure the rumours that have gone about amongst his associates. If it's been in the public arena, then there *is* a clear opportunity to do something.

MODERATOR

How should their name be cleared, Wendy Bacon?

BACON

I suppose if Mr Costigan made an announcement saying he really did come to the conclusions that there was nothing in it, well obviously it would get published in the press. But I think it would have to be a fairly clear case. If there were unanswered questions which made you wonder whether Mr Costigan might have been intimidated into making the statement, then I think the journalist would want answers to those questions.

MODERATOR

Senator Missen, a device for name clearing?

MISSEN

I think this is a greatly exaggerated problem. It is more important that Mr Costigan has the power to expose an enormous conspiracy in this country. Some people may be damaged by that, but if you tie his hands behind his back, you give the criminal in this country an enormous start.

MODERATOR

The end justifies the means?

MISSEN

No, but it's more important to get the real criminals than to cause a bit of stress along the way.

MODERATOR

Well, Diana Bryant, you're an associate of Teague and Lewis, about to be made a partner. If all goes well. Mr Costigan has subpoenaed a senior partner, Bruce Archbold, to give evidence and Bruce takes you along with him for moral support. The first question is: Does he know whether Mr Kleen has any connections with Vanuatu? Bruce answers, "I have no

of that at all," which is odd, because you saw the
.rust file on his desk only last week. What do you do?

ɔuld wait for an opportunity during an adjournment to speak
him. I would advise him of what I knew, and suggest he
answer the question again.

MODERATOR
He says, "Diana, there are some things it's better you don't talk
about."

BRYANT
I would be very concerned, and I would go back to the office
and talk to Mr Lewis.

MODERATOR
Talk to him.

BRYANT
Gordon, Bruce Archbold this morning denied any knowledge of
the Vanuatu trust that we're advising our client about. I have
brought it to his attention, but he won't reveal it. What should
I do?

LEWIS
What are the powers of the Commission, Diana?

BRYANT
They seem to be very wide as I understand it, Gordon.

LEWIS
Well if, on behalf of the firm, you have to go to prison—don't
you hesitate. (laughter) I think we had better have a meeting of
partners. Julian, would you come into my room for a moment?
Where's Teague?

DISNEY
He's down in the Sigh of Relief, Gordon. (laughter)

LEWIS
Julian, Archbold's lying to the Commission. What are we going
to do?

DISNEY
We will have to put the strongest pressure we can on him to

tell the truth in this situation. But there is a question, though, whether in fact the information still has the protection of professional privilege. I suppose we could ask Archbold to take it as far as he could without going to prison.

MODERATOR
Well, Bruce says, "Look, the Costigan Royal Commission is on a fishing expedition again. I am not going to tell them anything. As far as I am concerned, I don't know anything about any of my client's activities."

LEWIS
Julian, do you think there is a difference between lying positively to the Commission, and just making no statement at all? I don't mind if he stands there and refuses to answer their questions. I mean, if he goes to prison, how do we divide the profits up?

DISNEY
I agree. I think that if all he is doing is declining to answer them, that's a matter for him. If the information is protected by privilege, it may be that he is entitled to withhold it.

MODERATOR
Let's get back to William Sykes languishing in Pentridge, finally charged with murder. You are defending him, John Marsden. Sykes tells you he wasn't there at the stables on the morning Amanda was murdered—or presumably murdered, because the police haven't found her body yet. He was snug in bed with his girlfriend, Katie Bomschell, a model and masseuse who works at the Sigh of Relief, miles away from the stables. He didn't leave her bed until . . . well . . . Lester Gallop discovered the bloodstained clothes about six o'clock and Sykes tells you he didn't leave her bed till six-thirty. The police have an identification witness who says that Sykes was seen driving away from the stables at five o'clock. Pretty important that you interview Miss Bomschell, isn't it?

MARSDEN
Yes, certainly.

MODERATOR
What questions do you ask this vital alibi witness?

MARSDEN

I'd ask her straight-out: was the accused with her at such and such a time?

MODERATOR

You'd actually suggest a time?

MARSDEN

Yes.

MODERATOR

You'd say, "Weren't you still in bed with him at five o'clock"?

MARSDEN

Yes.

MODERATOR

Mr Galbally, would you ask the question that way?

GALBALLY

No. I would say, you have come to me on the basis that you can help Sykes. How can you help him?

MODERATOR

"Well, he was in bed with me that day the girl went missing."

GALBALLY

Thank you. How do you know it was that day?

MODERATOR

"Oh, I'm certain it was that day because he phoned me later and said he was going on the run."

GALBALLY

Very well, now would you tell me what happened for that twenty-four hours?

MODERATOR

"Everything?" (laughter)

GALBALLY

Leaving aside the sexual part.

MODERATOR

"Well, he stayed with me. He stayed with me till . . . what time would you *like* me to say?"

GALBALLY

I would not say . . .

MODERATOR

"What time does *William* say that I left him?"

GALBALLY

What time do *you* say you left him? I would cross-examine her myself to know whether or not she was in fact a reliable witness. This is a grave danger in any trial. If you produce a witness, they can be absolutely devastating for your own client unless they are totally honest, and it's your duty at first instance to cross-examine them in such a manner that you are totally satisfied they are telling the truth.

MODERATOR

And like the thorough solicitor that you are, you check the records at the Sigh of Relief. Victoria's licensed brothels have to keep very careful records, and you find that Katie, in fact, was on the early morning shift. She was at work at four o'clock, so Sykes has been lying to you.

GALBALLY

Yes.

MODERATOR

It was a close shave. If you hadn't checked those records you could have put up a false alibi witness and lost the trial. Isn't it time that Sykes now told you the truth?

GALBALLY

You'd go to Sykes and say, I do not propose to call your alibi witness. You make your own choice whether you want me to continue as your adviser, otherwise you can go elsewhere.

MODERATOR

Mr Lewis, you're Sykes' lawyer. Would you now put pressure on him to stop inventing, to start telling you the truth?

LEWIS

I'm satisfied that he's lying to me, and I would indicate to him that I could not continue to act for him in a situation where he expects to give sworn evidence that he didn't commit the crime.

MODERATOR

"OK, OK. I'll tell you the truth. I did go to Phar Out's stable that morning to see whether the cocaine had dropped. But I never killed the girl, honest. Her naked body was just lying there, stabbed to death. I panicked—I got rid of the cocaine packets—flushed them down the toilet. Then I put the body in the boot of my car, drove out to Ripponlea House and buried it in the rose garden. Then I went straight to Mr Marsden's office." What do you do? You know the body is in the rose garden at Ripponlea House. You're the first person to know. The police are still searching for Amanda. They're dragging the Yarra looking for her. Amanda's mother appeared on *Willesee* last night, saying that although a man has been arrested for the murder of her daughter, she's still hoping against hope that she's alive.

LEWIS

Thank heavens not too many people know about it then.

MODERATOR

Mr Marsden, would you tell the police? Given that Sykes can't go into the witness box at his trial because he'll be cross-examined about the cocaine.

MARSDEN

I'd have to think about it. Lawyers are not almighty Gods. They're not sitting up there in judgement. Their job is to do a case and protect the interests of their client.

MODERATOR

If you tell the police where Amanda's body is, that will be the first evidence that the prosecution had to connect Sykes with the burying of the body.

MEAGHER

It'd also be the first evidence they had that she's dead.

MARSDEN

That's right.

MODERATOR

It'll be devastating. You can get your client off if Sykes says nothing at his trial—the police haven't got the strongest of cases. The minute you notify them where the body is, that evidence will connect her death with your client.

MARSDEN

I would act entirely on my client's instructions. At that stage I would put to him the options that were open to him. I believe that I must act on instructions. I'm convinced that what he's told me is the truth and I'd put to him the options in relation to the body, the fact that the police case is not strong and that he's entitled to use every avenue at his disposal to protect his innocence or to ensure a verdict of acquittal.

MODERATOR
So you wouldn't tell the police where the body is?

MARSDEN
If they were my instructions, no, I wouldn't.

MODERATOR
They are your instructions, and the police are still looking for the body. One day your office door bursts open and Amanda's father comes in. "Please, Mr Marsden, your client must know what happened to Amanda. Won't you tell us if she's alive or dead. Can't you just tell us that?"

MARSDEN
No, I can't discuss it with him. I simply would not discuss anything with him whatsoever.

MODERATOR
These lawyers, Mr Newnham, are going to keep from you the fact that a missing girl is buried in the Ripponlea rose garden. When it comes out, as it undoubtedly will later on, that they didn't disclose the fact, are you going to criticise them?

NEWNHAM
At every suitable opportunity, as I do now. Their ethics are wrong.

MODERATOR
Why?

NEWNHAM
Because they have a duty to the community as well as to their client and one has to supersede the other. They've chosen to put the interest of their client above the interest of the community and that is a wrong value judgement.

MODERATOR
Senator Missen, are you as critical as the Commissioner?

MISSEN
No, I don't think so. It's not for me to determine legal ethics. I

think the lawyers are probably justified in this.

MODERATOR

Tom Hughes, was it an ethically correct decision not to disclose the existence of Amanda's body?

HUGHES

What the accused said to his solicitor was clearly a privileged communication. The solicitor is not at liberty to disclose the contents of that communication to anyone without his client's consent. If he had that consent, obviously it would be his duty to disclose that information.

MODERATOR

He didn't have the consent.

HUGHES

In that case, the solicitor's duty is to remain silent, regrettable though it may be.

MODERATOR

Of course Sykes' problem is that he can't go into the witness box at his trial, because in order to clear himself of the murder charge he would have to admit to his involvement in smuggling cocaine through the horse's intestines.

HUGHES

I think in that situation, when the chips are down and you're acting for a client in the predicament of Mr Sykes, you have to make with him an assessment of which is worse, the frying pan or the fire, and if he instructs you that he has a story which, if believed, would result in his acquittal of a charge of murder, then I'd be very inclined to tell him that if he gets out of the frying pan, the fire may be warm but not as uncomfortable as the frying pan. I'd advise him that his better option is to give evidence or at least make a statement from the dock.

MODERATOR

But if he does give evidence, he'll have to admit the involvement in importing cocaine. He might get off the murder charge, although even that's not certain. He'll certainly go down in a cocaine trial subsequently.

HUGHES

So be it. He's made his bed and he'll have to decide perhaps to lie in it. But the second bed may not be so uncomfortable as the first, and his period of incarceration on the drugs charge may be less than a life sentence for murder.

MODERATOR

Mr Lewis, were those lawyers right in not disclosing the whereabouts of the body?

LEWIS

I've just decided to brief Tom Hughes for the trial. I reckon he's good. (laughter)

MODERATOR

You've realised at last! But as the director of the Victorian Law Institute, would you say the lawyers were right in not disclosing it to the police?

LEWIS

Well, it does come back to the client's instructions and certainly without his instructions they couldn't do so.

MODERATOR

So their duty is to the client, not as Mr Newnham says, to society.

LEWIS

Yes, that's right.

MODERATOR

A year has passed, ladies and gentlemen, and Melbourne Cup time has come round again. Phar Out is the favourite, and he's to be ridden by Lester Gallop, Australia's top jockey. Lester's involved in divorce proceedings which are at a rather tricky stage, Miss Bryant. There's a custody problem and his wife, Mrs Gallop, is being represented by Gordon Lewis. It's going to be a tough battle. Lester has sooled a private eye onto his wife for evidence of her maternal unsuitability—to prove she's not a fit and proper person to have custody of the kids. He's come in today with photographs—photographs that show a woman who's undeniably Mrs Gallop, engaged in what is without doubt an act of sexual congress, with a person whom he confidently asserts is Mr Lewis. It's a back view only, but his confidence stems from the fact that it was taken through the window of Mr Lewis' house last week with a telephoto lens. How are you going to use that material?

BRYANT

It's relevant to the issue of whether she's a fit and proper mother, so I think it should be used. The person who took the photographs can be called to give evidence and the photographs can be produced.

MODERATOR

What about getting Mr Lewis off this case?

BRYANT

Then I might well approach him confidentially beforehand, and let him know.

MODERATOR

You're very flattered to be approached by Miss Bryant, Mr Lewis, because in fact the photographs are not of you, they're of your articled clerk who was minding your house while you and your family were on holiday last week. Has this pimply youth destroyed his legal career?

LEWIS

He might have just started it. (laughter)

MODERATOR

What advice would you give him?

LEWIS

Well, I'd get him in and I'd say that there are photographs about which show identifiable portions of him and of Mrs Gallop, and what the hell does he think he's doing by not pulling the blinds? (laughter)

MODERATOR

What about your duty to supervise and control your articled clerk?

LEWIS

Well, I acknowledge a responsibility, in a professional sense, to see that he doesn't cheat as an articled clerk but as for his sexual propensities, I draw the line.

MODERATOR

Doctors and dentists get struck off if they have relationships with their married clients. Why should solicitors be any different?

LEWIS
  Because to go and see a doctor, it's probably part of the game to
  take your clothes off at some stage. That's fairly unusual when
  you see a solicitor . . . (laughter)

MODERATOR
  The trial of William Sykes for the murder of Amanda Innocent
  begins next Monday. It's Friday afternoon, and Sykes is having
  his last conference with his counsel in Pentridge. "What should
  I wear, Mr Hughes?"

HUGHES
  Dress soberly.

MODERATOR
  "What, with a tie?"

HUGHES
  Yes.

MODERATOR
  So if I look like Mr Disney, in the dock, I'm more likely to be
  convicted?

HUGHES
  Far be it for me to penetrate the mysteries of Melbourne juries.
  The last one before which I appeared convicted my client in ten
  minutes. So I would tell him to dress quietly.

MODERATOR
  "What about some of my old friends? Should they come along
  for a day or so and sit in Court with the wife to show the jury
  that they're on my side? I could ask Graham Kennedy, George
  Negus and Susan Sangster . . . would that be a good idea?"

HUGHES
  I think that they'd be likely to be counterproductive.

MODERATOR
  Counterproductive, Mr Galbally?

GALBALLY
  No, not entirely. Mind you, my problem is usually to keep my
  clients sober rather than dressed soberly. I disagree with Mr
  Hughes to this extent; the more well-known people you can
  have there barracking for your client, the better.

MODERATOR

All right . . . we can get Susan Sangster and George Negus.
What about Russ Hinze?

GALBALLY

Oh definitely, and get Joh Bjelke-Petersen down here if you
can.

MODERATOR

Rachelle Lewiton, you are junior counsel to Mr Hughes and
you've formed quite a friendly relationship with William Sykes
in the time that you've been advising him. As Mr Hughes and
Mr Marsden are leaving, Sykes beckons you over. He says:
"Listen Rachelle, I'm not going to be there on Monday. I've got
a prison break planned. I'm going over the wall during the
chapel service on Sunday. But tell Tom not to worry, the wife's
got the money for his brief fee." What do you do?

RACHELLE LEWITON

Well, I'd immediately tell Tom . . .

MODERATOR

That the wife has the money for his fee? (laughter)

LEWITON

No, no, I'd advise Tom of what's been said to me.

MODERATOR

Advise him.

LEWITON

Well, Tom, the prisoner, Mr Sykes, has just advised me that he
plans to escape. It's something that I think I should bring to
your attention and perhaps we should get instructions on it.

HUGHES

Well, that would be the understatement of the year wouldn't it!
(laughter) Th⌐nk you very much for letting me know. What a
difficult client we have. I will get in touch with our instructing
solicitor and advise him to communicate as soon as he can with
our wayward intending traveller to tell him that if carries out
that proposal I shall return the brief and have nothing more to
do with the case.

MODERATOR

Mr Marsden?

MARSDEN

I'd tell Mr Hughes that he's not very pragmatic in relation to criminals and criminal practices. Obviously, when the pressures are on in trials, criminals will say that. I would go and see the client and implore upon him not to take the step.

MODERATOR

He's been doing the Jane Fonda aerobics course while he's been inside. He's very fit. He's going over the wall on Sunday.

HUGHES

It's not my job to go and see the client. The less I see him, the better for him.

MARSDEN

And this is why we need fusion in the profession, instead of having two sections.

HUGHES

Nonsense . . .

MARSDEN

The fact of life is that the barristers are prepared to just throw off the client to the solicitor and take no further interest in the matter.

HUGHES

Don't you realise we have different functions to perform?

MARSDEN

I don't think you do. You have an interest in protecting the client. I would talk to the client, I would ask him not to go, but if he decides to go that's a matter for him. We would still run the case and I'm sure that the barristers would be happy to know that their fees were protected. That's all that they're interested in.

MODERATOR

You're not going to inform the prison authorities?

MARSDEN

No.

MODERATOR

Even though there may be a danger to life if Sykes goes over the wall? He may kill someone while breaking out?

MARSDEN

You're dealing with someone who at that time is under immense personal pressure. He reacts to that personal pressure of being in a courtroom. He's a human being with feelings and emotions. You don't necessarily have to accept everything he says about breaking out. And I would just not be prepared to cause a stir in the community—a stir amongst the judge and everyone else by saying that this bloke's going to make a break on Sunday.

MODERATOR

Senator Evans, is that good enough? Is this the point at which the solicitor should break his client's confidence?

EVANS

I don't think it is good enough. I can't see that that kind of communication would be protected by privilege, and when you're out of the territory of privilege and protection I think you are in the zone where your responsibility to the larger community overrides what you might conceive to be your ethical responsibility to your client.

MODERATOR

What view do you take, Mr Costigan? Is the solicitor, where he's learnt of his client's prison break, obliged to tell the authorities?

COSTIGAN

Well I'd go along with Mr Marsden to this extent: that I'd go and talk to the client and really find out whether he was serious or just hot air. But if I felt that he was serious, I agree with the Attorney.

MODERATOR

You'd break your client's confidence?

COSTIGAN

Yes, I'd communicate the information. I'd tell the client I was going to do that.

MODERATOR

Sykes does not in fact try to escape, and on Monday he's brought from the prison to stand his trial. There's an air of expectancy about the court as we wait for the arrival of Mr Justice Nathan. Counsel are in their place—Mr Costigan and

Mr Meagher for the prosecution, Mr Hughes, Mr Castan and Mr Galbally for the defence. It's a sensational murder trial. The Sykes family have spent vast amounts of money to help Wiliam's defence. They have even hired a professional lip-reader, Lola la Bouche, to sit with Mr Marsden and watch the prosecution team of Costigan and Meagher, lip-reading what they whisper to each other. She'll be very helpful, Mr Hughes. She'll be able to tell you what Mr Justice Nathan is muttering to his clerk. Will you accept her services?

HUGHES

No.

MODERATOR

Why not?

HUGHES

It would be quite improper to use any means to penetrate the secrets of the other side.

MODERATOR

But if they whisper to each other publicly and you have a lip-reader there it might be very helpful to your client.

HUGHES

Of course it might be.

MODERATOR

What about your duty to your client?

HUGHES

Well, one has a duty to one's client; one also has a duty to the court and a duty to the system of justice.

MODERATOR

Lola has been very helpful already. The woman juror-in-waiting, in the floral dress, has been talking to another juror, and she's been saying, according to Lola, "It looks like we're on the Sykes trial—that dreadful man who killed the little girl!" Mr Marsden, Lola tells you that the juror in the floral dress has said that, and lo and behold the juror in the floral dress is the first called to the jury-box.

MARSDEN

I'd instruct the barrister to forthwith object to that juror.

MODERATOR

Mr Hughes, would you object to the juror on the strength of Lola's lip-reading?

HUGHES

It depends on how the information comes to me. If I'm instructed that there are good reasons for objecting to the juror, I will object.

MODERATOR

So you'll use Lola's information to object to the juror?

HUGHES

Yes, but I will not be a party to hiring a lip-reader.

MODERATOR

What about juror number two? He's a rather righteous-looking young man with a copy of the *National Times* under his arm. He'll believe everyone's guilty, won't he? Would you challenge him?

HUGHES

If he's got the *National Times* tucked under his elbow I'd be inclined to. One makes an intuitive judgement based upon such evidence as one has. There's really very little information and it's all an exercise in somewhat uneducated guesswork. You know their name and their occupation, and if you see a juror holding a particular publication which might give you an intuitive whiff of a suspicion that perhaps his tastes are towards a conviction, yes, you'd strike him off.

MODERATOR

Juror number three is clutching a crucifix. Amanda's body was finally found in the rose garden, and it was identified by the crucifix she was wearing. Would you challenge the Catholic juror?

CASTAN

Yes. For the same sort of reasons that Tom Hughes has indicated. I would challenge if I felt that there might be prejudice.

MODERATOR

Juror number four, Frank Costigan, looks as though he's been drinking— probably kerosene. He's been sleeping rough, you notice noses crinkle as he walks along to take his seat. Would you challenge him—one of life's unfortunates?

COSTIGAN

Yes, I think I'd challenge him. Not because he was one of life's unfortunates, but because he'd been drinking. What I'd really be looking for would be twelve people on the jury who would approach it rationally and come to the right decision.

MODERATOR

Juror number five, police tell you, is a member of the Painters and Dockers' Union. Would you challenge him?

COSTIGAN

I might return my brief at that stage. (laughter)

MODERATOR

How do you challenge jurors, Mr Galbally?

GALBALLY

By guess and by God.

MODERATOR

How does God help? (laughter)

GALBALLY

Inspiration. Generally you look for the fellow who probably has a bit of booze every now and again and who probably has not had to live up to fairly difficult standards in his life.

MODERATOR

By guess and by God, Attorney-General. Oughtn't we to have a more rational system of challenging jurors? Oughtn't we to be like the Americans and be able to ask them questions to find out if they've got any prejudices?

EVANS

I think there's a lot to be said for that.

MODERATOR

It would make trials longer, but it would be more rational wouldn't it?

EVANS

To the extent that you can ever impose rationality in jury deliberations. It would at least advance that if you could filter out some of the prejudices which do otherwise apply, yes.

MODERATOR

At the end of the day when the court adjourns, Wendy Bacon,
you catch the Melbourne tram back to your hotel and it so
happens that you are sitting next to a young woman who has
been selected for the jury on this trial. "You're Wendy Bacon,
aren't you? You're covering the Sykes trial. I'm writing a diary
of what goes on in the jury room during this trial. Would you
be interested in publishing it in your newspaper?"

BACON

Perhaps I would say, Contact me when the trial is over.

MODERATOR

"And here is my business card"?

DAY

After the trial is an entirely different kettle of fish.

MODERATOR

The Sykes trial is the most sensational trial in Australia since the
dingo baby case. After that trial would you publish that juror's
story?

DAY

If the juror came back to us.

MODERATOR

Ought there be a law against it, Senator?

EVANS

I don't think so; not in relation to after-the-event stories of this
kind. There's all sorts of very good reasons why jurors shouldn't
be put under any pressure or taken advantage of in any way
while the trial is pending, but I don't think the interest of the
community is such that jurors or those who publish their stories
should be threatened with contempt after the event.

MODERATOR

Ought there to be a law against it, Mr Costigan?

COSTIGAN

I would certainly make it a criminal offence for anything that a
juror said to be made public. I would make the jury-box
sacrosanct.

MODERATOR

But suppose a jury tells you that the question of guilt or innocence was decided by the toss of a coin. Isn't that something so discreditable that it ought to come out?

COSTIGAN

Yes, but hard cases make bad law. Of course if one had access to all jury decisions over a period, you would find in some cases you were troubled by the technique that the jury had used to come to its decision. I think the principle of having the jury room sacrosanct is so much more important.

MODERATOR

Free speech for jurors, Mr Castan? You are a great free speech exponent.

CASTAN

Certainly I am, but I am also a great exponent of the jury system. This practice of publication will destroy it.

MODERATOR

But maybe it should be destroyed if it can't stand up to the light of day.

CASTAN

It is not a process we want to have carried on in the light of day. That's why we have them carry on their deliberations behind the closed doors of the jury room; not interfered with by the processes of the press, or the processes of public pressure or political pressure or any other sort of pressure.

MODERATOR

What if something really discreditable happens in the jury room. Ought a juror not be entitled out of conscience to ring up talkback radio . . .

CASTAN

Definitely not. If something bizarre is happening, they have got access to the judge. The jury room should be sacrosanct, otherwise you could destroy the system.

MODERATOR

Senator Evans, how does it come down for you?

EVANS

One of the things that worries me most about the present jury system is that so little is in fact understood about its internal dynamics—the way the jury operates—because there has been so much secrecy in the past. It is accordingly possible for jurors not to know that they have a constitutional right to acquit, notwithstanding that they believe the person has in fact been technically guilty. I suspect it's only by these sorts of issues being aired and exposed in the way that they have been in recent times that we can get rationality and propriety back into the system, which sometimes lacks it.

MODERATOR

Mr Meagher, while Mr Costigan is making his opening speech for the prosecution you are rifling through your old papers to do with the police investigation, and you discover that in the very early days the police took statements from all the jockeys at "Squeaky" Kleen's stables. One of them happens to mention in his statement a rumour that Lester Gallop was having an affair with Amanda Innocent. That jockey isn't being called as a witness. Would you be under any obligation to disclose the statement to the defence?

MEAGHER

I don't see who would be interested in a rumour of that sort.

MODERATOR

Well, you don't disclose it. But it's a draughty old courtroom, and a little breeze wafts the paper over to Mr Marsden's desk, and he can't help reading it. A jockey says there was a rumour that Amanda Innocent, the dead girl, was having an affair at one stage with Lester Gallop. Lester is the first witness—purely formal evidence of identification—he was the person who found the girls' bloodstained clothing when he came to take Phar Out for an early morning canter. Are you interested in that statement?

MARSDEN

Yes, certainly. I would certainly show it to my client and I would certainly seek to cross-examine. I would want to establish what his relationship was with the girl.

MODERATOR

Your client wants you to go further. Sykes is very excited. He says: "That's it! Lester must have killed her! He was having an affair with Amanda. Perhaps she got pregnant and he killed her so she wouldn't complicate his divorce. Put that to him, Mr Hughes." Would you put that to Lester, on your client's instructions?

HUGHES
No.

MODERATOR
Why not?

HUGHES
Because I would have to be satisfied before I put such a suggestion to a witness that there was a proper basis for putting the question. From what I have been told so far there is not a proper basis.

MODERATOR
But you have got your client's instructions.

HUGHES
That's not enough.

MODERATOR
He wants you to allege that Lester Gallop murdered the woman that he's accused of murdering.

HUGHES
So be it, but he won't get me to do what he wants me to do unless there is sufficient basis for putting the suggestion. And even if there was some sort of a basis for it, it might be very bad advocacy to intrude such a virtually collateral question into the case. It might do my client no good in the jury's eyes.

MODERATOR
Your client is determined. He says, "Put it to him."

HUGHES
Well, I would tell him if you insist on those instructions, you better realise you would be hiring other counsel because I will seek an adjournment and return the brief. I am not bound by your instructions. I'm bound as your advocate to do what I think is proper to do in your interest.

MODERATOR
Mr Castan, you are Mr Hughes' junior; would you put that question?

CASTAN

No, not on the basis it's being put. It's quite apparent that Sykes has made up this allegation as the result of information that has come on the piece of paper you referred to, and that's not sufficient basis to put it.

MODERATOR

Miss Lewiton, would you ask the question?

LEWITON

No. Ultimately the responsibility of counsel is to determine for themselves whether the question should be put. In those circumstances I would not put it.

MODERATOR

You would put the question, Mr Marsden?

MARSDEN

Yes, I would. If my instruction was to put it, I would put it. I believe there is an element here of suspicion as to what could have happened. We have learned something about the deceased having an affair with a well-known jockey, we know he is married and we know that he might have placed himself in a very embarrassing position if it was found out. Obviously it is worthwhile acting on his instruction.

MODERATOR

Would you publicly destroy Lester Gallop's reputation?

MARSDEN

I don't care.

MODERATOR

On the strength of your client's insistence, and nothing by way of evidence?

MARSDEN

Certainly I would. I don't care. My client is charged with murder.

MODERATOR

He is indeed, and the main evidence that the police have against him comes from their discovery of Amanda's body in the Ripponlea rose garden. There were traces of fertiliser found in Sykes' car and on Sykes' trousers, a fertiliser imported specially from England and used only at Ripponlea. That forensic evidence is vital because it connects Sykes with the body of Amanda. And how did the police come to find Amanda's body? Well, way back last year, when Sergeant Doberman accompanied Mr Newnham to search Mr Marsden's office, he put an illegal bugging device under the decanter in the drink cabinet. Quite illegal, but it later picked up Mr Marsden agonising with his partner Mr Disney over whether they should notify the police of the whereabouts of Amanda's body. Mr Castan, are you going to object to the admission of the forensic evidence about fertiliser which has been indirectly obtained from the illegal police bugging?

CASTAN

Certainly.

MODERATOR

Object to Mr Justice Nathan.

CASTAN

I object to the evidence on the basis that it has been illegally obtained and is therefore not admissable against Sykes. In so far as you have a discretion you should exercise it against the police who have behaved so improperly, unlawfully bugging my client's solicitor's office.

NATHAN

A very powerful submission, Mr Castan. I will hear from the prosecutor, Mr Meagher.

MEAGHER

The answer to that submission is that the discovery of the body, and the matching fertiliser on Sykes' clothing, is fairly remote from the illegal bugging. And the importance of the evidence is of such magnitude that it should be allowed into the trial, notwithstanding the illegality. The information which led to it being obtained was illegal, but the evidence that has been put in is convincing evidence which was legitimately obtained.

MODERATOR

How does Your Honour rule?

NATHAN

The initial illegality taints all that flows from it. It's a fundamental principle in the law that we should not connive at or be part of any of the illegal processes which it is a part of the function of the court to resolve. In those circumstances I would rule that the illegality, albeit far removed in its result from the initial trespass, is such as to taint all that flows from it. I rule the forensic evidence inadmissable.

MODERATOR

Mr Newnham, are you happy with that ruling?

NEWNHAM

Not at all.

MODERATOR

Why?

NEWNHAM

I think that evidence which is relevant should be admitted. How it is obtained is not really relevant to the issues. If people have acted illegally in gathering that evidence, then they should be prosecuted in their turn.

MODERATOR

But unless rulings of that sort are made, the police will have open slather to act illegally—to tap telephones, to put bugging devices in people's homes and offices.

NEWNHAM

In Victoria, that is a nonsense.

MODERATOR

But you see you can't really discipline Sergeant Doberman. He's a hero in the police canteen, he'll be offered immunity by the National Crimes Authority, the *Age* will publish the "Marsden–Disney Tapes" for the next two weeks.

NEWNHAM

Not at all. He will be prosecuted for a breach of the Listening Devices Act.

MODERATOR

But what's the point of prosecuting someone on the one hand, and on the other hand saying, "Thanks very much for obtaining this evidence. We will use it to convict Sykes."

NEWNHAM

Because that's the only way we can resolve the dilemma to the satisfaction of the community.

MODERATOR
Are you satisfied, Attorney-General?

EVANS
I am certainly not satisfied. That there should be an absolute rule that all evidence goes in, however illegally obtained, and we rely simply on disciplinary sanctions down the track . . . that's not good enough.

MODERATOR
Ladies and gentlemen, the trial continues. There is still enough evidence to go to the jury. Sykes makes an unsworn statement, and there are very eloquent closing speeches from Mr Costigan for the prosecution and Mr Hughes for the defence. Mr Justice Nathan sums up all of Monday, he's going to send the jury out first thing Tuesday—Melbourne Cup day. Mr Hughes, you have a problem. Mr Kleen has booked you to appear for one of his companies in a tax assessment case in Sydney. Will you leave your client at this crucial juncture?

HUGHES
Certainly not.

MODERATOR
Mr Lewis, you are acting for Mr Kleen. Have a word with Mr Hughes.

LEWIS
Mr Hughes, the fee we agreed was a thousand dollars per day. We have a lot of work in the future, and Kleen's very taken with you. We want you to be there in Sydney tomorrow.

HUGHES
I know you want me to be there, Mr Lewis, but I can't leave a criminal trial until it's finished. The jury may come back and ask questions, and if they do I should be there.

MODERATOR
The jury does come back to ask a question. The question, Judge, is this: "Can we please have a radio to listen to the Melbourne Cup while we consider our verdict?"

NATHAN
Is this horse running in the race?

MODERATOR

You have drawn Phar Out in the judicial sweepstake. (laughter)

NATHAN

In this particular instance, being a murder trial carrying life imprisonment, no, I would not allow them to have a radio in the jury room.

MODERATOR

Even though they may be pressured to bring back a verdict early, so they can get out and listen to the Melbourne Cup?

NATHAN

No.

MODERATOR

It's Tuesday morning. Sykes has spent a sleepless night, and so has Lester Gallop, who is riding the favourite Phar Out, in the Cup later today. On his way to Flemington, he drops by the office of his solicitor: "I think we will have to drop the custody case, Miss Bryant. I can't take the risk. There's something I have to tell you. It was I who killed Amanda Innocent. I loved that girl. I destroyed my marriage for her. Then I read her diary and discovered she'd been having an affair with an articled clerk at Teague and Lewis. I went to the stable early that morning to confront her, something just snapped and I stabbed her to death. You won't tell anyone my secret?"

BRYANT

Well, I certainly think you should drop the custody case. (laughter) If you tell me that in confidence, then I think I am obliged to keep that confidence.

MODERATOR

You are obliged to keep that secret, even if Sykes, an innocent man, is convicted of murder in a few hours' time?

BRYANT

I think I am obliged to keep that confidence.

MODERATOR

Even if Sykes is convicted?

BRYANT

Yes.

MODERATOR

The jury is returning with a verdict. It's fifteen minutes before the Melbourne Cup is due to start. The foreman stands, the verdict is "guilty". How do you feel now, Miss Bryant, when you hear that on the radio?

BRYANT

I would feel terrible, but I would still be obliged to keep my privileged information secret.

MODERATOR

You would feel terrible, but your client, Lester Gallop, feels fine. Relief at sharing his guilty secret, relief that someone else has been convicted of his dreadful crime. He leaps to the saddle and rides the great horse so skilfully that he's lengths ahead in the home straight. And that, ladies and gentlemen, is where Phar Out stumbles and falls. Where Lester, his feet still firm in the stirrups, is trampled by the rest of the field; and where legal privilege finally dies with the death of the client.

In due course Miss Bryant's affidavit will be presented to the Appeal Court, and William Sykes will stumble blinkingly into the sunlight outside Pentridge, reflecting that the justice game, like the racing game, has its winners and its losers and that lawyers make sure that everyone gets a fair old crack of the whip.

THE FAST TRACK

The Minister for Enterprise has a pet Bicentennial project: he
wants to build the fastest train in the world, to service marginal
electorates along the fast track between Sydney and Canberra.
Business leaders, lobbyists and backbenchers share his enthusiasm,
but public servants have reservations which the press and the
parliamentary opposition are keen to exploit. Austrain will make
political capital for the government at the Bicentennial election—
but only if it makes the political capital of Canberra on schedule.

Politicians and public servants vie to outwit each other in an
Australian real-life version of *Yes Minister*, raising en route
important questions about the methods and quality of decision-
making in the corridors of power.

THE FAST TRACK
Participants

JOHN BROWN
Minister for Sport, Recreation and Tourism

ALAN CADMAN
Liberal Member for Mitchell, New South Wales

ELAINE DARLING
Labor Member for Lilley, Queensland

JOHN DAWKINS
Minister for Finance

DR MEREDITH EDWARDS
Second Assistant Secretary, Prime Minister's Department

SIR LENOX HEWITT
Former Permanent Secretary, Prime Minister's Department

DAVID HILL
Chief Executive, New South Wales Rail Authority

PATRICK LANIGAN
Former Director-General, Department of Social Security

MICHAEL MACKELLAR
Former Minister for Immigration

PETER PARAMOUR
General Secretary, Administrative and Clerical Officers' Association

ALAN RAMSAY
Political Correspondent, *National Times*

GRAHAM RICHARDSON
Labor Senator, New South Wales; ALP National Executive

PETER SEKULESS
Registered Lobbyist, Canberra

DICK SMITH
Businessman

REG WITHERS
  Former Liberal Senator and Government Leader in the Senate

Recorded at the Institute of Engineers,
Canberra,
August 1985.

THE FAST TRACK

MODERATOR
A new federal government has just been elected, ladies and
gentlemen, on a platform promising enterprise, reconstruction
and great national works—works like the Austrain project, the
fastest train in the world, speeding between Sydney and
Canberra in fifty-nine minutes flat. Australia has the technology
to build the engine, the labour to lay the fast tracks, the
passengers to make it a paying proposition. At least that's what
the election program said. Austrain would create forty thousand
new jobs, foster enterprise, encourage national technology,
service at least six marginal electorates and be a great boost for
the country during the bicentennial year. It would be good for
tourism too, John Brown?

JOHN BROWN
Absolutely. It looks like we were elected on a railway platform,
doesn't it?

MODERATOR
You've done rather well in your last portfolio and you can
expect promotion. What cabinet job do you think you deserve?

BROWN
I'd like to stay with tourism, if I could, particularly as you've
now given me an indication of this super-fast train and I've
always had a great fascination with trains. Australia is a vast
country and we need to get Australians seeing their country.

MODERATOR
You're sitting at home in your electorate in Sydney, a couple of
days after the election, and you get a telephone call from the
Prime Minister. She tells you (laughter) . . . that she's appointing
you Minister for Enterprise. The Department of Enterprise is
crucial to this government's plans for intervention to boost
industry and create new jobs. She's looking foward to your cabinet
submission on the Austrain project. "Get on the train, son," are
her final words. How do you start?

BROWN

Well, there's an old expression in politics, "When the gravy train leaves the station, make sure you have a seat." But first of all I'll need a very expert adviser.

MODERATOR

First of all you've got to get to Canberra. You rush to Sydney Airport first thing Monday morning, but your secretary hasn't had a chance to book, so you have to join the stand-by queue, behind Mr Ramsay who's the political correspondent for the *Australian Herald* and Dick Smith, the Chairman of Smith Industries, whose helicopters have all been grounded by the Department of Aviation. (laughter) I'm afraid, gentlemen, we only have one seat left for this plane. Who's going to get it?

BROWN

(to Ramsay) Would you please give up your seat, so the Minister can get to Canberra and see about this marvellous train, which I'm about to take over in my new Department of Enterprise.

ALAN RAMSAY

Why should I?

BROWN

Ah, well, in the interest of promoting jobs for young Australians I thought that, you being a journalist of some decency, you might just do that.

RAMSAY

I need to get to Canberra just as importantly as you do, because I want to cover the story in Canberra. Why should a politician have preference over the press, or anybody else in the community? Why should a politician seek to bump somebody else off a plane, just because he thinks, or she thinks, that their necessity to get there is more important than anybody else's?

BROWN

Because seventy-five thousand wise electors have elected me, two days ago, to go to Canberra and help run this nation.

MODERATOR

Your appointment as Minister for Enterprise hasn't been announced yet. It will be announced tomorrow. Maybe you could swap him some information. Offer him an exclusive.

RAMSAY

I'd accept that. (laughter)

MODERATOR

Well, you've got rid of Mr Ramsay. Mr Smith, will you give up your seat in the national interest?

DICK SMITH

Yes, I certainly would. I'd offer him the seat instantly because it would be a good way of keeping on side with the Minister—an honest way of keeping on side with him. It wouldn't matter if I went on the next aircraft.

MODERATOR

You've learnt the parable of Androcles and the lion. Do him a little favour, and he might be in a position to reward you handsomely some day?

SMITH

Possibly.

MODERATOR

Smith Industries is hoping to build the supertrain. Does that excite you?

SMITH

Yes it does, even though I know that the track record for railways has not been very good. I believe that there is going to be some very good profits in it.

MODERATOR

Well, you're going to license the technology from the French who have a very fast train running between Paris and Lyon, and you've hired Ben Lexcen and Ralph Sarich to improve it a little, and it will be the fastest train in the world by the time you've finished with it. You've got your submission in, but I'm afraid there's fog at Canberra Airport—as usual at this time of the year—and your plane is delayed, Mr Brown. You haven't been sworn in yet, so there's not a Commonwealth car. Is he likely to get a taxi, Peter Sekuless, at Canberra Airport?

PETER SEKULESS

No, very little chance, very little chance of that at all. They've just installed a new computer in the cab system here, so all the cabs aren't where they are supposed to be, and even if they were, they would all have been taken up by the public service, ferrying public servants to and fro. There certainly wouldn't be enough for the people who help run the country.

MODERATOR
Well, you walk to your office, Mr Brown, and there on your desk is Mr Smith's submission, a joint submission with the New South Wales government to build the supertrain. Have a word with your political assistant, David Hill, about this project.

BROWN
David, there's this proposition about a very fast supertrain. I favour it greatly. Given my abiding interest in tourism, and the need to improve the transport systems in Australia, I'd like to push ahead very strongly with this proposition.

DAVID HILL
Is it going to work?

BROWN
Well, according to the genius from Smith Industries, it will work. I think it's well-known that Smith Industries has a marvellous record of achievement. I'm inclined to believe their figures at this stage, yes.

HILL
Then I'd take a hard line. I'd say it was visionary stuff, I'd say it was the new Sydney Opera House, and I'd be in it.

MODERATOR
You'd be in it? What other advantages does it have?

HILL
Well, you would take a lot of coaches off the road. You would provide a much better service by rail between Canberra and Sydney than you do now. You'd cut the journey times from about four hours to just around an hour I think you said.

MODERATOR
That's right, fifty-nine minutes.

HILL
And you'd take a lot of cars off the road. Good visionary stuff.

And at some stage, incidentally, Australia has to link these capital cities on the eastern seaboard with a good, fast rail system.

MODERATOR

And of course it would relieve the congestion of Sydney Airport, so you wouldn't have to build a second airport in Sydney—the one they're thinking of building in your constituency. (laughter)

BROWN

I think there are secondary benefits that are hard to quantify, for instance all those wonderful towns on the central highlands of New South Wales—Mittagong, Bowral, Berrima, Moss Vale—screaming for new industry. Marvellous scenic places with historical interest.

HILL

And you're making them available to four million voting residents in Sydney.

BROWN

Great. There's another advantage.

HILL

As long as the government goes in with its eyes wide open, about the size of the subsidy you'd need to operate it, then I think you should go for it in a big way.

MODERATOR

Mr Lanigan, what's your view of this supertrain?

PATRICK LANIGAN

Wildly impractical. It'll never get off the ground.

BROWN

It's a train, not a plane, stupid.

LANIGAN

It would cost the earth. You are going to far exceed the benefits. Canberra's a small town and can't support a train like this. This is totally different from running between Paris and Lyon. You just can't do this sort of thing in Australia. What would have to be given up to pay for this train is just beyond contemplation.

MODERATOR

Mr Brown, Mr Lanigan is head of the Department of Enterprise.

Mr Lanigan, meet your Minister. (laughter)

BROWN

Mr Lanigan, congratulations on your appointment. I hope your association with me will raise your level of optimism.

MODERATOR

How are you going to dampen your Minister's enthusiasm for the supertrain?

LANIGAN

Well, we're going to tell him about when Sir Arthur Fadden was the Treasurer, and people would ask him, "Why don't you do this?" and "Why don't you do that?". And he would produce an enormous compendium of all the proposals and he'd say, every one of these is a wonderful idea, but if you put them all together, they'll cost something like one hundred million dollars. It was a lot in those days. But this is still the truth; you just can't do wild impractical things without abandoning things that are important. We're committed to doing countless things in government. If you want to do this, you have to stop doing something else. Or borrow the money and never be able to pay it back.

MODERATOR

How do you answer that, Mr Brown?

BROWN

The name of this department is Enterprise. I'm not prepared to be the head of a department called Enterprise that isn't prepared to take a gamble on Australia's future. Referring me to Arty Fadden is like looking back down a time tunnel. That was the forties and fifties; this is the eighties. We are the most innovative country on the earth and this train is going to be a manifestation to the world of that particular fact.

MODERATOR

Mr Lanigan, you're dining this evening with your old friend, Sir Lenox Hewitt, who is head of the Prime Minister's Department. He asks you how you're getting on with your new Minister.

LANIGAN

Well, Len, I'm really worried. He seems to have a particularly unsophisticated view of what's practical in this situation. How are we going to convince him? We've got to go along with

him, we've got to let him have his little idiosyncrasies, let him
have his dream, but somehow we've got to get him to face up
to reality. Have you got any ideas how we can convince him?

LENOX HEWITT

I don't think I see it quite that way. I've never thought that it
is the responsibility of a permanent head of a department to
frustrate the government, or frustrate the Minister, and I think
the thing we have to remember is that John Brown and his
colleagues were elected on a policy and that policy included the
construction of this rail line. That's our starting point. But who
are they going to blame if it doesn't work? Are they going to
blame themselves, or are they going to blame all the officials
who haven't told them all the details? This is the trouble, you
see. At the moment they are only seeing all the advantages of it.
What about the problem when they've got to pay for it? Are
they going to accept the responsibility then? There's always
been an element of dirt money in our remuneration, and we are
all familiar with being turned upon in times of stress by
Ministers.

LANIGAN

I'm worried about the whole thing. Somehow we've got to get
them to face up to all the implications of this project.

MODERATOR

Any way of delaying it, setting up an interdepartmental
committee . . . ?

LANIGAN

Well that's the obvious way.

MODERATOR

A Royal Commission! (laughter)

LANIGAN

A Royal Commission would be ideal for this, but it's not
sufficiently exciting at the moment to get that. Why don't we
have an interdepartmental committee?

MODERATOR

In fact you had an interdepartmental commission a couple of years ago
when this idea was first mooted. It said that there was no problem with
the engineering, but the costs might spiral alarmingly.

LANIGAN

Well the starting point is weakening. We prepare a report for the Minister. We must put the Minister in the position where if he goes ahead, then some day that report might surface. Then he'll have to carry the can for going ahead in spite of all the facts. I think Len, we could at least do that, couldn't we?

HEWITT

Oh, we must. You should give him a paper as quickly as possible. In fact you'll have it ready, I'm sure, already, because we all watch the policy speeches and prepare ourselves for the election of the alternative government. Push it into him, give it to him, show him the facts, and then the decision is his and his government's, not ours.

MODERATOR

Meredith Edwards, you are a middle-ranking public servant in the Department of Enterprise. You've just qualified for your free American Express card, and you're using it this evening to dine at the same restaurant as Sir Lenox and Mr Lanigan. You overhear snatches of Mr Lanigan's conversation: "Expensive folly . . . let's put a spoke in the wheel." Do you mention this plot to your Minister when you see him next day on another matter?

MEREDITH EDWARDS

If I'm seeing him on another matter, I will have no reason to raise this. I would want to speak first with the secretary, to argue with him as to whether or not we will be supporting the Minister on this particular proposal.

MODERATOR

Whether or not you would be supporting the Minister on this particular proposal! But isn't it your *duty* as a public servant to support your Minister, right or wrong?

EDWARDS

By support, I mean whether we are going to be whole-heartedly behind him.

MODERATOR

Sir Lenox, is a public servant's duty to the government of the day, or to a broader concept of the public interest?

HEWITT

It's to the Crown, not to the Minister. It is to the Crown. The sovereign, of whom for the time being, be it for today or be it for twenty years, is represented by this government.

MODERATOR

So you're in favour of the Westminster system—the anonymous, apolitical public servant?

HEWITT

I think it's the best that we have but it's passed into restful peace and it's no use reviving it.

MODERATOR

You think we've departed from the Westminster system?

HEWITT

Undoubtedly.

MODERATOR

Should we then move to the Washington system, where the incoming government awards people committed to its own programs and policies by appointing them to all the senior jobs in the public service?

HEWITT

I think the sooner, the better. This halfway house we've been residing in over the past ten years or so in Australia is very unsatisfying.

MODERATOR

What do you mean by halfway house?

HEWITT

The situation in which permanent heads and departments are nominally advising Ministers, who yet, because of mutual distrust and suspicion, have their own separate advisers, appointed in their private offices.

MODERATOR

Mr Dawkins, your proposals are taking us down the line to Washington, with more opportunities for Ministers to bring in their own consultants and advisers. Goodbye Sir Humphrey; hello Mr Haldeman, Mr Erhlichman?

JOHN DAWKINS

I just think it's inevitable that there has to be a more

contemporary and more relevant public service which does not
just give anodyne advice. It has to take into account what the
government wants to do and indeed the sooner in the decision-
making process it does, the better. You don't want to have a
situation where the department and the Minister's advisers are at
loggerheads. You do need to ensure that the way the
government thinks and the way in which the government is
moving has to be taken into account by the public service.

MODERATOR

Mr Smith, you're going to have some opposition to Austrain
within the public service—opposition from MPs whose
electorates won't benefit, opposition probably from the
opposition. Would you hire a lobbyist to help you find your
way around Canberra?

SMITH

Yes, I think I would.

MODERATOR

Hire Mr Sekuless.

SMITH

What I would like you to do, Peter, is to find out, first of all,
whether the senior bureaucrats are on side with this railway. I've
heard they're not. Try to find that out, through the normal
means in Canberra, on the grapevine and so forth. And then
possibly, I'd like to be able to talk to the secretary or take down
a submission to him, to see if we can convince the bureaucrats,
because the Minister's onside, but I have a feeling that possibly
the bureaucrats aren't.

SEKULESS

Thank you very much, Mr Smith. This is a wonderful proposal
and in the national interest I propose not to charge you any fee
for this. Because . . .

MODERATOR

You'll take a commission on the profits? (laughter)

SEKULESS

We'll discuss that later, perhaps.

MODERATOR

What can you do for him that he can't do for himself?

SEKULESS

Absolutely nothing, actually. But don't let him in to the secret.

MODERATOR

Are you a registered lobbyist? You're on the register?

SEKULESS

I hope so.

MODERATOR

What does it mean to be a registered lobbyist?

SEKULESS

What it means is that we comply with a funny sort of scheme that the government cooked up a couple of years ago. It means that when I get a new client—in this case, Mr Smith—I fill out a little form and I send it in to the registrar of lobbyists and that, as far as I know, is the last you ever hear of it.

MODERATOR

But it gives you a seal of approval?

SEKULESS

In a way. I haven't noticed it affecting the bank balance very much, but it was said at the time that this licensing would in fact give us a legitimacy that we didn't have before.

MODERATOR

So you now have a legitimacy. With your new legitimacy, try lobbying Senator Richardson.

SEKULESS

Right now, hang on. I have only been taken on to suss out the bureaucratic attitudes. Am I going outside my perimeter?

MODERATOR

No. Mr Smith is concerned that you should have some political supporters. This project is very important to the New South Wales Government. It will be a great boost for the Premier in the bicentennial election.

SEKULESS

Senator Richardson, there's a lot of opposition from the bureaucracy on this as you can imagine, and I think we will have a lot of trouble with Treasury. But they aren't the real problems. I think we'll probably prevail on that OK. But by gee, I'm worried about the greenies. I was at a restaurant the other night, and there was a conversation going on between a couple of permanent heads and they were discussing Austrain and on the next table there was one of those junior public servants, who I happen to know is a closet greenie, and she was all ears. Now what I'm really worried about is that she's going to go back to, you know, the environmentalists and they are going to kick up a big stink about this, and try and knock this thing on the head before it even gets off the ground.

GRAHAM RICHARDSON

I think you're right to worry about the greenies. They get in the way all the time and we've got to go through just on a hundred miles of national park. You are not going to convince the greenies that going through a hundred miles of national park is a good idea. You are just going to have to do it and wear the fact that flak is coming. When we started the proposal we knew we would get the flak, we allowed for the fact that we would get it, we got the overwhelming support of the people, so the greenies are just going to have to wear it.

SEKULESS

OK, Dick Smith is a well-known personality, the Minister's onside, we've got a lot of horsepower with this proposal—do you think we are going to be able to push it through?

RICHARDSON

Well, given that Dick Smith is always hanging around national parks, flying around them or skiing or something, he's pretty au fait with what greenies think, and what they do. I'd send him to go and smooth-talk the greenies—he's pretty good at that sort of thing—and tell them that we'll plant flowers along the tracks or something. (laughter) He'll come up with some proposal. I also suggest you go up to Sydney, see Wran, and perhaps we might get a little bit more parkland proclaimed somewhere else as some sort of compensation.

MODERATOR

A few bits on the Harbour do you think?

RICHARDSON

On the Harbour . . . but there's other places. There are plenty of areas along the coast where we might proclaim a national park and perhaps keep the greenies happy.

MODERATOR

You've obviously got the senator on side. What about the unions? Mr Paramour is General Secretary of the Shunters' and Fettlers' Union, would you have a word with him?

SEKULESS

Absolutely. I'll give him a call. These things are always done over lunch, so we can have lunch one day, Pete?

PETER PARAMOUR

Yes certainly, we can have lunch and discuss it. But we're very sceptical of the plan. Our relationships with the State Rail Authority and with Mr Hill haven't been very good in the past, and we'd want very clear assurances on what this would mean for our members—what conditions he intended to try and undermine. Until such time as we work those matters out fully I think our members wouldn't be very supportive of the proposal at all.

SEKULESS

(to Smith) And I thought the greenies were going to be a problem!

SMITH

Our proposal is a joint State government proposal, and we have to convince obviously the unionists that it is a good thing, that it's going to employ people. I think we should leak to the unions that we're very happy to pay very much over award payments to get this done because it's very important to get it finished. Possibly you could mention that to them?

SEKULESS

Oh, I think that's terrific. (to Paramour) Pete, we realise that your union and your members have got particular problems with this proposal and particularly that you've had a background of problems with the Rail Authority. But let's put that aside for one moment and look at the reality of the situation. I think that probably, if you're prepared at this stage just to stay neutral— we're not asking you to come out and say what a wonderful thing it is but don't sink it, don't undermine it, at this stage—I think the company would probably be prepared to work out very satisfactory industrial arrangements further down the track.

PARAMOUR

We have looked at it in many ways already, and we are concerned about the national interest, and the creation of jobs and we're willing to look at it with an open mind.

MODERATOR

Well you've got the unions coming to the aid of the party, you've got the party on side. What about the opposition? Mr MacKellar, you're leader of the opposition, which is rather more attracted, as far as Bicentennial projects go, to the Turn the Rivers Back project—the idea of turning the northern rivers inland. Instead of flowing out to sea, they would enrich the grazing land of northern New South Wales and Queensland. You've just had a forty-five per cent of the vote. What prospects do you have of convincing the government to go with that scheme?

MICHAEL MACKELLAR

Very little I would say. They didn't put into practice any of their promises that they made before the previous election and they got a bit of a belting during the last election, so they're more wedded to the party policy this time than previously was the case. I know it's a particular interest of the Minister responsible, because he loves playing with trains—he has been doing it for years—and this is something that appeals to him. It's got a lot of publicity value, he will travel a lot, which he likes, and so we'll have a lot of trouble convincing him. Obviously the Prime Minister has a strong commitment to this thing too, so I don't see any real prospects at this stage. Unless we can demonstrate to the public that this is an absolute nonsense.

MODERATOR

Your leader in the upper house is Senator Withers.

MACKELLAR;

Reg, this looks like a typical government scheme and wildly impractical. The word I get around the traps is that there has been a lot of work done on it before and there's an IDC report. If we can get hold of that, it might give us a lot of information which we could use to demonstrate very clearly that it really is a nonsense. Have you got any ideas how we could . . . ?

REG WITHERS

Oh Mike, it's one of those Sydney socialist cons. I mean here we all are, the sons of convicts and the Rum Corps, about to steal the wealth dug up by decent people in Western Australia and Queensland to be spent on weekend jaunts for those harboursiders. It's not on, pal.

MODERATOR

You don't quite have the numbers to throw out the budget this time. (laughter) Mr Lanigan, the frontbench opposition spokesman who is most vociferous in his support of the Turn the Rivers Back scheme is Bill Gladhand MP. He used to be your Minister and you remember years ago, when you first discussed with him the Turn the Rivers Back scheme, you remember vividly his reaction. He said, "That's the most preposterous idea I've ever heard. Who does Malcolm think he is? King Canute? (laughter) Are you going to tell Mr Brown that Bill Gladhand, who's making a speech in parliament at this very moment, saying that he would have implemented the Turn the Rivers Back scheme, is lying?

LANIGAN

No. We don't play politics like that. Once there's a change of government, what's been said beforehand is confidential.

MODERATOR

Even though Bill Gladhand is lying to parliament, saying he was on the verge of implementing the Turn the Rivers Back scheme?

LANIGAN

Lies are relative in politics. I don't think you can worry about that, you've just got to leave the politicians to worry about their relations with the public and their consciences. But what you can do is let the facts come out in reports to the government.

MODERATOR

But the facts aren't going to come out unless you tell Mr Brown that his opposite number is lying.

LANIGAN

No, that's not something that you do. You hold back. You say to yourself you'd love to tell them, but you don't.

MODERATOR

You'd love to tell them but you don't. Is that the correct

approach, Sir Lenox, for public servants? Even if they know
their former Ministers are lying, they keep their peace.

HEWITT

Their responsibility, as I said before, is to the sovereign government of
the day. I don't think it's any part of the duties of the public servant
to be turning up the records of the previous government.

MODERATOR

But if politicians act as hypocrites, why shouldn't public servants
expose them?

HEWITT

No, no. That would be a breach of proper standards of conduct.
What a previous government has written and done is their
business and not that of the successor government.

MODERATOR

Dr Edwards, you've been seconded to the Austrain task force
and as you're going back over the old files you find a
memorandum from Bill Gladhand when he was Minister,
putting in writing what he said so vividly to Mr Lanigan—
"Preposterous idea. I veto it." Do you take the same view as Sir
Lenox, or would you show Mr Brown the memorandum?

EDWARDS

I would take the same view. I'd be intensely interested in the
back files in general and that note in particular, but I would see
it as none of my business to be passing it on.

MODERATOR

None of your business to be passing it on to show that the
former Minister is a hypocrite and lying to parliament.

EDWARDS

That's right.

MODERATOR

David Hill, you're prowling the corridors of the department late
at night as the political assistant to Mr Brown, and you go
through a few files and you find this memorandum. Will you
show it to the Minister?

HILL

Yes I would.

MODERATOR

What do you do with it, Minister? How can you make political capital out of it?

BROWN

Well, fish swim and politicians tend to be political, and I guess, given an opportunity in the debate, I'd drop this right on Mr Gladhand.

MODERATOR

Elaine Darling is one of your backbenchers. Perhaps she'll give you an opportunity by asking you a question in parliament?

BROWN

Dorothy Dix is often a very useful tool in politics, yes.

MODERATOR

Ask Elaine Darling to play Dorothy Dix.

BROWN

Elaine, I've got a bit of information on Bill Gladhand and I wonder if you would be so kind as to ask me a question in the parliament so the hypocrisy of the man can be revealed?

ELAINE DARLING

John, you may be aware from questions like this put to me before, that I don't like to ask questions that tip the bucket on someone. I'm running on a line of credibility in my electorate and therefore I don't ask a question like that. Austrain is an excellent project, when we think of being stuck in that rotten airport in Canberra. I think that we should turn the spotlight onto our superb project, not play dirty tricks on the opposition.

BROWN

Very high flying and laudable sentiments, but the political realities are that we have to get this through the senate and if that involves turning an argument back against the opposition so that we can achieve our ends, which we believe to be in the national interest, well, that's the way we play politics, Elaine. I think the electors of your electorate would be more than pleased to see you acting your role as a politician as well as the local statesman.

MODERATOR

Join in this conversation, Senator Richardson.

RICHARDSON

Look, Elaine, this is a pretty fair opportunity for you to get a run for yourself. Your seat has not always been safe, we don't know what will happen in a few years' time. If you really want some good publicity this is not a bad time to do it. If you don't want to do it I can find twenty volunteers in the next five minutes who would love to, because they'd get a front page and they've never been on a front page, and they'd love it. So for God's sake, get off your high horse and ask the question.

DARLING

Well, I'd like to challenge that. I know that some of you wheelers and dealers see this as party wisdom, but I'd point out that I have been holding this seat of mine on the credibility line for three terms running—the first time we've held it that long—and you have to learn, I think, to count the numbers.

RICHARDSON

Oh we will, but given that you're one of those in the forefront for future Ministerial position, and given that you'll be looking around for support I'd have thought that if you did this you'd be able to expect some support from quarters where perhaps you would not have got it before. So it might not be a bad opportunity on two fronts for you.

DARLING

You are kidding. (laughter)

RICHARDSON

I never kid on matters like that, Elaine . . . (loud laughter)

MODERATOR

While Elaine Darling is running on the credibility line, you've got to get your cabinet submission together.

BROWN

. . . I want that train running on a railway line.

MODERATOR

Mr Lanigan, how are you going to write this first draft?

LANIGAN

We've got problems, haven't we? Because if the objective evidence is that this is going to cost far more than it will be worth, if the evidence is that it will never pay, if the reasonable assumption is that with all this vast expenditure the government is going to have a millstone round its neck in a few years, are we really serving the Minister if we just pander to his short-term political advantage by saying this is a good thing?

MODERATOR

So you put in all the pros and all the cons.

LANIGAN

Indeed.

MODERATOR

There are an awful lot of cons in Mr Lanigan's first draft, Minister. Are you going to tidy it up?

BROWN

I don't necessarily accept the advice of my department. I always believe in going to the practitioners in an industry. I must say, the upper echelon of my department are very, very efficient people and while their advice is often times given in the most honest and sincere fashion, it often is not based on proper knowledge of how industry works. So I'd be seeking counter-advice from Mr Smith.

SMITH

I think your bureaucratic heads are being a little concrete-minded on this matter. I would like to get the top people from my company to come down and talk to you and the heads of your department to explain the feasibility . . . to explain that it's going to be a very profitable railway line.

MODERATOR

You've got Mr Lanigan's cabinet submission. Are you going to change it to reflect the weight of the argument you've heard from Mr Smith?

BROWN

Of course.

MODERATOR

Your draft comes back with all sorts of instructions from the Minister, which you think are going to produce a misleading cabinet submission. He wants you to overstate the benefits and understate the costs. What do you do?

LANIGAN

Well I've got some problems really because under these new rules they're planning to have less security for permanent heads and I'm tired of worrying about my own status now. On the one hand if I go along with the Minister he's not going to thank me if this blows up in a couple of years' time; on the other hand, there's going to be the Finance Department knocking the proposal. If our proposal doesn't face up to reality the Minister's credibility is going to fail. What I think I'd have to do is to write him a very careful submission, but I won't push it too far because he's going to become resentful.

MODERATOR

Mr Dawkins, you're the Treasurer. How does it come down for you?

DAWKINS

We've had to deal with some fairly extravagant proposals from John in the past. We had to put them under the microscope fairly closely. I have to acknowledge the fact that I was on the platform applauding the leader when she made this commitment to build this railway line, but I also have to say that we have the next election to contend with and if this thing becomes an albatross we won't be thanking ourselves for embarking on something that doesn't work. The whole basis of the submission is on the assumption that fifty per cent of the people that now travel by plane will travel on this railway line. Now I just think that is an assumption which has no basis, and what we want to do is contest that in the first instance. The other claim that's made is that it is going to develop Berrima and the towns on the route, but if the train has to stop, then the duration of the trip is going to be doubled or trebled even, so that is obviously a fanciful proposal. So there are a number of problems with this particular submission, and we've got to protect the Prime Minister.

MODERATOR

Mr Ramsay, as political correspondent of the *Australian Herald* can you get hold of cabinet submissions?

RAMSAY

No. But I've heard a bit about this round the Parliament House, journalists keep talking about it, and they feed off one another, so we know that there is a submission on this proposal going on. We also know there is criticism from the public service. I'd first probably try and get in touch with Minister Brown, because he got my seat on the plane. (laughter)

MODERATOR

Call in the favour.

RAMSAY

I gave you my seat on the plane John, and you promised sometime in the future you'd pay me back with a story. What can you tell me about this business that's going on that Dick Smith's put up? I know he's a big supporter of the party, he kicked in the can for the election campaign, so you know what's going on here.

BROWN

Well, what's going on here Alan is a proposition that I favour as the Minister for Enterprise. It's certainly in line with how we view Australia's future, particularly in terms of mass transportation.

MODERATOR

Mr Ramsay, you're dining rather late this evening at Khemlani's, the fashionable Canberra restaurant, (laughter) and it's packed, but they find you a table. It's just been vacated by Mr Brown. He pats you on the back as he goes out—the way cabinet Ministers do to journalists—and as you take the seat something crinkles underneath you. It's a large brown envelope marked "Department of Enterprise—Cabinet Submissions". What do you do?

RAMSAY

I pick it up and I put it in my pocket and I say nothing.

MODERATOR

You can see Mr Brown through the glass of the restaurant window signalling to his Commonwealth car driver. You've just got time to rush out and give it back to him.

RAMSAY

No, I don't. I've had a discussion with him earlier in the day; he hasn't given me much joy. I hadn't expected much mind you, but he hasn't given me much. I still am a bit resentful about the fact that I'd given up my seat originally and I still haven't got much for it. Here's an opportunity perhaps to get a story. At least I'll look at it before I give it back.

MODERATOR
It's sealed.

RAMSAY
Yes, that's what I mean. I'll open it.

MODERATOR
You steam it open and there is a paper headed: "Bicentennial Great Works Project. Cabinet Submission on Austrain. Cabinet in Confidence." Going to read any further?

RAMSAY
Yes I am. I'm going to read the lot.

MODERATOR
What's going to happen to him, Sir Lenox, if he not only reads it, but publishes it?

HEWITT
He will get a higher salary, and public acclaim. (laughter)

MODERATOR
Unfortunately these cabinet submissions from Mr Brown and from Mr Dawkins are rather boring, particularly those from Mr Dawkins because there are a lot of facts and figures. But there is one line in his submission that captures your eye. "We're not satisfied," says the Treasury, "that all safety tests can be completed on Austrain before its bicentennial inauguration." Is that a factor that you want to play up?

RAMSAY
Well it's interesting, but what is more interesting quite clearly, is the very strong public service opposition to this whole proposal.

MODERATOR
In your research into fast trains, you read that the Paris to Lyon fast railway was so successful that the lucrative airline that used to fly the route had to close down. The proprietor of the *Australian Herald*, Sir Rupert Fairpacker, happens to own one of the airlines that flies between Sydney and Canberra. Does that

make you play up the doubts about Austrain's safety?

RAMSAY

Oh yes, I see what you mean. It's in the management's interest
in fact to knock it, because it competes with their own airline.
This story is going to carry itself. Quite clearly it's also going to
be in the management's interest, so they are going to be as
interested in publishing it as I am going to be in writing it.

MODERATOR

In your story criticising Austrain, would you mention the fact
that your newspaper had a conflict of interest?

RAMSAY

I think the story would make it clear. The fact that it was
going to damage the airline would become clear in the story.

MODERATOR

There would be no need to spell out the fact that the proprietor
of the *Australian Herald* owns an airline?

RAMSAY

Exactly.

MODERATOR

Why not?

RAMSAY

Because we know that everybody else is going to make this
known. Our publisher is a very well-known figure, everybody
knows that he owns the airline. You can't hide the fact.

MODERATOR

Is that good enough reason, Mr Dawkins, for the press not
revealing conflicts of interest in editorials and stories like this?

DAWKINS

It's not always the case, with the highly centralised media as we
have, for the proprietors to be as candid as they might be.

MODERATOR

Surprisingly, no editorial critical of Austrain appears in the
Australian Herald. Who should appear in Canberra but Sir
Rupert. He's off to play a game of mixed doubles with the
Prime Minister (laughter) and he calls you, John Brown. Can he
see you for breakfast?

BROWN
Of course.

MODERATOR
You were going to give a breakfast address to the Amateur
Train Spotters' Association, but you will cut it short in order to
see Sir Rupert?

BROWN
Oh yes. I think it's fair to say that if a newspaper proprietor
wanted to see a Minister, no matter which government was in
power, he wouldn't have too much difficulty.

MODERATOR
He says, "Mr Brown, you're obviously a man of great
vision. You're a man who's supported sport, particularly the sport
of skiing, and your Austrain project particularly appeals to me.
I'd like you to build a branch line to the snowfields up Mount
Ainslie, just out of Cooma." Are you going to support the idea?

BROWN
Well, funnily enough the snowfields happen to be a very
important industry. Because of my abiding interest in sport, and
my abiding interest in leisure industries and the employment
they create, of course I'd be prima facie attracted to that
proposition.

MODERATOR
"And you'll come and lay the foundation stone at my luxury ski
lodge at Mount Ainslie next month?" (laughter)

BROWN
I'd consider that.

MODERATOR
Three days before the vital cabinet meeting, a much loved
government backbencher dies. He'd held the seat of Steedman
in the outer Canberra suburbs, and he died from stress brought
on by the long sitting hours in Parliament House. The by-
election is not going to be easy for the government — he
scraped in last time with a strong personal vote. But Austrain
is very popular in his electorate, Senator Richardson. There's
nothing Canberra people seem to like more than getting out of
it.

RICHARDSON

The by-election is obviously going to do Austrain a hell of a lot of good in cabinet. Now that we have a by-election and the people are desperate to have an Austrain, that's strengthened John Brown. He's a good friend of mine, and I'm happy about that.

MODERATOR

Mr Dawkins, it looks as though you are going to have a tough time in cabinet.

DAWKINS

Yes, I think that's right. We've got a Prime Ministerial commitment, we've got a by-election where this could be a key issue, we've got to find a way of kind of saying that we are very enthusiastic about this particular project, at least until such time as the by-election is out of the way.

MODERATOR

You fight a valiant battle in cabinet, but the numbers are against you. Your opposition to Austrain doesn't succeed, and cabinet decides to go ahead. You've got a press conference later in the day. Mr Ramsay, what questions do you have for the Treasurer?

RAMSAY

Treasurer, quite clearly you're getting a lot of opposition from your own departmental advisers that this is a waste of money and a very costly enterprise. How do you publicly respond to that?

DAWKINS

The government made a decision, it was an election commitment, and we are very enthusiastic about proceeding with the project.

MODERATOR

Are you personally very enthusiastic, Mr Dawkins?

DAWKINS

No.

MODERATOR

Did you vote against it in cabinet?

DAWKINS

Yes. I think that unless we're prepared to cut the road program in half in order to pay for this scheme, then I think we're going to be in a great deal of trouble coming up to the next election because after all . . .

MODERATOR

Are you really going to attack a decision that your government has just made?

DAWKINS

No, of course not.

MODERATOR

But you just have, you've just given the media today's headlines.

RAMSAY

I was interested in whether he was talking to the press when he was saying "no", or whether he was talking to you.

MODERATOR

Ah—he was talking to me. If the press had asked you those questions, would you have answered the same way?

DAWKINS

No, of course not. (laughter)

MODERATOR

How would you have answered if the press had asked you "Are you personally opposed to it? Did you vote against it?"

DAWKINS

I would have said that the arguments that I put forward in the cabinet and how I lodged my vote in the cabinet is my business, and as far as I'm concerned the government has made the decision which I fully support.

MODERATOR

But you don't fully support it. (laughter)

DAWKINS

Senator Withers says that consistency in a politician is a sign of a small mind, and that's advice which he himself has taken to heart on many occasions.

MODERATOR

So you, having a large mind, tell the press that you're fully in support of the project—but you don't support it. Privately

you've argued very strongly against it in cabinet. Obviously
cabinet is the place where the vital decisions are made. Why
shouldn't it be open to the press? Why should we have this
farce of Ministers violently opposing something in cabinet one
day and then telling the press they support it the next?

MACKELLAR

I think it's important that governments do make decisions rather
than shilly-shallying around, and that it be a government
decision as such.

MODERATOR

You agree with Sir Humphrey Appleby that open government is
a contradiction in terms. You can be open, or you can have
government.

MACKELLAR

I do think that cabinet solidarity is important under our system
of government.

MODERATOR

Why should cabinet be closed, Sir Lenox. Isn't that the place
where the real decisions are made?

HEWITT

Is is the place where decisions are made, but they are made in
the star chamber, not in public.

MODERATOR

But why should they be made in the star chamber? Wouldn't
they be made better if they were made in public?

HEWITT

That would be a very novel proposal, and a very interesting
one.

RAMSAY

The problem with it is that you'd end up with two cabinets.
You'd have a secret cabinet where you rowed and made the
decisions, and then you would go into an open cabinet and
make the decision in public. That in fact tends to happen with
both the major political parties in this country at their annual
conferences or their federal conferences. When they're held in
secrecy you row in secret; now you row in private and agree in
public.

MODERATOR

The Austrain project has been approved by cabinet. You've got your green light, and the first thing you have to consider is *which* of the fast trains you should go for. The Paris–Lyon train or perhaps the British train that runs from London to Bristol. Mr Lanigan, it's rather important that the Minister should travel to Paris and London to see for himself—with his departmental head, of course.

LANIGAN

I think it's terribly important. (laughter)

BROWN

Does Alan Ramsay think it's a good idea?

MODERATOR

Alan Ramsay thinks it's a wonderful idea because he gets to go with you.

BROWN

Well, maybe that puts a different aspect on it . . .

MODERATOR

I see from the rules that govern these trips that you're entitled to take with you "a nominee with whom you have established a *bona fide* domestic relationship". Would that include your wife?

BROWN

My wife of twenty-four years is also the mother of my four children. Of course, I have very old-fashioned views about bona fide relationships. Yes.

MODERATOR

Your wife is very keen to go. She runs a boutique in Sydney called "The Micturating Marsupial" (laughter) and she would very much like to see the new Paris fashions, and do some buying for the boutique. Is that all right?

BROWN

Why not?

MODERATOR

So you have a very productive trip, Mr Brown. You travel the railroad between Paris and Lyon, you work out a draft agreement with the French Minister of Transport, you come back via the Grand Canyon where you see some of the earth moving equipment that the Ausrail Corporation are using, then you catch a seminar in Honolulu—"Life on the Fast Track: the future of the supertrain." Mr Ramsay is at the airport to interview you when you return.

RAMSAY

Do you think the expense of the trip was justified in going over to look at this favourite project of yours, Minister?

BROWN

As in all the three trips that I have taken for this government, yes, I think I have come back with the goods on every occasion.

RAMSAY

But the cost of this trip for four weeks has been sixty-four thousand dollars. You've travelled first class everywhere, you've stayed in five-hundred-dollar-a-night hotel rooms. Looks to ordinary people like you have had a damned good time. Sixty-seven thousand dollars for your four weeks surely is a bit much?

BROWN

Well I could have done it more cheaply I guess. I could have put a haversack on my back, or ridden a bike.

RAMSAY

You think sixty-seven thousand dollars for four weeks overseas is a reasonable amount of money, particularly public money, not your money?

MODERATOR

But countries that are much poorer than Australia send their Ministers first class—to stay in five-star hotels and drive Mercedes.

RAMSAY

That's why they are poor. (laughter)

MODERATOR

Minister, wouldn't it be better for you to show the government's new austerity program in action by travelling economy, staying in two-star hotels, hiring cheap rent-a-cars?

BROWN

Is that the way the management of the ABC travel, or large

business corporations, or journalists and public servants travelling abroad? If that was the general rule, I'm sure that most politicians would be most happy to accede.

MODERATOR

The French Transport Minister with whom you negotiated the draft contract, is so keen to seal the agreement that he pays you a return visit. There's a reception for him in Canberra the night before he's due to sign the deal. You're there, David Hill, talking animatedly to him, and he tells you that it's the custom in his country for foreign politicians who visit without consorts, to be provided with ladies from Madame Claude's. He's staying in room 511 of the Lakeside Hotel, and he wonders whether a suitable lady might visit him there at about eleven-thirty pm. Can you arrange that?

HILL

No way.

MODERATOR

Why not? Because you can't get anything in Canberra after eleven o'clock? (laughter)

HILL

I don't know whether it's the done thing in Canberra; I really wouldn't know how to go about it. I would probably ask Senator Richardson what the conventions are in Canberra. Politicians are far more adept at this sort of thing.

MODERATOR

Ask Senator Richardson.

HILL

Senator Richardson, I have just been proposed to by the head of the SNCF Railways. He wants a woman. Over to you.

RICHARDSON

If the French consul wants a woman, he'll have to find one himself. We don't do that sort of thing here. We don't procure for foreign legations.

MODERATOR

But you don't want to miss the licensing of the agreement being signed tomorrow. You've got to keep the French Minister of Transport sweet.

RICHARDSON

Oh, I think most people here, whether they would be advisers
to a Minister or a Minister or public servant, wouldn't get into
that sort of thing.

MODERATOR

Well, you go so far as to help him by looking up the yellow
pages of the Canberra phone book, and sure enough there is an
escort agency called "the Transport of Delight". (laughter)
"Twenty-four hours visiting service", with an address out in
Steedman. He calls the agency, and the woman who turns up at
Room 511 is Lavinia Upright, a legal assistant in the Crown
Solicitor's office (laughter) working part-time as an escort. Mr
Paramour, you're her union representative and she rings you the
next morning just to check that her new part-time job is in
order. Is it?

PARAMOUR

No it's not, because we wouldn't be in favour in the current
economic climate of her having a second job. We'd see it, first
of all, as taking away job opportunities from other individuals.
(laughter)

MODERATOR

If she were in your department, Mr Lanigan, would it be
improper for her to have this second job?

LANIGAN

It would be improper if we knew about it. The chances are, we
wouldn't know about it.

MODERATOR

Ladies and gentlemen, the remuneration tribunal, which sets
public service salaries, has just reported. It reports that salaries at
the top of the public service lag very far behind private
enterprise, and it's time for parity. Departmental heads should
receive a salary equivalent to managers in big business—about
$130,000 a year. The chairmen of the Ausrail Corporation and
of Qantas should receive a salary equivalent to the chief
executive of other big transport organisations—about $140,000;
the general manager of the Commonwealth Bank should receive
what other banking general managers receive—$150,000; the
general manager of the ABC should get what other managers of

communication networks get, which is believed to be about $250,000, although Mr Whitehead will probably settle for less. (laughter)

DAWKINS

I would say this is a fine recommendation—but not now.

MODERATOR

When?

DAWKINS

There are clearly serious problems here. The public sector is being plundered by the private sector for what are essentially very bright people, very capable people. There has been a very huge brain and capability drain from the public sector. So at some stage, governments are going to have to confront the issue. We have to at some stage bring about some greater equality between the public sector and the private sector.

MODERATOR

What's the opposition's view, Mr MacKellar?

MACKELLAR

I think the essential difference between the public service and private industry is that public servants have permanency, and that puts them in a very different category to private industry.

MODERATOR

Sir Lenox, should public servants get equivalent to their opposite numbers in big business?

HEWITT

Yes, without doubt. The remuneration tribunal has never done the job for which it was appointed.

MODERATOR

It has now.

HEWITT

Yes, for the first time. It was established to take the odium off the shoulders of parliamentarians, grasping at this problem. It was conceived twenty or more years ago. And the problem is even greater today than what it was then. It is, with the utmost respect, nonsense to talk about permanency in the civil service. I, having been disposed of twice by Prime Ministers, can assure you, Mr MacKellar, that there is no such thing as permanency for permanent heads.

MODERATOR

Come, come, Sir Lenox, you would do the job that you've done for the basic wage, wouldn't you? It's the *power* and the *pleasure* and the *privilege* of public service that attracts you.

HEWITT

Not the power, no. The sense of vocation that I suppose calls people at times to a career, does exist for a few. But I did not continue as long as I could have continued.

MODERATOR

What's the *Australian Herald* going to say about this, Mr Ramsay?

RAMSAY

The *Australian Herald* would probably agree with most of what's been said. The private sector has been bleeding the public service of all the good people. The salaries are about half the level, but it's a political decision, you see . . .

MODERATOR

A political decision, Senator Richardson. You're a member of cabinet, how are you going to vote on this?

RICHARDSON

I will try to find a scheme to phase in the increases . . . over a period of time because I think it's acknowledged generally we've got to do it. And since we've got to make a start sooner or later, it may as well be sooner.

MODERATOR

Austrain is going ahead. The project, Elaine Darling, is very important to your electorate, because you're the member for Gorton, which is about halfway between Canberra and Sydney. And your constituents are very keen that you should get a whistle stop at Gorton Station. Unfortunately, that will add about ten minutes to the trip between Sydney and Canberra. How would you go about convincing the Minister that the train ought to make the stop?

DARLING

First of all I would look at my constituency and see what

reasons there would be for the train to stop at Gorton.

MODERATOR

Unfortunately, the Ausrail Corporation vetoes the idea, and the editor of your local paper, the *Gorton Advertiser*, is very angry about your failure to convince them. He writes an editorial which says, "What's the point of electing people to this reptile pit of carpetbagging and corruption? It would be an act of good citizenship to dynamite the VIP carriage of freeloading MPs as Austrain crosses Gorton Gorge." What are you going to do about that editorial?

DARLING

If the editor was a reasonable person . . .

MODERATOR

The editor, Eric Bombast, is by no means reasonable. He's so pleased with his editorial that he runs it again the following week. The Attorney-General is extremely angry—he points out that it's a contempt of parliament, encouraging the mass murder of MPs. Do you think, Mr Cadman, you ought to punish Bombast for contempt?

ALAN CADMAN

The parliament should, every now and then, when the most intemperate and vicious attacks are made on MPs, be prepared to stick up for their rights.

MODERATOR

There is a big debate in the house, a joint sitting that happens to occur during the experimental period for television. Are you in favour of television proceedings in parliament, Senator Richardson?

RICHARDSON

No.

MODERATOR

Why not?

RICHARDSON

I worry that people will never understand what goes on in Parliament if you have television recording its proceedings. It's going to be very hard to convince the public that we're out there on committees. Half of them think we're at the bar.

MODERATOR

The Fairpacker television network has just abandoned televising cricket, and it needs some Australian content. (laughter) It wants to put *Highlights of Today's Play in Parliament* on every evening in place of the late movie, with a commentary by Kate Fitzpatrick and George Negus. Is this going to be helpful in bringing parliament to the people? Save all those schoolkids catching the train to Canberra to see their representatives at work?

RICHARDSON

If they are to do that, then I hope they are going to be showing question time, where at least all of the Greats and the Gods are present and doing battle, rather than some of the quieter moments that we find in the Pig Meat Eradication Bill or something. You've got to be a bit choosy and careful about what you show.

MODERATOR

Senator Withers, would you be happy for parliament to be televised?

WITHERS

Yes. Our ancestors opposed the print media one hundred and fifty years ago, and I don't think it's done parliament much harm. It hasn't done it much good, and in fact, I'd rather have the viewers see it direct, than get it second-hand from a print journalist. But question time is futile; it's not questions without notice, it's questions without answers. They should see us warts and all.

MODERATOR

You don't mind them taking a commercial break, during your speeches. (laughter)

WITHERS

No, no.

MODERATOR

The Fairpacker television network is very keen to take commercial breaks. In fact they are offering a large sum of money—one million dollars—for exclusive rights to televise parliament. Does that appeal to you?

DAWKINS

It might be OK if the exclusive rights were held by the ABC. I'd look with a little jaundice on giving it to a major commercial operator.

MODERATOR

The ABC doesn't have the money to make a bid, Mr Treasurer.

DAWKINS

Oh, we could perhaps talk about that. (laughter)

MODERATOR

Let's go back to the Austrain project. The secret of this train's speed is the metal coating used on its wheels. It's a compound, and part of it is cryptonite, a metal which has been discovered recently in South Africa and which is only mined in South Africa. It comes from a mine that falls below international standards in treatment of black labour. Could this be a problem for you, Mr MacKellar, if you were the Minister for Enterprise?

MACKELLAR

It could be a problem, depending on the government's policies in relation to importing goods from South Africa.

MODERATOR

There has not yet been a trade embargo applied to South Africa and in fact the cryptonite that the Ausrail Corporation is importing comes from France. The French railways have bought it from South Africa, they've done a bit of reprocessing at Cherbourg, and the cryptonite is at this moment on the SS *Carte Blanche* steaming towards Sydney. Unfortunately the waterside workers have taken a more aggressive view than the government and have put a ban on all South African originated goods.

MACKELLAR

This metal is required, and there is no government policy that prevents us acquiring it. We should acquire it.

MODERATOR

You get a question in parliament—"Are there any South African companies directly involved in the Austrain project?"

MACKELLAR

If they are not directly involved, the answer is "No".

MODERATOR

Dr Edwards, you're a member of the Austrain taskforce. You rather support the waterside workers' action in not unloading any goods which originated in South Africa. You are aware that the cryptonite on board the SS *Carte Blanche* is in fact originally from South Africa, even though it had been bought by the French government railways and reprocessed there. Would you feel it necessary to leak that fact to the press?

EDWARDS

No. I would find a conflict between my personal views and my professional interests. But I would not let my personal views override. On principle, I wouldn't do it. I would also not do it because I might be found out.

MODERATOR

Put your personal view aside. Do you think that's easy to do?

EDWARDS

No. It's not easy. No.

MODERATOR

You're having a drink with Mr Paramour, the secretary of the Waterside Workers' Federation. He asks you about the Austrain project, and whether there are any South African goods involved. What do you say?

EDWARDS

(long pause) It might depend on how much I've had to drink. (laughter)

MODERATOR

You've had a very small martini.

EDWARDS

I'm not prone to telling untruths and if at the time I could think of a white lie, I would use it. I would try . . .

MODERATOR

A white lie about South Africa? (laughter)

EDWARDS

About the origin of the component.

MODERATOR

You would say it came from France.

EDWARDS

If I could tell it that way and I didn't feel that it was a blatant lie, I would do it that way.

MODERATOR

Suppose that the question to the Minister had been, "Are there any South African originated goods involved in the Austrain project?" and the Minister had said "No" or "Not to my knowledge". If he'd lied to Parliament, would that change it for you?

EDWARDS

I think in a sense it would make it easier. I would feel an obligation.

MODERATOR

An obligation to do what?

EDWARDS

Not to disclose the truth. I would feel the need to protect my Minister.

MODERATOR

The need to protect your Minister who has lied to parliament. Shouldn't you protect the people from the Minister's lies?

EDWARDS

If I were to do that I would find another mechanism for doing it.

MODERATOR

You could tell Mr Ramsay, so he could tell the world that a Minister had lied.

EDWARDS

I could do that, but I would think there were other mechanisms by which the truth needs to come out. That's what I would explore.

MODERATOR

Who would you explore them with?

EDWARDS

I would go to my head of department.

MODERATOR

Go to Mr Lanigan.

EDWARDS

I find myself in a difficult position, Secretary. I have been approached by the media and approached by the union movement. They are onto the scent of the fact that our Minister has lied to parliament on this issue. What do you advise me to do?

LANIGAN

Well, that's none of our business. We must maintain confidentiality. I don't know that we can do anything other than say it is important in government that any Minister should have a confidential source of permanent advice based on continuity of experience. We destroy that if the Minister can't rely on us to be loyal to him.

MODERATOR

And so you as a public servant stand silently by, while the Minister lies to parliament.

EDWARDS

It's his responsibility.

MODERATOR

That's his responsibility, not yours? Sir Lenox, is this the right approach for a public servant to take or are there times, in extremis, where a public servant should speak out and expose the Minister?

HEWITT

The first part of your question I would answer by saying it's dreadfully wrong. But the answer is not to do as you have said in the second part and expose the Minister. The permanent head in these circumstances has an immediate responsibility to give to his Minister a draft statement to make in parliament correcting the error that he previously made. And indeed he has a greater responsibility in the first place to have drafted the correct answer to the parliament question. This is not altogether a hypothetical question. It has happened in Australia in the past. I believe myself that the disappearance of one Prime Minister arose from an error of judgement caused by being hounded to death by worry. The origins of that lay in an incorrect answer to the parliament, which his official did not advise him to correct.

MODERATOR

Mr Dawkins, the costs of the project are spiralling alarmingly. The trains are being manufactured on time by Mr Smith, but the cost of laying the tracks has almost doubled.

DAWKINS

I suspect that we are so far committed to it that we just have to come clean and say that the project is now costing a lot more than we thought and we're terribly sorry but that means that certain other proposals which we had will be deferred and taxes will have to go up.

MODERATOR

The Prime Minister had hoped to hold a "Summit of National Reconstruction" to consider other great works just before the bicentennial elections. Now there won't be the money for other projects.

DAWKINS

I assume there is still eighty-five per cent of people who are in favour of this train.

MODERATOR

No, it's dropped to forty-five per cent.

DAWKINS

Along with government standing, no doubt. I would say, "Well, I told you so."

MODERATOR

There is a select committee of parliament that is having some public servants before it to discuss the increasing expenditure. Mr Lanigan, as secretary of the department, is available for examination. What questions are you going to ask him, Mr Cadman?

CADMAN

What was the original advice to the Minister of this project?

LANIGAN

That would be privileged. You wouldn't be entitled to have that.

MODERATOR

Can you ask the question, Senator Withers, in a way that will extract some more information?

WITHERS

No, you can't go beyond Mr Lanigan's answer.

MODERATOR

Ladies and gentlemen, the bicentennial election is coming soon. It will be a very interesting election, for this reason: the High Court, in the first test case under the new Australian Bill of Rights, has struck down that old 1924 law that requires compulsory voting. The Chief Justice said the "right to vote" implies the right not to vote and the "right to travel freely" implies the right not to be forced to the polling stations. Mr Richardson, what is this going to mean for your party organisation?

RICHARDSON

A great deal of difficulty. Traditionally, when one looks at election results, Labor voters have been worse at turning out than conservative voters. Therefore we have to reorient the last ninety years of our campaign techniques, to getting them out to vote on the day.

MODERATOR

You will have to start kissing babies.

RICHARDSON

It's not a matter of kissing babies, it's a matter of rounding bodies up. To round bodies up we are going to have to do more research to make sure we can identify Labor Party voters. We are going to have doorknocking teams on the day to get out there and really drag them to the polls. That's going to have to be our new role.

MODERATOR

Do you support the High Court's decision, Mr MacKellar?

MACKELLAR

Certainly I support the High Court's decision.

MODERATOR

You wouldn't pass amending legislation to override the Bill of Rights if you got back in the next election?

MACKELLAR
I think the right to not attend and not to vote is obviously a liberal philosophy.

MODERATOR
It's a liberal philosophy—because it will help the Liberal Party?

MACKELLAR
I'm talking about small-l liberal philosophy. But I think that Senator Richardson has given us a very frank explanation as to why the Labor Party is against non-compulsory voting.

MODERATOR
Mr Dawkins, do you think we ought to conscript people to go to the polls?

DAWKINS
Well it's not quite as absolute as that. If they are prepared to pay the very trivial fine for not turning up, if they're in fact caught up with, then I think it's OK.

MODERATOR
But it is an invasion of civil liberties, isn't it?

DAWKINS
I'm not sure about that. I think the obligation to participate in the process of choosing a government can hardly be described as conscription.

MODERATOR
Senator Richardson, it's going to mean a great deal of administrative effort for your party in this coming election. You are going to need quite a lot of money, I suppose.

RICHARDSON
No doubt.

MODERATOR
See if Mr Smith will make a campaign donation.

RICHARDSON
Dick, you did the right thing last time, and I know you've got some problems with the train, but really, if you don't elect us it will never get built. You're too far in to get out, far too far. That being the case, how about giving us some sort of reasonable donation to make sure that, whatever weaknesses it has, we will at least get Austrain finished?

SMITH

Well, I'd have to put that to my board and let them look at that, but the most likely thing we'd do would be to make an equal donation to each of the political parties.

RICHARDSON

If all businesses did that, my party would be very happy! (laughter)

MODERATOR

Sir Rupert Fairpacker is in Canberra again, to play a game of singles with the Prime Minister. You've noticed some antigovernment editorials in his papers recently, John Brown. Does that concern you?

BROWN

Not particularly.

MODERATOR

He's a bit worried about your failure to complete the Austrain branch line from Canberra to Mount Ainslie. Do you apologise?

BROWN

Not in the least.

MODERATOR

He plays tennis with the Prime Minister and loses. So he comes to see you, Mr MacKellar. He says, "Look, Austrain from Sydney to Canberra and up to Mount Ainslie is all very well. But now the Prime Minister is talking about running it on to Melbourne in time for the Victorian elections, and on to South Australia on the new standard gauge to help Mr Bannon. If God had meant us to travel everywhere by train, he wouldn't have given us the Boeing 737." (laughter) Are you sympathetic to Sir Rupert's views?

MACKELLAR

As leader of the opposition, yes I am. I've campaigned on the slogan "No More Austrains". We'd be extremely sceptical about these new proposals.

MODERATOR

With an election coming up, would you ask Sir Rupert for a donation?

MACKELLAR:

In the Liberal Party matters of money are not handled by

politicians, they're handled by the party organisation. So I wouldn't be involved at any stage in soliciting donations. Sir Robert Menzies layed it down very clearly that no member of parliament was allowed to touch money. I'd give Sir Rupert the post office box number of the party organisation, and say, "Send it off." (laughter)

MODERATOR

Ladies and gentlemen, ASIO has completed its move from Melbourne to Canberra. The city is full of men in trench coats enquiring into the private lives of diplomats and public figures. ASIO's most productive enterprise has been to establish the Transport of Delight, that visiting escort agency out in Steedman. It's been very popular among the embassies since the French Transport Minister recommended its services. (laughter) You're acting Prime Minister, John Dawkins, when the head of ASIO tells you that Barry Borgia MP, the Minister for Ethnic Affairs and Women's Rights, uses the Transport of Delight regularly. What do you do with that information?

DAWKINS

That depends. I would ask whether there is a security issue involved.

MODERATOR

There is, to this extent; Barry has a small sexual bent. He likes to dress up in Nazi uniform and impersonate the Prime Minister.

WITHERS

That's well understandable. (laughter)

MODERATOR

The problem is that the woman he favours for these exploits is Lavinia Upright, the assistant in the Crown Solicitor's office who's still working at the escort agency. But she's also the favourite escort of Maxim Smirnoff, the cultural adviser to the Soviet Embassy, whom we suspect is the top KGB man in Canberra. Does that mean there's an important security implication?

DAWKINS

Quite clearly, yes.

MODERATOR

Barry Borgia might spill cabinet secrets while he's impersonating the Prime Minister. (laughter)

DAWKINS

Barry Borgia sounds a bit of a dope to me. I think he should
certainly be counselled. (laughter)

MODERATOR

You're not going to remove him from the Ministry?

DAWKINS

I think that would depend. This is becoming a much more
serious matter. It depends what kind of secrets Mr Borgia might
have, whether he has access to sensitive government information.
But basically it's conduct unbecoming of a Minister, and he
shouldn't be doing it.

MODERATOR

So he should be warned, and Smirnoff should be deported?

DAWKINS

I'm not sure whether you'd want to have a diplomatic incident
which would reveal the indiscretions of Mr Borgia.

MODERATOR

Mr Ramsay, Lavinia bumps into you at the bar of the Lakeside
Hotel. She wonders whether she might make rather more than
her meagre public service salary by selling the story to the press.
There is an election coming up, what's it worth?

RAMSAY

We'd need a lot of proof. We'd need an awful lot of proof.
You have got no idea how much proof we'd need. (laughter)

MODERATOR

What about a statutory declaration?

RAMSAY

No.

MODERATOR

What about photographs?

RAMSAY

You're getting closer. (laughter)

MODERATOR

She does have some photos taken aboard a love boat on Lake

Burley Griffin. (laughter) They're a bit fuzzy and you can't tell one Minister from another from the back. (laughter) Any help?

RAMSAY

No, that's not good enough; not fuzzy photos. Nice sharp clear ones maybe.

MODERATOR

"I know," she says brightly. "I've got the Minister's new identity card. I slipped it out of his pocket when we were in a passionate embrace last night." Starting to get there?

RAMSAY

It adds a little bit to it. You would certainly be interested.

MODERATOR

Suppose the story of Barry and Lavinia—leave out Smirnoff—is published. Has this ended his ministerial career, Mr Dawkins?

DAWKINS

Having counselled him to stop it, then not having stopped it, I would have no alternative.

MODERATOR

Senator Withers, you don't know anything about the security angle. Forget that. All you know is that he has been patronising the agency. Would you make political capital out of it, with an election coming up?

WITHERS

I would hope I could restrain myself from doing so. I do not agree with getting into other people's bedrooms or bank accounts. That's their business.

MODERATOR

Could you restrain him, Mr MacKellar, would you tell Senator Withers to go right ahead?

MACKELLAR

No, I would try to restrain him. We should really try to get away from this sort of gutter stuff.

MODERATOR

It's time for the inauguration of Austrain. It will be a red-carpet, red-letter day. There will be brass bands and ticker tape at Sydney's Central Station. The Premier of New South Wales

will make a speech, saluting his government's vision in
supporting the project. Engine driver Ken Chifley will blow the
whistle, and Austrain will rocket off to Canberra in fifty-nine
minutes flat. At Canberra Station the Royal bicentennial visitor,
Prince Andrew, will be there to meet it and the Prime Minister
will make a speech saluting her government's vision in
supporting the project. Mr MacKellar, as leader of the
opposition you have at least been allocated a seat in the VIP
carriage. It's not a window seat, and it's next to the toilet. Are
you going to accept?

MACKELLAR

No. We've been mounting a vigorous campaign against the
waste and extravagance of it. I would almost certainly refuse.

MODERATOR

There's a great deal of television interest in this historic event.
The Fairpacker network offer the Ausrail Corporation two
hundred thousand dollars for the exclusive right to broadcast it.
The ABC can't offer any money, but it can put up Jill Wran
and Molly Meldrum as commentators. Who do you go for?

HILL

Everybody. You wouldn't sell exclusive rights, because given the
finances of this thing you need every bum on the seat you can
get and we would be after every skerrick of publicity. So you
wouldn't accept two hundred thousand dollars. The publicity
itself would be worth more than that.

MODERATOR

The Fairpacker network won't screen it unless they have
exclusive rights, so it goes to the ABC.

HILL

It goes to anybody who's interested.

MODERATOR

A great day for government politicians, Mr MacKellar. Are they
exploiting the Bicentennial?

MACKELLAR
Absolutely.

MODERATOR
Anything you can do or say to stop them?

MACKELLAR

No. And just you watch it happening over the next few years.

MODERATOR

Perhaps you can get at Mr Hill. He's the head of the Ausrail Corporation. It's a quango—does parliament have any power over him?

MACKELLAR

We can get the head of a quango or statutory authority along to a select committee if there is one formed for a particular purpose, yes.

MODERATOR

There is, and you're chairing it. What questions do you have?

MACKELLAR

We grill him as extensively as possible to demonstrate the absolute extravagance which is associated with this project.

MODERATOR

Grill him, Mr Cadman.

CADMAN

Mr Hill, in the arrangement for the opening of this railway, who is picking up the tab for the celebration of this great occasion?

HILL

We've decided to launch this great publicity machine because we want everybody to use this railway, instead of cars and aeroplanes and road coaches. Now, quite separately from our organisation of this wonderful festive promotion, the Minister in his wisdom has decided that he too would like to participate in this event. We welcome that because, indeed, it is his government that has put up the money, and it's his government that will be covering the subsidy to operate it.

CADMAN

Did you invite the Minister?

HILL

I have invited the Minister.

CADMAN

It was your initiative to have the Minister there?

HILL

Certainly, on the basis that we couldn't have got away with it any other way. (laughter) But we think since it's a government decision, the Minister should represent the government.

CADMAN

So this is a government occasion rather than an Austrain occasion?

HILL

It's an occasion for Australia.

MODERATOR

It is indeed an historic occasion, as the great day dawns at last. You feel a surge of pride, John Brown, as you climb into the cab of the engine alongside Ken Chifley. Of course, you weren't to know that millions of television viewers would miss the start because the ABC ran out of film; you didn't realise that Eric Bombast had chained himself to the track just beyond Gorton Gorge and several hours would be lost cutting him free; you could hardly have foreseen that during the long wait at Canberra Station the Royal bicentennial visitor Prince Andrew would strike up a conversation with an official representative of the Crown Solicitor's office, Lavinia Upright, leading to complications which the Palace is still trying to unravel. (laughter) And it wasn't your fault that just outside Steedman a switching mistake diverted Austrain onto the unfinished branch line which led it up Mount Ainslie but not down again. (laughter)

BROWN

Nobody's perfect, are they?

MODERATOR

Nonetheless, your party scrapes home in the bicentennial election, and here you are a few days' later anxiously awaiting that call from the Prime Minister. What position do you think you deserve this time?

BROWN

Given all those disasters, if the train got there in the end I think

I should be made Minister for Miracles.

MODERATOR

You should be promoted. Well, the telephone rings, and it's the Prime Minister's press secretary calling to congratulate you on your new appointment: as Tourist Commissioner in Vancouver. (laughter)

WE NAME
THE GUILTY MEN

A distinguished judge contracts AIDS; a girl is expelled from a private school because Matron suspects she's using drugs; a top model faces public execution in Malaria for smuggling heroin; the Minister of Police has suspicious dealings with a prominent Sydney business identity. Where there's smoke there's usually fire, but sometimes there's only a smoke-machine. Can the Australian media be trusted to tell the difference? And when it does, will the law allow it to tell the people?

Some of Australia's top journalists and judges are confronted with the ethical and legal dilemmas of reconciling the public right to know with the individual's right to privacy, reputation and fair trial.

WE NAME THE GUILTY MEN
Participants

PETER BOWERS
  National Columnist, *Sydney Morning Herald*

PAT BURGESS
  Reporter and Member, Australian Press Council

GERALDINE DOOGUE
  Current Affairs Presenter

JOHN DOWD
  Shadow Attorney-General, New South Wales

JULIE FLYNN
  Current Affairs Producer, Radio 2GB Sydney

DAVID HICKIE
  Journalist, *Sun-Herald*

JONATHAN HOLMES
  Executive Producer, *Four Corners*

STUART LITTLEMORE
  Barrister

IAN MATHEWS
  Editor, *Canberra Times*

WENDY McCARTHY
  Deputy Chair, Australian Broadcasting Corporation

ANTHONY McCLELLAN
  Chief of Production, *60 Minutes*

JAMES McCLELLAND
  Former Judge and Royal Commissioner

RICHARD NEVILLE
  Television Commentator, Channel 9

BERNARD TEAGUE
  Solicitor and Vice President, Law Institute of Victoria

OWEN THOMSON
Publisher, Melbourne *Truth*

BRIAN TOOHEY
Editor, *National Times*

HAL WOOTTEN
Chairman, Australian Press Council

Recorded at ABC Studios,
Sydney,
August 1985.

WE NAME THE GUILTY MEN

MODERATOR:

Once upon a time, ladies and gentlemen, in a land where press is free, trial is fair and news is plentiful, there descends a much publicised pestilence which afflicts a small number of people. It's an incurable virus, it kills within eighteen months and it's believed to stem from indulgence in highly unconventional heterosexual practices. We don't know exactly what causes Zenger's syndrome, but we do know who has it — thanks to blood tests done in total privacy, their results returned to doctors with complete confidentiality, all sufferers registered with the Department of Health under conditions of utter secrecy. An impeccable source tells you, Peter Bowers, that a judge of the Supreme Court — Mr Justice Benchmark — has just contracted Zenger's syndrome. Is that a matter of some public important?

PETER BOWERS

It is.

MODERATOR

So you'll publish the fact that there will soon be a vacancy on the bench?

BOWERS

Probably not.

MODERATOR

Why not, probably?

BOWERS

I think I'd pass it on to my colleague Brian Toohey who is more used to these things. (laughter)

MODERATOR

Will you publish, Ian Mathews?

IAN MATHEWS

I'm not sure that we would. We'd very likely mention that he was ill; that he was taking time off from the bench to recover.

MODERATOR

But you wouldn't publish the name of his disease?

MATHEWS

I'm not sure at this stage that it's relevant any more than it's relevant if he's got influenza.

MODERATOR

Would you publish it in *Strewth*, Owen Thomson?

OWEN THOMSON

Yes. Very, very quickly and we would try to find from the judge exact details of the sexual adventures in which he got this disease. (laughter)

MODERATOR

If he publishes it, Peter Bowers, would you publish then?

BOWERS

No.

MODERATOR

Even though his readers will know, your readers won't?

BOWERS

He's got his readers and I've got mine.

MODERATOR

And never the twain meet?

BOWERS

Maybe they do take a sneak at one another now and again, but just because somebody else has published . . . if you make your decision you stick to it.

MODERATOR

Let me make it a little more interesting for you . . .

BOWERS

Juicy.

MODERATOR

Not so much juicy as important. The information you have is that the judge, although ill, is not resigning from the High Court, because if he does he thinks the government will replace him with a political appointment. By that he means they will appoint a judge who doesn't share his politics. If he hangs on another year, there will have been an election which the opposition may win, and it will appoint a judge who shares his

political philosophy. Does that make it more important to
publish?

BOWERS

I think the only grounds for publication would be if Zenger's
syndrome was somehow affecting his judicial capacity and he was
going crazy.

MODERATOR

How do you tell when a judge is going crazy? (laughter)

BOWERS

Perhaps we should ask Jim McClelland. You look to see whether
there's obviously some extraordinary conduct on the bench . . .
some quite peculiar, inconsistent decisions that are clearly
indicating he isn't in command of his mental faculties and should
be removed.

MODERATOR

Your lawyer friends tell you that his associate is writing all his
judgements and they've improved enormously.

BOWERS

I'd need to be convinced that there was clear evidence of
incapacity.

MODERATOR

There's no evidence at this stage of incapacity—other than the
fact that pre-senile dementia is going to affect most sufferers
from Zenger's syndrome late in the development of the disease.

BOWERS

I think then, at that later stage, you could probably make out a
case why he should step down from the bench without saying
he's got Zenger's disease.

MODERATOR

Suppose Mr Bowers has passed his information on to you, Brian
Toohey. What do you do with it?

BRIAN TOOHEY

We'd publish it, and then put up with the outcries from all the
people who are the judge's supporters, who'd say, "Where would
we get another jurist who's lived such an interesting lifestyle as to
get Zenger's syndrome." I agree with Owen Thomson that

the public has an interest in knowing whether or not a High Court judge has got Zenger's syndrome. And particularly how he got it and whether or not he was attempting to pervert the course of justice in the process of getting it. (laughter)

MODERATOR

Of course, if you do publish it, people will think that these secrecy conditions don't work, that the press can find out who has Zenger's syndrome, and potential sufferers will take fright. They won't go in for medical tests, so they won't learn that they have Zenger's syndrome, and in their ignorance they will pass it on to others. Hundreds of people could die as a result of all the publicity you will generate about this one man having the disease.

TOOHEY

If the secrecy provisions have broken down, it's important that the public should know that the secrecy provisions aren't working.

MODERATOR

Even though by telling them you may cause potential sufferers to take fright and to avoid taking the tests? And so you may actually indirectly cause the death of some people by publishing that story?

TOOHEY

What benefit comes from this secrecy? I can't follow how it stops the spread of the disease, the fact that it's a total secret who's got it.

MODERATOR

Because it may deter people from taking the tests, and if they don't take the tests they're more likely to pass it on if they do have it.

TOOHEY

But plenty of people who take tests still go ahead and indulge in the activities that give you Zenger's syndrome, surely.

MODERATOR

Suppose the State government makes it an offence to publish the names of sufferers from Zenger's syndrome. Will a five hundred dollar fine deter you?

BOWERS

A five hundred dollar fine wouldn't deter me if I believed it was in the public interest that the public should know that there's a judge on the Supreme Court who's got Zenger's syndrome and has gone off his head and should be removed from the bench forthwith. Five hundred dollars wouldn't stop me, five thousand dollars wouldn't stop me.

MODERATOR

Fifty thousand?

BOWERS

Well it might stop the proprietor. It wouldn't stop me. (laughter) Look, before we decide on publication we privately went to the Premier, and placed all the evidence before the Premier, so he could take some action to remove this judge.

MODERATOR

You would approach the Premier and ask him to remove the judge?

BOWERS

Yes.

MODERATOR

Approach Mr Dowd; he's the Premier.

BOWERS

Mr Dowd, we have these documents that prove quite conclusively that this judge you appointed has Zenger's syndrome, and you must yourself have become aware of his extraordinary conduct. Here's the folder with our material. I put it to you in the public interest that you should remove this man very quietly. You should have people speak to him to get him to step down. If he doesn't step down voluntarily then you should remove him in the interests of justice in this State.

JOHN DOWD

This is a matter that would have to go to the inner cabinet steering committee, to make a decision as to how quickly we can relieve ourselves of this troublesome judge.

MODERATOR

If the judge is removed quietly, you won't say why he's been removed?

BOWERS

I'm worried about publication. I think we should exhaust all other means before we resort to publication, because as you pointed out there are competing public interest factors. Only if the Premier refuses to act would we publish.

MODERATOR

But if he does act by quietly removing the judge, you won't say why?

BOWERS

Having confidentially gone to the Premier and asked for his removal, I think you're obligated to say nothing if they do remove him.

MODERATOR

Ian Mathews, your confidential source in Canberra—a doctor's receptionist—gives you the name of a second sufferer from this disease. It's Senator Bill Gladhand, a high-ranking cabinet Minister. Will you publish that story?

MATHEWS

No. First of all you've got to find out what effect it's going to have on the government of the country and his performance. If, like the judge, he's going around the twist, then you do what Peter Bowers said. You go and see the leader of his party. If he's behaving in a strange way in public, then of course you're going to mention it, but you don't necessarily mention what he's suffering from.

MODERATOR

Well you see him in the non-members' bar late one night, making advances to an Amanda Autocue, a television journalist from the opposition network. He shouldn't be drinking with Zenger's syndrome; it brings on delusions of grandeur. (laughter)

MATHEWS

I would have a swift word with the young lady.

MODERATOR

She's delighted that you do so. She's looking for a scoop—and she scoops you with your own story. (laughter) Would you try this "behind the scenes" approach, Owen Thomson?

THOMSON

No. I never thought I'd live to see the day of such morality in our press. (laughter)

MODERATOR

Richard Neville, the law once deemed you an immoral journalist. Now you're editing an alternative journal — *Woz.* (laughter) Is it a story for you?

RICHARD NEVILLE

I'd be much more interested in finding out the antics that led these people to get this strange heterosexual disease which we know nothing about. No-one's raised the point of whether they're still spreading it. Is the judge still actually involving himself in these delightful parties?

MODERATOR

So you would make a moral judgement about his conduct, and if you think his conduct is immoral, you'd publish?

NEVILLE

No, I didn't say that. I'm saying that I know very little about this disease and people keep saying, "Maybe he's going around the twist," but just because people go into the non-members' bar and behave rather eccentrically, I don't think that's any reason to rush off to the Prime Minister with documents. More people should be doing eccentric things in our society. That wouldn't worry me either.

MODERATOR

What you do know of is the evidence that most sufferers from Zenger's syndrome develop pre-senile dementia — mood shifts, loss of memory, occasional delusions. Is that enough?

NEVILLE

How is that actually affecting his work?

MODERATOR

Well, he's Minister of Defence. His finger's on the button. (laughter) He could invade another country. He could invade Tasmania. (laughter) Jonathan Holmes, there's a third name that a source gives you. It's one of those Englishmen who are running the ABC on a seven years contract. What do you do?

JONATHAN HOLMES

Is it the Managing Director of the ABC we're talking about?

MODERATOR

Yes. He's been acting very oddly. He listens to the early morning program on 2BL. (laughter)

HOLMES

I'm not sure that that's important, the fact that the Managing Director of the ABC has Zenger's syndrome. I think the other two cases are much more clearly in the public interest.

MODERATOR

Is it important, Brian Toohey?

TOOHEY

What I certainly would never, ever dream of doing is going to the Premier or the Prime Minister, as a journalist, wheeling and dealing behind the scenes to get rid of a judge or a Defence Minister. It's nothing to do with journalism. You're in the business of information, and it's going to be published. It doesn't have to be the most important story on earth to publish it. That's just ridiculous. Millions of words are published every day, not all of them are important. It's an interesting story. And it's particularly interesting as to how they got it. It sounds quite intriguing.

MODERATOR

So you would publish the story about the Managing Director of the ABC. You'd say that Zenger's syndrome was never heard of in Australia till he arrived. (laughter) Suppose, Peter Bowers, the third name was the name of your proprietor, Sir David Murfax. Does madness really matter in media proprietors? He's been known as "Mad" Murfax ever since you were a copyboy.

BOWERS

It matters if he's going mad from Zenger's disease, because he's going to get madder with each month.

MODERATOR

It matters to your job?

BOWERS

It may well. How is it communicable? Should we be washing

his crockery? I'm getting a bit nervous about having someone with Zenger's disease so close to me.

MODERATOR

We've seen, John Dowd, that some sections of the media will publish the names of important people who suffer from this disease. Do we need a law that prevents them from doing so?

DOWD

Yes. If the whole policy of not allowing press reporting in order to avoid deterring people from having tests is going to work, then we have to prosecute editors like Mr Thomson and Mr Toohey.

MODERATOR

You're prosecuted, Owen Thomson. Does that make you lose sleep?

THOMSON

I wouldn't sleep much if it did. No, no; I mean you know what a joke politicians are regarded as in this counry.

MODERATOR

He's not worried about paying a fifty thousand dollar fine; his proprietor had pre-tax profits of twenty million last year. How big will the fine need to be to stop the press from publishing?

DOWD

Well, if it's clear that your one-off prosecution is not going to attract a big enough fine, that they're just going to get a slap on the wrist, then you must impose an on-going daily fine, a continuing fine for every day they mention the name, and eventually the little gremlins on the board of directors will make editors see sense and see that the law is enforced.

MODERATOR

Jim McClelland, is that the sort of law we should have?

JAMES McCLELLAND

I would not allow the press to publish the names.

MODERATOR

Why not?

McCLELLAND

It's not a matter of public interest, it's a matter of privacy. And there's a greater public interest, I believe, and that is that the publication of names will discourage people who would otherwise be assured of anonymity in reporting their complaint.

MODERATOR
But that's the argument that Mr Toohey doesn't understand.

McCLELLAND
I disagree with him on that. It's a matter of deciding between competing public interests. And the greater public interest is that people should report their disease as soon as possible.

MODERATOR
But you've seen that some sections of the media don't buy that argument. Sooner or later, they will publish these sensational facts about public figures.

McCLELLAND
Well, the media would have to be dealt with.

MODERATOR
How do you deal with them?

McCLELLAND
By putting Brian Toohey in gaol. (laughter)

MODERATOR
For how long?

McCLELLAND
Until he publicly repents. (laughter) We're looking at a great public menace, a communicable disease that could reach epidemic proportions. The fate of any one, or any one hundred editors, is a small consideration compared to that.

MODERATOR
The only alternative to gaol and fines is the Press Council, and there's a complaint to the Press Council about Mr Toohey and Mr Thomson publishing the names of public figures with Zenger's disease. Do you uphold that complaint?

HAL WOOTTEN
We approach these things by starting off with the fact that it's a problem of balancing the public's right to know matters of importance and interest against a reasonable right of privacy on the part of individuals. We look at it after the event and

consider whether the media have gone beyond the bounds of a responsible press. Things that affect public figures, doing important jobs, are matters of public interest and I wouldn't be prepared to say that a journalist who published this had done the wrong thing, and equally I would respect a journalist who decided not to publish it.

MODERATOR

There's another concern in Sydney at the moment, and it's cocaine. Cocaine coming in cheaply from South America via New Zealand. It's the latest craze. It's in the schools, it's in the streets, it's in Sydney in a big way. Geraldine Doogue you're a reporter on the program that replaced *The National*. It's called *30 Minutes*—*60 Minutes* without the advertisements. (laughter)

GERALDINE DOOGUE

I'm sure we would do a story on the cocaine craze.

MODERATOR

You're an old girl of Cranbala, an exclusive Sydney girls school, and you hear on the old girl network that some fourteen-year-olds have been expelled for sniffing cocaine. Is that part of your story?

DOOGUE

Yes.

MODERATOR

One of them is Melissa Nott, the daughter of Judge Nott who is chairing a Royal Commission into organised crime and drugs racketeering. Will you name her?

DOOGUE

It would depend on whether we were naming all the expelled girls. Since they are minors, probably not. The story would be treated as a symptom of the problem, without names.

MODERATOR

Would you name Melissa, Owen Thomson? She's been expelled because Matron suspects that she was sniffing cocaine in the dorm.

THOMSON

We would name her with great pleasure.

MODERATOR

Because she's the daughter of a judge?

THOMSON

Yes, of course. But I think any teenager being expelled from school for sniffing cocaine is a story in anybody's paper, even the dull ones we're surrounded with here. (laughter)

MODERATOR

Richard Neville, would you name her?

NEVILLE

I'm not sure—not at the age of fourteen. I mean many of us have been suspected by matrons in our time, and it turned out not always to be the truth. So I can't see any justification for naming fourteen-year-old girls who are suspected by matrons for sniffing cocaine, and doing what most of their peers were doing anyway.

MODERATOR

What's your justification, Owen Thomson?

THOMSON

Because these are matters of public interest. The public are interested in these things.

NEVILLE

But why? Why should that justify you ruining the lives of four young ladies?

THOMSON

Well they've done a fair job of ruining it themselves haven't they?

MODERATOR

Your exposure of Melissa Nott will go into the press-clippings files, and will dog her throughout her life. Her father complains to the Press Council.

WOOTTEN

I would think that a paper that published the names went beyond reasonable bounds. I can't see the element of public interest. What Owen calls public interest is just public curiosity. This is not something that affects any public matters; there's no reason to think that her father is implicated. So I would uphold the complaint.

MODERATOR

So you'd censure Mr Thomson.

THOMSON

They can't censure us, because we won't join their Council. We won't play their little games.

MODERATOR

Consider yourself censured, Mr Thomson. Does that make you lose any sleep or lose any money?

THOMSON

We give a nice smile. That's all.

MODERATOR

What is the point then of the Press Council, if it issues these censures and no-one takes any notice?

WOOTTEN

Owen Thomson may not take any notice but we do help to establish the standards of the press and my experience is that journalists, apart from Owen, are really a very moral lot of people, and they're very concerned at their professional ethics.

THOMSON

Are you saying I'm immoral? If your lot isn't immoral I don't know who is. I mean the Press Council has been handing around unction for years. I've never heard such nonsense.

MODERATOR

Brian Toohey, do you take any notice of Press Council censure?

TOOHEY

Not really. It's mealy-mouthed nonsense for the most part. You shove their judgements in the paper because you've got to and that's it.

MODERATOR

You are a member of the Press Council, Pat Burgess. Are you in the habit of issuing mealy-mouthed nonsense?

PAT BURGESS

No, certainly not.

MODERATOR

But the editors don't take any notice of you.

BURGESS

But they do take notice of us. News Ltd withdrew from the

Council because they were getting so many judgements against their papers.

MODERATOR

But the Press Council has no power. You don't make editors or proprietors lose sleep or lose money, so what's the point?

BURGESS

Well, that's what they say, but I have yet to see an editor who fronts before the Press Council and does not defend his publication and his reporter very vigorously, hoping to avoid an adverse judgement.

THOMSON

When I was an editor of various News Ltd publications, I used to front quite regularly, but I didn't take any notice of their judgements. I don't think their arguments count for much. They come down on the side of trying to sound reasonable and balanced and that sort of thing, and they give you a bit of a cuff over the ear every now and then . . .

MODERATOR

The Press Council doesn't seem able to protect privacy, Stuart Littlemore. As a lawyer would you want firmer sanctions against this sort of conduct?

STUART LITTLEMORE

In the case of the fourteen-year-old girl, yes, of course — anybody would — but turning it to practicalities is another matter. I wouldn't recommend that anybody in Melissa's position went to the Press Council because there is no remedy. If she and her parents came to see me I would have to say to them that there's no point, we're not going to get it taken out of the paper. If the editor takes the attitude that Brian Toohey takes or Owen Thomson takes there will be no redress for you.

MODERATOR

Is there any practical step she can take? Is there a law that protects privacy?

LITTLEMORE

No.

MODERATOR

Should there be a law, Jim McClelland?

McCLELLAND

Yes. Especially in a case like this. How can the publication of a peccadillo by a fourteen-year-old child be justified in the public interest? There's no public interest involved in the publication of that name. There's a right to privacy which should be protected by law and at present is not.

MODERATOR

John Dowd, would your government bring down a law to stop Owen Thomson publishing these names?

DOWD

We've always had child welfare legislation to protect people under the age of sixteen when they are charged with criminal offences. If in fact that act doesn't cover the names of children who are suspected but never charged, of course we will act to protect children from publication of their names in circumstances where it is likely to harm the moral well-being or reputation of the child.

MODERATOR

Do you worry, Owen Thomson, that your sort of journalism is going to bring laws like this rather too close for comfort?

THOMSON

It's not only my sort of journalism; it's what made journalism before it was overtaken by television and radio. The drying out of vigour in Australian journalism over the past ten years has been so noticeable, because the vigour has been transferred to television. Now the allegedly serious newspapers are just full of what people think. The public doesn't want to know what people think, it wants to know what people do.

MODERATOR

If there's one faster way to die in Sydney than from Zenger's syndrome, it's from a Melbourne hit man. Your information, Peter Bowers, is that there is a Melbourne hit man in town at this very moment, stalking Judge Nott, who is chairing the Commission into organised crime. Will you publish that story?

BOWERS

Why shouldn't I? Of course, after checking the facts with the police who are meant to be guarding him.

MODERATOR

Superintendent Doberman says: "I don't know how you got that story, but for heaven's sake don't publish it."

BOWERS

Why?

MODERATOR

"We have laid a trap for this hit man. If you publish that story, it will blow our whole operation."

BOWERS

You mean the Royal Commissioner is going to be the patsy and . . .

MODERATOR

"I can't tell you the details, but please don't publish."

BOWERS

Are you going to let us in, exclusively, on this story?

MODERATOR

"We will issue a press release as soon as the hit man is arrested, giving information to all the newspapers in our normal way."

BOWERS

See you later, I'm going to publish. (laughter)

MODERATOR

Geraldine Doogue, on *30 Minutes* you get this story from a very high source. The judge is being used as a patsy, as a decoy. The security of the judge and his family is not what it should be.

DOOGUE

This is from somebody sympathetic to the judge, who fears that he's being set up?

MODERATOR

That's your tip, from a highly confidential but very reliable source. So you send your *30 Minutes* camera team to take a look at security outside the judge's home in Bluegum Avenue, Killara. When they arrive, what they see, and what they film, is difficult to describe in words. The body of the judge's wife, shot in the head, on a stretcher being loaded into an ambulance. Melissa, screeching with grief, clutching at her mother's body. That's on your film. Does it go out at six-thirty tonight?

DOOGUE:
Yes.

HOLMES
It depends how horrifying it is. At six-thirty you've got to think about the kids watching. It may be that you would cut out the really gruesome parts but the essence of it would certainly go out. Here's a judge's wife who's been shot down by a hit man. I mean that is the biggest story in Sydney this year. We don't just ignore it because it's a bit frightening. I mean we didn't not shoot the Vietnam War.

MODERATOR
And you have it exclusive to the ABC.

HOLMES
Well, great!

ANTHONY McCLELLAN
We want it too; for Channel 9.

MODERATOR
It's an ABC exclusive, so how do you get it?

ANTHONY McCLELLAN
You ring up Jonathan Holmes and say, "Do you want to broadcast it to a mass audience or not? (laughter) We're very interested obviously in running some of that film that you've got—we go to air before you."

HOLMES
You've got to be joking. You've got to be joking. Come back after we've gone to air. I'll put it in a cab half an hour after it's gone to air with us, how's that?

ANTHONY McCLELLAN
Not interested.

MODERATOR
Would you offer money for that film?

ANTHONY McCLELLAN
Well, the ABC certainly needs it, so . . .

DOOGUE
You'd offer it. (laughter)

ANTHONY McCLELLAN

Yes, we would. Yes. It would be a commercial transaction.

MODERATOR

The ABC aren't selling it to you, but they're using it on their six-thirty news. Your program is at seven.

ANTHONY McCLELLAN

Once it's gone to air we'd get it anyway. It's in the public domain.

LITTLEMORE

It's not in the public domain because you have to take it off air at Channel 9 by plugging into the ABC's frequency and putting it onto a videotape, and it's copyright in the ABC.

MODERATOR

So the ABC or any other media network can have copyright in news? In the biggest story in Australia?

LITTLEMORE

They cannot have copyright in news as such, but they can have copyright in the work that they have prepared. That is the film, the videotape. That is theirs and nobody may take it from them without permission. They can stop other networks from using their film, because it's their property.

MODERATOR

Melissa is sent down to stay with her aunt and uncle in Dapto. You get a call from her aunt. Do you want to interview the girl?

ANTHONY McCLELLAN

Yes.

MODERATOR

The aunt says that for five thousand dollars you can have an exclusive interview with fourteen-year-old Melissa about the murder of her mother. You speak with Melissa and she is clearly upset. She'd weep on camera but she's articulate and clearly would give you a very moving interview. Would you have any ethical inhibition about paying five thousand dollars for that interview?

ANTHONY McCLELLAN

No.

MODERATOR

None at all?

ANTHONY McCLELLAN

No.

MODERATOR

Would you, Richard Neville?

NEVILLE

I think it is difficult because it's very, very soon after the event and she's completely freaked out by the tragedy. She might not be in a position to make a reasonable judgement about whether she ought to be doing that interview.

ANTHONY McCLELLAN

But you've no right to make a reasonable judgement about her reasonable judgement, have you?

NEVILLE

No, I guess not. But in each case, in the end, it comes down to your own feeling about the situation; whether you feel within yourself that it is exploitative to go ahead with it. If somebody's in a very vulnerable situation, and you are going to expose their vulnerability to the world . . . I'm not saying that I'm more moral than anyone else, but there comes a moment when you're actually there at the doorstep with a weeping and wailing victim of a tragedy, and the feeling that you are exploiting them through the power of your chequebook just overcomes, perhaps, your hard-nosed judgement as a journalist.

ANTHONY McCLELLAN

I don't think there's a difference between chasing ambulances and trying to interview people who've been mangled in a car accident, and the situation that we're discussing.

MODERATOR

So you see no ethical inhibition in paying money to the girl's aunt and uncle to make the girl available to weep on camera.

ANTHONY McCLELLAN

No, on the strict precondition that I'm convinced that Melissa is not being coerced into giving the interview by her guardians.

MODERATOR

Judge Nott's wife's funeral is tomorrow, Mr McClellan. The

family have requested no flowers, no reporters. Would you send a camera team, against the family's wishes?

ANTHONY McCLELLAN

Yes.

MODERATOR

You'll photograph members of the family weeping at the graveside, as the coffin is lowered into the ground?

ANTHONY McCLELLAN

Yes.

MODERATOR

Why won't you respect the wishes of the family?

ANTHONY McCLELLAN

I think it can be done with some degree of respect. I'm not talking about a camera crew jumping into open coffins or open graves. I think it can be done from a distance with available technology.

MODERATOR

Telephoto lenses that will pick up the tears running down the cheeks?

ANTHONY McCLELLAN

I think it's important that this judge's wife has been assassinated by a Melbourne hit man. I think it's important the public understand the degree of organised crime in this State, and this is a visual method of making that point very clearly.

MODERATOR

The sorrow and the pity?

ANTHONY McCLELLAN

Yes.

MODERATOR

And the anger?

ANTHONY McCLELLAN

Yes, the anger.

MODERATOR

Richard Neville, would you go to the funeral with a camera team, against the family's wishes? They don't want television cameras intruding into their private grief.

NEVILLE

That's a really difficult question. If I did go, it would be with extreme reluctance and I don't accept that you can be non-intrusive. The press is always saying, "Oh, we'll go and we won't intrude." That's a contradiction in terms. The very presence of the press, and of television especially, is intrusive. I would just try and weigh up the particular situation and ask whether the fact that this woman is being buried by her family at this particular moment really adds anything to our understanding of organised crime.

MODERATOR

The judge will be there, and so will the Minister of Police, Mr Andrew Angel. His press office rings you and lets you know he'll be available for interview afterwards.

NEVILLE

Yes, I think I would concede that it does make it a bit more likely I'd go to the funeral.

MODERATOR

A big tear will form in his eye and trickle down his cheek, and he'll speak powerfully about the need to stop organised crime in this State.

NEVILLE

And he could be questioned as to why, if they knew that there was a hit man in the territory, they allowed the hit man to get so close to the judge as to murder his wife. You would have access to him at a very delicate time, for some very delicate questioning.

MODERATOR

So we'll take a close look at Mr Andrew Angel, a rising star in the political firmament, a Minister of Police who is expected some day to be Premier. David Hickie, you're writing a profile on Andrew Angel; what sources do you use?

DAVID HICKIE

All sources available to you. The reporter goes for broke, getting as much information as he can together, and leaving the legal and moral judgements to his editor. Let's get the information first and exclusively, and then let's discuss what are the problems.

MODERATOR

When Andrew Angel was nineteen, he was involved in a car accident and was prosecuted for dangerous driving. The case was thrown out by the magistrate. Would you mention that in the profile?

HICKIE

That'd be the sort of thing you'd put to Mr Angel when you interviewed him.

MODERATOR

He says there's nothing in it. The case was thrown out.

HICKIE

If it was a simple answer like that, it probably just wouldn't be something that's interesting.

MODERATOR

If it were a fatal accident, but not his fault?

HICKIE

I can't really see much newsworthiness in it. If I was writing the profile, I'd be seeking a lot more newsworthy things than that or I'd have a very boring story!

MODERATOR

The magistrate who threw the case out was convicted a few years later for taking bribes. (laughter)

HICKIE

Right. That's the sort of thing. You'd be discussing with your editor what in fact may be the implications, and what we're actually trying to get out here.

MODERATOR

Brian Toohey is your editor.

HICKIE

Brian, we've got evidence that Mr Angel was in this accident and put on a charge of negligent driving, and that the case was thrown out by a magistrate who's fairly notorious for taking bribes. The way I see it, we've really got to establish whether there's any evidence that this may have been one of the specific cases where bribes may have passed.

TOOHEY

I don't think we have to establish that. I think we can report that he was let off this case by this magistrate, who's subsequently been convicted. If you can come up with the other information . . .

MODERATOR

Reported in the same paragraph?

TOOHEY

Well and good.

MODERATOR

Isn't that guilt by association, to mention the fact that the magistrate was convicted of bribery several years later? No evidence that Andrew Angel or anyone associated with him bribed him to throw the case out.

TOOHEY

You never know; somewhere down the track, by publishing this material, you might get someone to come forward. Someone might come out of the woodwork and make some interesting links.

MODERATOR

Richard Neville, you're writing this profile for the *Sydney Morning Bugle*, and you remember Andrew Angel from St Jude's College at Sydney University. He used to have a lot of wild parties in his room, exotic cheroots were passed around, and sometimes he was generous enough to pass them to you. He is now Minister of Police, twenty years later. Would this feature in your profile?

NEVILLE

If you were trying to convey his personality or his character or paint a vivid picture of his university days, and you remembered these parties with a certain amount of affection, perhaps you would mention it. I don't think it's particularly crucial.

MODERATOR

As Minister of Police he's just imported from Sweden, at great expense, a "potalyser", a device which detects cannabis traces in urine. He's proposing random urine sampling to catch drugged drivers.

NEVILLE

Yes, well I think in that case I'd have a certain amount of

mischievous pleasure in pointing out that he was an old pot-head from way back.

MODERATOR

Peter Bowers is your editor. Are you going to let that paragraph stand?

BOWERS

I certainly wouldn't allow it to stand. I'd go back to Andrew Angel and say, "Listen, you smoked pot when you were at university; what's made you change your mind?" And I'd want to interview him on that in great detail.

MODERATOR

He denies it. "I never did. Neville must be hallucinating."

BOWERS

Listen, Richard and six others of your university cronies have told us that they've been to the parties with you, I mean . . .

MODERATOR

"Their minds have been damaged." (laughter)

BOWERS

It seems to have been standard conduct at university, from what I've heard of it. The fact is going to be reported, and Andrew Angel needs to be pressed on it; now that he's the Minister in charge of "potting" others or testing others for pot, and he'd been into it himself some years ago.

MODERATOR

Well, you've got a lot of *old* dope on Andrew Angel, but nothing recent. Except, David Hickie, you discover that two years ago, when he was Minister for Lands, he went against a departmental recommendation and granted permission to a prominent Sydney business identity, Len Borgia, to redevelop an old kindergarten as a massage parlour. Borgia made a vast amount of money out of it. Does that interest you?

HICKIE

Great story.

MODERATOR

Great story?

HICKIE

Of great public interest.

MODERATOR

You track down his former secretary. Philida Phickle, who signs a statutory declaration that she saw Borgia hand over twenty thousand dollars to Andrew Angel, two weeks after he granted that development permission.

HICKIE

Very good start of a great story.

MODERATOR

What more do you need?

HICKIE

It's likely to be her word against two other persons. But it's the sort of thing you obviously want to get all the information you can about.

MODERATOR

You find that Borgia was in the Minister's office on that day; his name is in the appointments book. You discover from your sources at the bank that twenty thousand dollars was paid into Angel's account on that day. What more do you need?

HICKIE

Well Brian, it seems as though we've got a fairly publishable story here. We've got the witness, who's signed a statutory declaration and is prepared to appear in court to testify, and we've got photostats of the bank documents showing that the money was paid. I assume that neither party at this stage will talk to us. What do you think is our next step? As I understand it from all the sources, the story's looking good.

TOOHEY

We have a written instruction from the management, that we have to show this to the lawyers. The lawyers will say it's defamatory, and it'll be a dead duck of a story. Undoubtedly it happened; this man'll continue to take millions off other people because he's a corrupt politician; and he won't be written about because that's how the law stands.

MODERATOR

You don't have those written instructions from your management, Peter Bowers. Will you publish?

BOWERS

Before I'd publish I'd go and put it very hard on Andrew

Angel, and if he denied it, and if my investigation of Philida Phickle suggests that she didn't make up the story, I would publish and probably the night before I published, present all the documents to the Commissioner of Police.

MODERATOR

Why not present the documents to the Commissioner of Police, and not publish? Wouldn't that be the proper course?

BOWERS

We're in the business of publishing newspapers and publishing news, and this is a top story. Now the law can take its course and we're going to publish it.

MODERATOR

But you went to the Premier about the judge; why not go to the Commissioner of Police about the Minister of Police? (laughter)

BOWERS

This is a much clearer case.

MODERATOR

So you publish it on the front page of the *Sydney Morning Bugle*. Andrew Angel comes to you, Stuart Littlemore, and he's *very* angry, "These people have libelled me disgracefully. I fired Phickle because of bad work, and she swore she'd get back at me. The twenty thousand dollars that went into my bank account on that day was a cheque for my last defamation action against the *Bugle*. I did see Borgia, but in his capacity as Grand Visor of the Holy Knights of Gozo, a charitable organisation that raises money for a trust to help victims of Zenger's syndrome. He handed me the cheque because I'm the honorary treasurer of the trust. What do I get?"

LITTLEMORE

You get an action for defamation fairly smartly.

MODERATOR

"How *much* do I get? This is a most dreadful libel. What could be worse? Saying of a politician that he's corrupt."

LITTLEMORE

Nothing. No, I'm totally sympathetic with you, Mr Angel, but they may not settle this one.

MODERATOR

They may have to settle. Bernard Teague, you're legal adviser to the *Bugle*. Philida Phickle breaks down after the story is published and recants.

BERNARD TEAGUE

Stuart, before this story was published our newspaper went to your client and was only given a blanket denial. The opportunity was there for him to lay it to rest completely and the matter would never have gone further. We're prepared to consider an apology, but another option would be for us to publish a story which would give Angel's side of the matter entirely.

LITTLEMORE

Well I've got his instructions. He's not interested in that. He just wants an immediate acknowledgement that your story was completely wrong, without foundation, and hugely damaging. That's number one. But no apology has the same force as the first story. As you know, Bernie, you're talking about a bucket of butterflies. If you tip out a bucket of butterflies and they fly away, you can never get the same butterflies back in the bucket. How can it be presumed that the people who read the retraction are going to give it the same credence as they gave the original story? No, we want the fullest and most humiliating retraction, correction and apology, but much more importantly, we want a great deal of money.

TEAGUE

Well, it seems there's an issue there as to whether his motives are the right ones. Does he want the story corrected? Surely that's the most important thing?

LITTLEMORE

We've already sent you the apology we want. It's to be run on page one, there is to be a photograph of the Minister, and under it the headline "We were wrong." The copy reads: "The *Sydney Morning Bugle* acknowledges that the story about the Minister for Police, Mr Andrew Angel, was entirely wrong, without foundation, and we unreservedly apologise to him for all the distress this has caused. We have no excuse for it, we acknowledge it is a grave mistake, and a *substantial* amount of money has been paid to the Minister in settlement of his defamation action against us."

MODERATOR
How much money?

LITTLEMORE
It's likely to be fifty thousand dollars or more, but if it's handled the right way it can be up to two hundred thousand.

TEAGUE
(to Bowers) In view of the treatment that it was given in the first place, and the difficulties that we find ourselves in, and the potential cost of going to court and the attitude of the advisers on the other side, I think the prudent thing to do is pay fifty thousand dollars now.

BOWERS
Offer him twenty-five thousand dollars and go up to fifty thousand if necessary, but not a cent more! (laughter)

MODERATOR
Andrew Angel gets fifty thousand dollars from the *Sydney Morning Bugle* and an apology. Unfortunately, the libel was published by Megamedia in America. Andrew once had a relationship with an American film star who has just written her biography, so he's the one Australian politician Americans know about. Can he sue in America?

McCLELLAND
It's extremely doubtful, because the libel law in the United States in relation to public figures is quite different to ours. In America, in order to succeed in an action for defamation if the facts are wrong, the plaintiff has to prove that the publisher acted maliciously by publishing them *knowing* that they were wrong. That's a problem that a plaintiff would not strike in Australia.

MODERATOR
Would you recommend that Australia adopted the American position, whereby public figures can't recover damages against newspapers which make honest mistakes?

McCLELLAND
Yes, I certainly would. I think that public figures should bear in mind what Harry Truman said, "If you can't stand the heat, keep out of the kitchen." Once you become a public figure, you're in a sense, public property.

MODERATOR

John Dowd, would you adopt the American libel laws?

DOWD

No, because you end up with only virgins as public figures. People who want to protect their families, friends and so on, will tend to be deterred from going into public office. If they are not protected by libel laws, you will stop decent people coming forward and standing for public office.

MODERATOR

Stuart Littlemore, you've got a lot of money for Andrew Angel. Len Borgia comes to you as well. Can you get some money for him?

LITTLEMORE

It depends, Mr Borgia, whether your reputation is such that it deserves protection.

MODERATOR

"A lot of people think I'm a bit shady, but I've never been convicted of anything. The police didn't object when I got a TAB licence in Surfers Paradise the other day." (laughter)

LITTLEMORE

I'm not going to advise you unreservedly to go ahead, because we're going to have to see what sort of defence would be available to the other side. If they defend on the basis that what happened did no further harm to your reputation, then we'll have to consider what sort of evidence they could call of your actual reputation. If you bear a reputation as being a briber and a crook, then you might well find that running this action would do more damage to your reputation than it would be worth.

MODERATOR

"So, if I've got a bad reputation already, it's not much point my suing; even though the story was totally wrong?"

LITTLEMORE

That's what I would have to advise you.

MODERATOR

There's a lot of interest, ladies and gentlemen, in Judge Nott and his Royal Commission, and in how he's coping after the

death of his wife. I'll tell you, Owen Thomson, exactly how
he's coping. I'm Ken Papparazzi, freelance photographer for
Playpen, one of your stable of sophisticated adult magazines. I've
got some pictures here of Judge Nott coping, with the help of
Kerrie Bombschell, the famous film star. They're in a private
pool at Palm Beach; she's topless and he's breathless. You want
to buy them?

THOMSON
Yes. How much?

MODERATOR
Ten thousand dollars.

THOMSON
Five.

MODERATOR
You buy them for five thousand dollars and put them in *Playpen*
and your sales soar. There's a complaint to the Press Council,
Hal Wootten, about the press publishing pictures taken by
telephoto lens of a couple in a private pool.

WOOTTEN
Well I find that . . . quite a difficult one. What do you think
about it, Pat?

BURGESS
Once again the people are in the public eye, and therefore their
private life becomes intermingled with their public life and they
are therefore fair targets.

MODERATOR
Fair targets for a telephoto lens from a private house some
distance away?

BURGESS
Yes, I'm afraid so.

MODERATOR
Geraldine Doogue, Kerrie's latest film, *Picnic at Snowy River*, is
opening next week, and you're doing an interview with her.
Would you ask her about her relationship with the judge?

DOOGUE
Given that *Playpen* has published the pictures, yes, I would ask.

If she gave me instructions before the interview that she wasn't in any circumstances going to talk about her private life, I'd respect that, too. But I'd ask her. She might be quite happy to talk.

MODERATOR

You'd ask her because this picture of her in a private pool was published in *Playpen*?

DOOGUE

She may have a perfectly reasonable answer. (laughter) It's possible.

MODERATOR

If the picture were not of Kerrie Bombschell, but of Geraldine Doogue, how would you feel about your privacy being invaded in that way?

DOOGUE

Well, it has been. (laughter) I know all about it. To some extent it's part of the penalty of being a public figure. It depends whether malice is involved, I think.

MODERATOR

Not malice, just circulation.

THOMSON

It's a peculiar moral view that people take that newspapers shouldn't increase circulation, they should all go broke and sack all their journalists. I mean, we're presenting true facts about human failing.

MODERATOR

There's another dimension to this story, because Judge Nott has just completed his Royal Commission into organised crime — he was relaxing after three years' arduous work. The first draft of his report has just been completed, and it comes to you, Brian Toohey, in the usual way (laughter) . . . in a brown paper envelope through the post. It's dynamite. It says that allegations were made to the Commission that senior government Ministers were involved in rake-offs from heroin trafficking. Would you publish it?

TOOHEY

Yes. Yes, of course I'd publish the report.

MODERATOR

You'd publish a *draft* report?

TOOHEY

A draft report, yes. I think it's important; obviously the government thought it was important; the subject seems to be reasonably important. Yes.

MODERATOR

Mr Dowd, you're the Attorney-General. The judge comes to you and says, "Look, they've got a copy of my draft report—not the final report—and it's tremendously important that we find out who leaked that document because, as you know, we have some enormously sensitive information, and there's clearly someone on the staff we can't trust. We think we can trace that traitorous source if only we can get back the numbered copy that's leaked."

DOWD

Well, we'll help you find the source of the leak, but we can't stop publication. We've just got to let it run. The best thing now is to get the report finished, publish it, and then we'll announce a new entertainment centre or whatever to take the heat off the following week. (laughter)

MODERATOR

"Superintendent Doberman thinks that when we get the photocopy back we can trace it to whichever photocopying machine was used to make the copy, and this will help us to identify the source. So I want that document back."

LITTLEMORE

In which case you can get it back. It's an item of property—the Commissioner's property—and it's been stolen.

MODERATOR

"How can I get it back?"

LITTLEMORE

By the intervention of the police, as if it had been a stolen bicycle.

MODERATOR

The police can just go into Mr Toohey's newspaper and uplift the document?

LITTLEMORE

That's the law.

TOOHEY

They have to find it first, don't they?

MODERATOR

They can't find it. Is there any other way we can get it back?

LITTLEMORE

You could take injunctive proceedings in the Supreme Court.

MODERATOR

The government takes injunctive proceedings in the Supreme Court, and gets a court order that the newspaper should hand back to the Commissioner what is his property—namely the copy of the draft report. You have it, Peter Bowers. Do you hand it back?

BOWERS

I would have had several copies made of the original photocopy, and I may hand back one of the copies. I'd be very careful about handing back the original copy because, like Brian, I'd be very careful and would want to do everything humanly possible to protect the anonymity of my source.

TOOHEY

If you hand it back, Peter, I hope no-one ever gives you another story—ever. It's outrageous that you should even think of handing it back.

BOWERS

What I'm saying is, if you're obliged by court injunction to hand it back . . .

MODERATOR

And you are.

BOWERS

You first hand back a copy of it, not the original copy that you've received direct from the source.

MODERATOR

You'd better have a word with your lawyer, Mr Teague. There is an injunction, an order by the Supreme Court to hand back the original document that came in the brown paper envelope.

What's your advice? The document was given to you for safekeeping. You have it in your law office safe.

TEAGUE

My advice is to obey the court order. I'd hand back the report on the basis that it is the subject of the court order, and the only way you can comply with that order is to hand it over.

MODERATOR

Do you take that advice Mr Bowers?

BOWERS

Oh, I'd take the advice, but I'd be telling him if he hands back the original report, he'll never get another brief from me.

MODERATOR

Well, you're the client. You could take it back.

BOWERS

I'd take it back.

MODERATOR

He wants to take it back, Mr Teague?

TEAGUE

He gets it back. (laughter)

MODERATOR

And you get another brief. A brief to explain to Mr Bowers and his senior management what the consequences will be of not handing it over; of defying the court order.

TEAGUE

Well, it will amount to a contempt. If you continue to disobey it will be a continuing contempt, and not only will it be a matter of continuing fines, but more likely, if a dim view was taken by a judge of the failure to hand it back, it could mean continuing imprisonment.

MODERATOR

The proprietor certainly doesn't want continuing fines, although he's not too much bothered about Bowers going to prison.

BOWERS

But, see, I can't hand it back because as soon as I got it back, I put it through the shredder. Now I've got five copies of that original photocopy, and I hand them all over, and I tell the court that for all I know the original might be one of these. These are all I've got. You're welcome to them.

MODERATOR

Superintendent Doberman's forensic sicentists do tests, and find out that what you've handed back is not the photocopy, but a copy you created from it. The court doubles the fines, and sends you to prison for contempt of court; for deceiving the court.

BOWERS

It's through the shredder, and I can't do anything about it!

MODERATOR

Not. from prison. (laughter) Suppose Mr Mathews has the document. You're his adviser, Mr Littlemore.

LITTLEMORE

Your original document is the only thing you've got to bolster your story. It's the only thing that can protect you from a libel action, so really you've got to keep it. I would advise you, Ian, that it isn't necessary for you to hold onto the thing to protect your position. You can release it to the custody of the court and keep a photocopy so that the evidence can't be changed. There's no necessity to put your head on the block unless you want to make a martyr of yourself.

MATHEWS

I'm not particularly keen to make a martyr of myself.

MODERATOR

The court has ordered you to place the original photocopy into the custody of the court. The judge is going to decide whether it should go back to the government.

MATHEWS

The advice of my legal adviser is that we have some protection if we do that, so yes, I hand it over to the court.

MODERATOR

The court decides that the document is the property of the Commission, and hands it over to the Commissioner. Superintendent Doberman traces it to the photocopying machine used by Miss Sara Mole, a twenty-three-year-old typist who confesses, is prosecuted and convicted and sent to gaol for six months. Mr Neville, you're a reporter on Mr Mathews' paper. What do you do?

NEVILLE

I'd feel very responsible if the source was in gaol. I would resign.

MODERATOR

There's more to the report than I've told you about so far. It deals with organised crime syndicates, and it deals in particular with the importation of heroin by one syndicate from Malaria, a country to Australia's north. The heroin is produced in the hills by an Islamic terrorist group. It's sold to an Australian syndicate who recruit young couriers to carry it down to Sydney in their luggage. Mr Littlemore, you are the Solicitor-General, and you're asked to advise the federal government on how they can stop leaks about top secret and highly sensitive negotiations with the Malarian authorities about this importation racket. There's a secret section of the report which details the syndicate's operation, and publication would perhaps put at risk the lives of some informants.

LITTLEMORE

The federal government can try the voluntary procedure of the "D" notice, which is about as much use as the Press Council. Which means that it's a lot of use so long as people respect it.

MODERATOR

It might be a lot of use, because the story hasn't come to Mr Toohey, it's come to Mr Holmes of *Four Corners*. Would it be more help against the ABC?

LITTLEMORE

Without question.

MODERATOR

Mr Holmes, you have a story and you have a "D" notice on it. What do you do?

HOLMES

Well, I'm afraid on this one I'd have to consult my superior, unfortunately.

MODERATOR

Your superior is Wendy McCarthy. She's Acting General Manager.

HOLMES

(to McCarthy) I think the story is in the public interest, but we'll have to consider this "D" notice. If lives of Australian federal policemen or undercover agents or whatever are at risk, in our judgement as well as in the judgement of the government issuing the "D" notice, then we would have to give some consideration to not doing the story.

MODERATOR

There's more at risk than that; the ABC's budgetary allocation is coming up next month, which is a government decision and this is a government "D" notice. Will the ABC comply with it?

WENDY McCARTHY

No. If I'm the Acting Managing Director and I'm assured by my team of investigative journalists that this is very significantly in the public interest—and I would need to be assured that's the case—I think there would be sound reasons for letting them proceed with the story.

MODERATOR

The ABC, where it thinks it's in the public interest, should break a "D" notice?

McCARTHY

Yes. Are you asking me to allow you to go ahead, Jonathan?

HOLMES

I've referred it to you, Wendy. My advice as a journalist is it's a damn good story and we should publish, but I accept ultimately in matters that are going to jeopardise the ABC's relationship with the government, that there can be wider considerations. I think we should go with it, but I'm not going to jump up and down if you told me we shouldn't. I'm not going to resign, and I'm not going to run to the papers about it. But I can't guarantee my staff won't.

McCARTHY

I think the essential thing is that we deal with every case on its merits and if I decide that in my judgement there's a story to be told that may well benefit the public interest . . .

MODERATOR

But what qualifies you to decide? You don't have the

information available to the government, which in its wisdom
has issued the "D" notice?

McCARTHY

The very essence of being an independent public service
broadcaster . . .

MODERATOR

But you're not independent. You're reliant upon government
funds; and, as a national broadcaster, can't you rely upon the
government to decide the national interests?

McCARTHY

I rely upon the government to decide the national interest, but
the interests of broadcasting and the national interest don't
always coincide.

MODERATOR

Jim McClelland, you've just been appointed Chairman of the
ABC, and this matter comes to the board. Should the ABC
break the "D" notice?

McCLELLAND

I think this raises a fundamental philosophical question. Is any
organ of the media, whether newspaper, television station, radio
station, entitled to publish anything that comes into its
possession? Now the ultimate test of that would be if an item
came to the ABC, or to Mr Bowers, which would obviously be
damaging to the security of the country. Is it seriously put
forward by media people here, that that doesn't matter? That
they can publish anything that they get? Well I certainly can't
go along with that and I don't think that the media proprietors
generally do believe that. As Wendy said, you judge the facts in
each particular case. But I would hope that the people in charge
of our media are responsible enough to know that there are
some things which they just should not publish.

MODERATOR

You are in charge of this particular branch of the media.
Government experts have formed the view that this story
shouldn't be published.

McCLELLAND

That's the dangerous part of it, because governments are inclined to hide behind what they proclaim to be matters of national security. I wouldn't accept the "D" notice merely on the government's say-so. But I would examine the matter on its merits, and if I decided that it was something which, on balance, was against the public interest — for instance, if publication were to hinder suppression of the heroin traffic — I would not publish it. I wouldn't just act on the government's word, I'd make my own investigations. But if it's clear from the story that it would damage efforts to destroy the heroin traffic, I would withhold it. I wouldn't publish it.

MODERATOR

If the story came to you, Anthony McClellan, as producer of a commercial television program . . .?

ANTHONY McCLELLAN

I'd publish the first story and then commission the second story about the attempt to suppress the first one.

MODERATOR

Your proprietor has had a word with the Prime Minister, and he's satisfied the "D" notice should be complied with.

ANTHONY McCLELLAN

If I felt that it was journalistically a story that should go to air, I'd have to obey him, but I would resign.

MODERATOR

You'd resign, and go to Mr Toohey with the story?

ANTHONY McCLELLAN

Yes.

MODERATOR

(To Toohey) And you'd publish it, "D" notice or not?

TOOHEY

I'd hopefully publish it — more nonsense is talked about national security than anything else. Some of the greatest scoundrels on this earth have hidden behind it. For instance when President Kennedy was engaged in preparing for the Bay of Pigs, the *New York Times* got onto the story. He got onto the phone, begged them not to run it and they didn't. He later wished to his dying day that they had run it because it was such a disaster for him. But he appealed to national security and the *New York Times*, to their shame as a newspaper, accepted his pleadings. Similarly when the Chairman of the ABC says he'd make his own investigations . . . how's he going to find out? They will say, "Sorry, we can't tell you that; that's a matter of national security." You will end up taking their word for it because they're grave, serious men who . . .

MODERATOR

But aren't they the experts?

TOOHEY

No, they're not. They're not experts at all. They're fools.

MODERATOR

They may be fools but they were elected by the public to decide the national interest.

TOOHEY

The fools I'm talking about were not elected. They're the head of the Defence Department and head of Defence Intelligence and the head of the Joint Intelligence Organisation. They're not elected at all.

McCLELLAND

I would decide it on the face of the documents that I had. I would make my own assessment as to whether it was genuinely in the public interest that the story should be suppressed. I wouldn't take it on the say-so of the Prime Minister or anybody else. Now surely it's not an impossible task to decipher from the facts in your documents whether, in your view, it would or would not be damaging to the public interest. You're not entitled to be Chairman of the board, or Managing Director of the ABC, if you can't do a thing like that.

TOOHEY

The motives that they express publicly for these things are never their real motives. They're motives to cover things up, to save embarrassment to the government. It is not our job . . .

McCLELLAND

Brian, could I ask you: do you concede that there could be a story which you should not publish?

TOOHEY

I can concede these things in a vacuum of course, but in reality,

when you get down to it, you nearly always find that the
reason people don't want things published are petty, horrible
little reasons. Like it might cost them two percentage points in
the next opinion poll or whatever.

MODERATOR

The Malarian government has taken a very hard line against
heroin traffickers. It's imposed the death penalty for possession
of heroin, and that's the charge facing Gail Jones, a Sydney
model and former *Playpen* playmate, who was arrested at
Nirvana airport with a large amount of heroin in the false
bottom of her suitcase. She's in prison in Malaria and she hasn't
been brought to trial. Julie Flynn, will you want to interview her?

JULIE FLYNN

Yes.

MODERATOR

The Malarian prison authorities have no objection to you
interviewing her. Her story is that she met a handsome New
Zealander on the beach, fell in love with him during her three
day holiday in Nirvana. He lent her his suitcase because hers was
battered, and he was going to collect it from her in Sydney
some weeks later. That's her story.

FLYNN

We let her tell her story on radio. But we'd also want to check
what the other side of the story was—from the police in
Malaria—and put their questions to her.

MODERATOR

You'd cross-examine her?

FLYNN

I'd play devil's advocate, and cross-examine her. You just can't
allow her to go on air and have free rein.

MODERATOR

She hasn't been tried yet, and the death penalty's in force in Malaria.

FLYNN

Yes. She knows that.

MODERATOR

She's been in Nirvana prison for a few months; not a pleasant experience. Do you cross-examine her about her story, Anthony McClellan?

ANTHONY McCLELLAN
Absolutely. You'd be very derelict not to.

MODERATOR
And you'd press her on her answers?

ANTHONY McCLELLAN
Yes, I would.

MODERATOR
She's not very intelligent. She doesn't have a journalist's IQ.

ANTHONY McCLELLAN
If she voluntarily submits to the interview, I would ask her whatever questions I thought appropriate at the time. I would play the devil's advocate to her, as Julie Flynn would.

MODERATOR
You cross-examine, and she breaks down sobbing and says, "I needed the money, because I was hooked on heroin. I'm just so sorry, so dreadfully sorry." You've got a great film. Do you show it?

ANTHONY McCLELLAN
. . . Yes.

MODERATOR
Before her trial?

ANTHONY McCLELLAN
Yes.

MODERATOR
Even though the Malarian Embassy will video your program and use it in evidence against her?

ANTHONY McCLELLAN
Yes. I would tend to think that if she broke down in front of a television interviewer, and he's a skilled cross-examiner, then a courtroom cross-examiner would have no problems in getting the same admissions from her.

MODERATOR
She's got the right of silence in Malaria. She doesn't have to go

into the witness box. She could escape the death penalty if you withhold that film.

ANTHONY McCLELLAN

I'd still show it. Our publication of it is irrelevant to her commission of the act.

MODERATOR

It's her fault for trafficking heroin? Her fault for giving the interview?

ANTHONY McCLELLAN

Not her fault, her decision. There'd be no problems.

MODERATOR

You'd put it out. Would you, Jonathan Holmes, on *Four Corners*?

McCARTHY

(to Holmes) And don't ask *me* this time! (laughter)

HOLMES

I don't think we'd have any particular right not to show it. I mean, if she'd said anything else we would have run it. Why are we suddenly not going to run the truth?

MODERATOR

Because if you do, she's going to be executed.

HOLMES

That's not my responsibility—that's the law of the land in which she's committed the crime.

NEVILLE

Yes, but it's no good us hiding behind their responsibility. You as a person would be aware that if you broadcast that confession, a human being will be swinging on the end of a rope. Wouldn't that make you feel uncomfortable?

HOLMES

Well, it would, certainly. I mean, I don't think it's easy. I don't know what I'd do, in fact. I think in principle probably it ought to be published. But you could wait until after the trial is finished?

MODERATOR

You certainly could. In about a year's time.

FLYNN

    She did it; she's guilty; she confessed. What's the problem?

MODERATOR

    You'd run the interview?

FLYNN

    Of course.

MODERATOR

    It goes out—Julie Flynn's interview, Anthony McClellan's interview. Jim McClelland, you've been appointed to a job you've always wanted, the television critic of the *Sydney Morning Bugle*. (laughter) What do you write about these interviews?

McCLELLAND

    Well, I wish I had the instant wisdom of all the journalists here. I think it's a much more agonising question than any of them seem to face up to. Frankly, I don't know what I would do in the circumstances.

MODERATOR

    The trial of Gail Jones for attempting to export a large amount of heroin takes place in Malaria. The prosecution's prime exhibit is the television interview of her confessing to the crime. The judge accepts the prosecution's case, and sentences Gail Jones to death. The death penalty will be carried out by firing squad in the yard of Nirvana prison. The Malarian government, in the hope of deterring other Australian heroin couriers, will permit you to televise the execution, Jonathan Holmes. Will you?

HOLMES

    No.

MODERATOR

    Why not?

HOLMES

    I simply don't see any justification for it. It would be purely sensational interest. Sure there'd be public interest in it in the sense that the public would be riveted, but no. I mean, we don't have public executions in this country.

MODERATOR

    But they have them in Malaria and they execute Australians in

Malaria. They're about to execute Gail Jones in Malaria.

HOLMES

I don't think I'd put it on my program. I can't see it fitting into a *Four Corners* format, I could tell you that.

McCLELLAND

It's not much more indecent than what appeared on the ABC a few nights ago, is it? An interview with those condemned prisoners in Malaysia, asking how they felt about their imminent deaths?

MODERATOR

It's much more indecent than that; because the girl will be brought out in a white dress, she will be tied to a post, the execution squad will raise their rifles and shoot, an officer will walk up and hold a pistol to her head and finish her off . . .

HOLMES

And it's not going to achieve anything, for her or for anyone else. I can't see the point of it.

MODERATOR

The ABC has turned it down. Anthony McClellan, you're the producer of *Good Morning Today*. You can have an Aussat enhanced simulcast of it at eight o'clock in the morning.

ANTHONY McCLELLAN

I would not put it to air live. I would put it after a warning.

MODERATOR

What time?

ANTHONY McCLELLAN

I'd put it to air in what's deemed to be adult viewing time; in other words, after eight-thirty.

MODERATOR

You're not worried about the thrill some viewers will get out of this beautiful woman being killed . . .?

ANTHONY McCLELLAN

It's reality. It's news; it's happening; it's not invention. I think we have an obligation to report news. It is news.

MODERATOR

The government is banning what are called "video nasties",

which will pale into insignificance beside this real life snuff movie.

ANTHONY McCLELLAN
That is fantasy. This is reality.

MODERATOR
Doesn't that make it all the more dangerous, if viewers are turned on by it?

ANTHONY McCLELLAN
No, it makes it all the more dangerous to suppress it. The fact that people might get a prurient thrill out of it is not our responsibility.

MODERATOR
Would you film it, Richard Neville? You are there with a camera crew.

NEVILLE
I just personally would be incapable of being present at that event.

MODERATOR
Mr McClellan is your producer. You are the only reporter with a camera team we have in Malaria. He orders you to go.

NEVILLE
I'd race straight back to being a guest on a daytime television talk show in Australia. Personally I would not want to witness that execution. I would turn it off if it was on TV. Other people have to make that decision as to whether to film it or not, but if you do I think that you're aiding and abetting something basically inhuman.

ANTHONY McCLELLAN
The broadcasting is not the inhumanity. It's the actual act that's the inhumanity; the execution itself.

MODERATOR
Eighty per cent of the Australian public, according to the last opinion poll, approve of the execution of Australian heroin traffickers in Asian countries. By showing this barbaric act, aren't you going to make them confront their opinions by showing them what an execution is really like?

NEVILLE
That is exactly the sort of justification that the executive of the

program would make for showing it. But I'm just saying that an individual journalist has the right to refuse to become implicated in an obscenity.

MODERATOR

Would you, Wendy McCarthy, having heard those arguments, think it right for the ABC to show it?

McCARTHY

Well, as a viewer, I'm not interested in watching it. I'm sickened by it and I hate the journalists for showing it, but as a person with a responsibility in a media organisation I accept the right of the journalist and the executive producer to make the decision to show it.

McCLELLAND

If I had any say as to whether it was shown or not, I would allow it to be shown.

BURGESS

There were at least ten executions which I covered in Vietnam for the ABC, and they were shown.

MODERATOR

You'd make the film and show it.

BURGESS

Certainly. I would show it before eight-thirty because I presume children are not as timid as we make them out to be. The execution itself might well diminish all of us, but the suppression of it, I say, would diminish us much more. I would have covered at least ten executions by firing squad and every one of them was shown around the world.

MODERATOR

Gail Jones is executed. Some channels show it and some don't. At last there's some good news in Sydney. At least for some. State politicians have been so impressed by the licensed brothels that they've been visiting in Nevada and Amsterdam that they decide to legalise brothels in New South Wales. Brothels can operate under licence, and can advertise. Len Borgia has a brothel that he built on the old kindergarten site. It's called "The Upper House" and he wants to advertise it in the *Bugle*.

BOWERS

As far as I'm concerned he can. If it's legal, you advertise it.

MODERATOR

You will really carry a large advertisement: "The Upper House, licensed by Jim McClelland; celebrity nights Thursdays and Saturdays; Sunday brunch on our Love Boat leaving Darling Harbour at eleven o'clock." (laughter)

MATHEWS

Yes.

MODERATOR

And you'll take it, Brian Toohey. No problems about your readers being upset?

TOOHEY

There's an extraordinary proposition here that if something's happening and you don't report it, or you don't let an ad in, then somehow it doesn't happen. If something nasty happens in the world, like someone's executed, and you don't report it, you can all feel a lot better about it, because it didn't happen after all. It's an extraordinary proposition. These events are not created by the media, they happen out there. And if you report them or don't report them it doesn't alter the objective fact of their being there.

DOOGUE

But isn't it too easy to say, "I never have to make a moral judgement, I'm just there observing." You've got to come in with moral judgements.

TOOHEY

I don't want to make these judgements on behalf of other people, and I think it's particularly wrong that the Chairman of the ABC should impose his standards of decency or whatever . . .

MODERATOR

Owen Thomson, you have no hesitation about publishing brothel advertisements?

THOMSON

Well, we have hesitation. (laughter) We carry their advertisements but we have hesitation about it.

MODERATOR

Why are these advertisements different from, say, cigarette advertisements?

THOMSON

Well, I don't think a brothel can kill you, but a cigarette can.

MODERATOR

Smoking is still marginally more dangerous than sex? (laughter)

THOMSON

It's less enjoyable.

MODERATOR

So why do you hesitate then?

THOMSON

Because of the nature of some brothels.

MODERATOR

You go and inspect them yourself before you carry their ads? (laughter)

THOMSON

We send our brothel critic.

MODERATOR

Your brothel critic, unfortunately, has just caught Zenger's disease; probably by working too hard. And all the recent publicity about Zenger's syndrome, particularly the latest speculation that it's contracted by having group sex on waterbeds under the influence of cocaine, is a great boost to crusaders against the permissive lifestyle. It's a great boost to people like Mrs Lily White, the charismatic and formidable leader of the "Right to Exist" campaign, which opposes abortion under any circumstances. Julie Flynn, you're doing an interview with Mrs Lily White, and you discover just before you do it— it's not live—that twenty years ago, she herself entered an abortion clinic. She's in their records, under her maiden name. Would you ask her about it?

FLYNN

I would ask her would she consider having an abortion. I would ask her had she had one.

MODERATOR

She says, "Yes, when I was twenty-five I went to an abortion clinic. I'd been raped, you see, and I fell pregnant as a result. It's not generally known and I hope you won't make it generally known."

ANTHONY McCLELLAN

If in fact her position was that she was opposed to abortion in toto, I would lead with that question.

MODERATOR

The position of the Right to Exist organisation is they oppose abortion under any circumstance.

ANTHONY McCLELLAN

I would lead with that question. She's in the public domain, she's put herself up as a public spokesman for a moral issue and she's been hypocritical and the public has a right to know that.

MODERATOR

Do you agree with that, Richard Neville?

NEVILLE

I tend to. I would go even further and ask her to try and analyse her feelings about abortion now in light of her past experience.

MODERATOR

You ask the question and instead you get this answer: "Yes, I went to an abortion clinic twenty years ago. I had been raped, you see. I stayed in that place one night. I couldn't bear it. I couldn't go through with the operation. I left it. My boyfriend, Peter White, stood by me and married me. My daughter is now twenty, studying at Sydney University. She doesn't know that her real father is a rapist. Please don't publish."

NEVILLE

I think I'm going to change professions! (laughter) There's no hypocrisy, because Mrs Lily White didn't have the abortion after all. There's no justification for publishing that information.

MODERATOR

No hypocrisy here, Anthony McClellan. Her behaviour then was perfectly consistent with her beliefs now. Are you going to publish the fact that her daughter is the result of a rape inflicted upon her mother twenty years ago?

ANTHONY McCLELLAN

I would have thought that's the sort of information about her life history that she should have thought about before she entered the public domain. This sort of information may become public through the work of some journalist.

MODERATOR

Your source told you that she had an abortion, that she entered an abortion clinic. Your source was correct . . . up to a point. She entered the clinic, but she didn't have an abortion. She decided to have the baby.

ANTHONY McCLELLAN

Yes.

MODERATOR

So you alert the twenty-year-old daughter to the fact that her real father is not Peter White, but is a rapist?

ANTHONY McCLELLAN

That is one of the tragedies that families of public people take with them when their parents decide to go into public life.

MODERATOR

Do you publish, Peter Bowers?

BOWERS

I should, but I wouldn't.

MODERATOR

Why not?

BOWERS

I think that girl is entitled not to know that. It could ruin her life.

MODERATOR

But we ruined Melissa Nott's life by publishing her expulsion from school because she was the daughter of a public figure.

BOWERS

Well, you make a judgement . . . you just make a judgement.

MODERATOR

Yes, but how do you decide which person you're going to ruin and which you're not?

BOWERS

You make one judgement, he makes another.

MODERATOR

If he publishes it, will you publish?

BOWERS
It doesn't matter, does it.

MODERATOR
Once it's out, it's out. In these matters, media ethics are reduced to the lowest common denominator.

BOWERS
Afraid so.

MODERATOR
Can anything be done by the Press Council?

WOOTTEN
Not once it's over, no.

MODERATOR
Not once it's over. You can never restore to that twenty-year-old girl the belief that Peter White was her father.

WOOTTEN
Well, all we're concerned about is the observance of standards by the press, not redressing remedies to individuals. We have no way of doing that.

MODERATOR
Ladies and gentlemen, at last there is a suspect for the murder of Judge Nott's wife. His name is John Smith, and does he have a record! A member of the Nazi party in the sixties, Melbourne hit man in the seventies, in the eighties he moved to Sydney and, after a brief spell in the New South Wales police, he got involved in heroin trafficking from Malaria. He is believed to be the man who recruited Gail Jones to do the heroin run that ended her life. Some man, Peter Bowers. Some story. An arrest warrant has been issued. You have a photograph and you have that background information. Do you publish?

BOWERS
Of course, in the public interest you would publish, no problems. If he's on the run and dangerous, you publish at the police request.

MODERATOR
All that background detail? Including the fact that he's the man who sent Gail Jones to her televised execution?

BOWERS

You publish all that's relevant to the fact that he's a danger, that he's a menace to the public. This is why he's a menace. Look out for him.

MODERATOR

Would you publish all the background detail, Brian Toohey?

TOOHEY

Are you asking would I willingly be in contempt of court? (laughter)

MODERATOR

This background information comes to you from the police.

TOOHEY

This information comes from everywhere. It's a question of whether the information is interesting or not. Yes, I can see no problems in publishing this. Will it stop him getting a fair trial?

MODERATOR

Will it, Stuart Littlemore?

LITTLEMORE

Of course it will. It doesn't much matter whether they publish it while he's on the run, when the press seem to think, and they are probably right, that they can say anything alleged about him. It doesn't matter if they publish what the police say about him before he appears in court, because the police will say all those things opposing bail for him. No matter whether they are later substantiated or not, the police will poison the minds of a potential jury at every opportunity. That's the only intention one can infer on the part of the police when they give prejudicial material to the press, and that's why there are such moves to stop it.

MODERATOR

He is still on the run and the one advantage of the sensational publicity is that someone may recognise him. And someone does. He telephones Mr Hickie. "This fellow John Smith, he looks exactly like my neighbour, who disappeared in a rush just after that judge's wife was murdered. Should I call the police?"

HICKIE

Call the police? Wait, where do you live? I'll rush out and talk to you straightaway.

MODERATOR

You rush out, and the helpful neighbour points out the house. It seems locked up, but there is a window that is open just a fraction of an inch around the back. Would you think of entering?

HICKIE

I would certainly have no pretensions of trying to make myself a public hero and risk getting shot. (laughter)

MODERATOR

Mr McClellan, the window is slightly opened. This man is on the run. He is wanted by the police. He is believed to have murdered the judge's wife, to have been involved in Gail Jones's recruitment. Sensational story, and the window is open.

ANTHONY McCLELLAN

No, I don't think I would go in, but that would be more on grounds of cowardice than morals.

MODERATOR

Do you go, Pat Burgess?

BURGESS

Yes, I think I certainly would, if I had a very courageous camera team and that the window was half open. I would be inclined to put a sun gun through the window and have a quick look around. All you are risking is a break and entering charge anyway.

MODERATOR

But what gives you the right to go into his house?

BURGESS

Once again, the public interest.

MODERATOR

Anyone can go into anyone else's house?

BURGESS

No, no. As I say, you are breaking the law and you must take the consequences.

MODERATOR

Are you seriously saying that you, with a Master's Degree in Public Interest, decide when you are justified in breaking the law?

BURGESS

Yes, I make the judgement and morally perhaps it's wrong, but considering all the other things that journalists may or may not do, I think that a simple break and enter in order to get information and pictures which will inform the public is justified . . . in my own warped moral sense.

MODERATOR

You see a Nazi uniform hanging in the closet.

BURGESS

Great! Marvellous film. (laughter)

MODERATOR

You open the drawers. There's a picture of someone who seems to be Gail Jones on a Malarian beach. Would you take that?

BURGESS

I'd prop it up somewhere where it could be lit and I would film it.

MODERATOR

You publish it to the world and Mr Peter Smith, a travelling salesman, who is watching your television program from a motel in Broken Hill, sees his home and his habits put onto Aussat enhanced pictures in Mr Burgess's film. He rushes back to you, Mr Littlemore. "I am very upset by the implication that I'm a murderer and heroin trafficker." What can you do to redress his hurt and grief?

LITTLEMORE

Well, his premises have been trespassed upon for a start. And if Burgess has put it to air with the suggestion that he's the wanted man, then it's libel as well.

MODERATOR

What sort of damages would you expect a jury to award in this situation?

TEAGUE

About twenty-five thousand dollars. But you always have to add a nought to that if the case is heard in Sydney rather than Melbourne.

MODERATOR

Why is that? Do Sydney juries dislike their newspapers more?

TEAGUE

Yes, it may be that they dislike their newspapers more. It may be that they are just a more generous population.

MODERATOR

John Smith is finally captured, and brought to trial for the murder of Annabell Nott, the judge's wife. It's a sensational trial, and the ABC, to boost its flagging ratings, is re-enacting highlights of the day in court with a transcript edited by David Williamson. Stuart Littlemore, do you object? You're defending John Smith. And you are being played by Mel Gibson. (laughter)

LITTLEMORE

Thank you. You can only object in so far as it is inaccurate or gives a prejudicial impression, but if it were going out every night, I'd ask Mr Justice McClelland to stop it, or else to discharge the jury and give us a retrial when things are calmer.

McCLELLAND

I'll reserve my decision and talk it over with my brother judges. What would you do, Hal? (laughter)

MODERATOR

Judges these days simply don't talk to each other. (laughter) Are you going to stop this dramatic re-enactment? You're being played by Max Gillies; and so is everyone else. (laughter)

McCLELLAND

It would depend on whether I formed a view that what was being done was prejudicial to a fair trial. I see no objection to television cameras in courtrooms. In fact, when I was a judge, I regularly had them in my court.

MODERATOR

American lawyers say that since television has been allowed in the courts, the lawyers are better prepared, the judges better behaved and the public better informed.

McCLELLAND

That's true. But be warned; the ratings of such shows would be abysmal.

MODERATOR

Richard Neville, you've been a defendant. Would you have

welcomed television coverage of your trial?

NEVILLE

I think I would, in my own case, because I think the more people view the proceedings in court, the less people will be mystified at what goes on.

MODERATOR

Would your clients want their trial to be televised, Stuart Littlemore, to let the public see them cowering in the dock?

LITTLEMORE

In some cases, clearly, it would be seen as being undesirable, but in other cases it may be appropriate. It's very much a matter on which all the parties, including the accused, would have to be considered. I have only ever known one client who wanted that sort of publicity. Everybody else is terrified that people will know they have been on trial. Let alone convicted.

MODERATOR

There's a sensation at the John Smith trial. He's on trial for the murder of Judge Nott's wife, and Geraldine Doogue is subpoenaed to give evidence. She's asked by the defence for the name of the source who tipped her off about the danger to the judge's security. The very high, very reliable source, to whom she gave an undertaking of absolute confidentiality. Will you break that undertaking?

DOOGUE

No.

MODERATOR

Even though it may mean being sent to prison for contempt?

DOOGUE

Yes, I would keep that confidence, even at the risk of prison.

MODERATOR

Are you sure?

DOOGUE

I would be petrified and I'd be working my damnedest to try to put it off, but I would uphold the principle that underlies my actions as a journalist.

MODERATOR

At the end of the day, you would protect the confidentiality of your source, even if it meant going to prison?

DOOGUE
  Yes, I think I can say I would.

MODERATOR
  We will deal with you at the end of the trial. (laughter) And
  the trial does end, ladies and gentlemen, with the conviction of
  John Smith for the murder of Annabell Nott whose husband,
  Judge Nott, is appointed to the High Court to fill the vacancy
  created by the death of Mr Justice Benchmark. He died, alas,
  just before the cause of Zenger's syndrome is discovered. It's a
  new ingredient in printer's ink, absorbed into the bloodstream
  through the skins of newspaper readers who get their editions
  hot off the presses. The discovery comes just in time to save Sir
  David Murfax, who celebrated his new lease of life by falling in
  love and marrying the glamorous film star, Kerrie Bombschell.
  To while away the long and lonely hours as the wife of a
  busy media proprietor, Kerrie Murfax writes a novel — *We Name
  the Guilty Men* — an improbable story of journalists who wrestle
  with the law, their consciences and each other. The Murfax
  newspapers, publishing houses and television stations fall over
  themselves to publicise, review and mini-serialise it. Meanwhile
  Andrew Angel weathers the last corruption storm by marrying
  Mrs Lily White's daughter, and goes on to become Premier of
  New South Wales.
  Geraldine Doogue, like the good journalist she is, refuses to
  reveal her source and goes to prison for contempt — fortunately,
  during a non-rating period. (laughter) She alone knows who her
  source was, the man who tipped her off to the danger to the
  judge and his family, the man who knew she'd never betray a
  source. It was Judge Nott, setting up a media cover story to
  divert suspicion from himself on the day he murdered his wife.

UNTO US
A CHILD IS BORN

William Shockley, the first Nobel Prizewinning scientist to donate his semen to a celebrity sperm bank in order that his intelligence might be propagated, had already fathered within marriage three extremely dull children. When asked how this squared with his controversial theories about genetic inheritance of IQ, he explained that his wife was stupid.

This study of science, sex and insemination, hypothesises the availability of certain technqiues of genetic diagnosis and in-vitro fertilisation which are already on the scientific agenda. How will they affect the relationships between men and women in an Australia of the not very distant future? Can we predict antisocial consequences with sufficient certainty to ban experimentation now, or is censorship of scientific knowledge inevitably counterproductive? Can there be effective legal or ethical limitations on techniques which benefit individuals but which may damage the social fabric, when private enterprise allows medical entrepreneurs to give some people what they want, or at least what they are prepared to pay for? Who should decide where to draw the bio-ethical line, and upon what principles?

A Royal Commission is meeting to discuss what life will be like after the Bicentennial. A leading experimental scientist is worried about his wife's inability to conceive, the increasingly bizarre behaviour of his bandicoots, and a tempting career offer from the University of the Deep North. A plane crashes, a fridge defrosts, a gramophone plays "Send in the Clones". In a court of last resort, a litigant will one day ask, "Who am I?"

UNTO US A CHILD IS BORN
Participants

BETTINA ARNDT
  Clinical Psychologist

HELEN COONAN
  Litigation Lawyer

ROSEMARY CROWLEY
  Labor Senator, South Australia

DR PETER FARRELL
  Bio-Medical Engineering, University of New South Wales

PROFESSOR TIMOTHY GLOVER
  President, Fertility Society of Australia

BRIAN HARRADINE
  Independent Senator, Tasmania

DR ROBERT JANSEN
  Gynaecologist

DR JOHN KERIN
  Reproductive Medicine Unit, Adelaide University

PROFESSOR CHARLES KERR
  Preventive and Social Medicine, Sydney University

EVA LEARNER
  Social Worker

FATHER BRIAN LUCAS
  Sydney Catholic Archdiocese

RUSSELL SCOTT
  Barrister and Deputy Chairman, New South Wales Law Reform
  Commission

THE VERY REVEREND LANCE SHILTON
  Anglican Dean of Sydney

PROFESSOR PETER SINGER
  Philosopher, Monash University

IAN TEMBY Q.C.
  Director of Public Prosecutions

DR ALAN TROUNSON
  In-Vitro Fertilisation Team, Monash University

FREDA WHITLAM
  Moderator, New South Wales Synod, Uniting Church

Recorded in the Great Hall,
Sydney University,
December 1985.

UNTO US A CHILD IS BORN

MODERATOR

Where better, ladies and gentlemen, to solve the sweet mystery of life than in the Great Hall of a great university; the place where Germaine Greer learnt English, and Enoch Powell taught Greek. Let us imagine it today as the meeting place of Australia's latest Royal Comission—a Royal Commission into the future of human relationships, established to answer the momentous question: "What will life be like after the Bicentennial?" (laughter)

Ian Temby, you're a member of this Royal Commission and because of the Treasurer's latest crackdown on perks you're travelling to the meeting by bus. It's a rather crowded Parramatta Road bus, but you do find a seat—which is more than Bettina Arndt does, who gets on at the next stop. She's standing in the aisle beside you; are you going to offer her your seat?

IAN TEMBY

No.

MODERATOR

Why not?

TEMBY

Unless she's got some particular disability—and being female is not a disability—she's not in need of particular assistance from me.

MODERATOR

You're going to sit there in comfort for twenty minutes while the bus lurches and sways and she tries to stop falling into your lap?

TEMBY

If she asked me to give up the seat I might do so, but I would assume otherwise that she can look after herself.

MODERATOR

Weren't you brought up to stand up for women?

TEMBY
Yes, I was when I was young.

MODERATOR
But now you're old, you've overcome the temptation. (laughter)
Suppose it were Freda Whitlam in the aisle; would you stand up
for her?

TEMBY
At the risk of being offensive, I think I would; yes.

MODERATOR
Why?

TEMBY
Bettina Arndt is apparently as fit as I am—probably fitter—and of my
age or younger. At least the latter can't be said of Freda Whitlam.

MODERATOR
When did Australian men stop standing up for women, Bettina Arndt?

BETTINA ARNDT
I think when women started standing up for men, which was
approximately ten years ago.

MODERATOR
As a result of the Whitlam government?

ARNDT
No, as a result of the women's movement. Making people realise
that that sort of chivalry wasn't doing us very much good in
terms of the issues that are important for women.

MODERATOR
So men were able to overcome their instinctive and their learnt
desires to stand up for women, in order to show that women
really are equal. Professor Glover, you're going down in the lift
this morning with Helen Coonan. The lift stops at the ground
floor, you're both getting out; would you stand aside and let
her go first?

TIM GLOVER
Yes.

MODERATOR
Why?

GLOVER

I was brought up to do that kind of thing and I think chivalry is important.

MODERATOR

But she is a much younger woman, you've got a test tube full of freshly donated semen you are anxious to put in the refrigerator, she's going shopping. You'd still let her go first?

GLOVER

Yes, I think I would.

MODERATOR

Because of the way you've been brought up or because perhaps of something instinctive, something in the "Y" chromosome— the male chromosome—that predisposes men to be more avuncular to women, more protective of them?

GLOVER

I wouldn't say it's genetic. I think the way you're brought up is important, but it has a much wider social connotation too. There is a wider philosophical reason for that kind of behaviour on the part of males.

MODERATOR

Professor Singer, do you detect a wider philosophical reason?

PETER SINGER

No. I have to say that I can't really see that there is one. It would depend entirely on the priority of the business that Helen Coonan and Professor Glover have as to who should get out of that lift first.

MODERATOR

Helen Coonan, he's an older man. Would you let him out first?

HELEN COONAN

Yes, I would turn and let him out first.

MODERATOR

So no-one's going to get out of this lift? (laughter) Well, we have a Royal Commission meeting this morning to plot our biological and bio-ethical future. It has a bottomless cornucopia of federal funds to give out to worthwhile scientific research projects. The first project to come before you is from Dr Peter

Jekyll of the Dapto Institute of Technology. Dr Jekyll's work on monoclonal antibodies makes him think that he can perfect a sex selection gel, so couples can decide whether they want a boy or a girl. Before you have intercourse, there will be a pink gel you can use if you want a girl and a blue gel you can use if you want a boy. Dr Farrell, would this be a valuable chemical breakthrough if it were safe and could be patented?

PETER FARRELL

If you had a woman who had four boys and wanted a girl, I think most people would say it's nice to have that choice available.

MODERATOR

So people could have legitimate reason for using the sex selection chemical to have a balanced family?

FARRELL

Right. On the other hand if somebody wanted to create an army—all boys of a certain size, weight, et cetera—I think you'd question that application.

MODERATOR

But if you're going to patent it and put it on the market, you can't tell for what reason it would be used.

FARRELL

Correct. Taking the entrepreneurial approach, if you were going into this to give people the choice—and if you were an entrepreneur you'd have to make money—you'd worry about the moral climate more than the morals.

MODERATOR

So, if it were safe, you would sell it?

FARRELL

I would sell it if there was a definite clientele; if there was a viable market.

MODERATOR

Do you feel any qualms about supporting Dr Jekyll's research, Bettina Arndt?

ARNDT

I think there are distinct dangers in terms of the future market

because of our society's appalling preference for male children.
There's a great danger we wouldn't have any women left to
experiment with in the years to come.

MODERATOR

But we've seen how Ian Temby can overcome self-regarding
male desires; isn't it possible that in the future Australian men
will cease to want sons?

ARNDT

We'd have to have a re-education process to convince them of
the value of having female children.

LANCE SHILTON

I'd be very careful about it because I believe that we ought not
to interfere with the balance of nature. And we don't quite
know what complications arise in the long run if you had the
choice in the sex of a child. It could be a disadvantage to the
whole of the human race.

MODERATOR

So you'd be dubious about it because it seems unnatural?

SHILTON

Yes.

MODERATOR

I suppose all drugs in a sense are unnatural. Cosmetic surgery is
unnatural, but we cope with that.

SHILTON

Yes, but other drugs are supposedly there to provide for health
or some need. I don't see that chosing whether a child is to be
male or female is actually contributing to a particular need.
Nature can do that for itself.

MODERATOR

Nature can't, if you've got three boys and you want a girl. Or
if you want to produce a child who will grow up to become an
Anglican priest. It would have to be a boy.

SHILTON

In the family context that would be so. But I think we have to
look at the broader community context rather than personal
desires within one family.

MODERATOR

Dr Jansen, do you see any dangers in the sex selection chemical?

ROBERT JANSEN

I think it has to be recognised that medical indications for it would be rare, and in most instances it would be somewhat similar to "cosmetics".

MODERATOR

But what's wrong with giving Australians the opportunity to have balanced families? It's a question of freedom of choice, isn't it?

JANSEN

Oh I agree, but let's not call it medicine.

MODERATOR

In fact, there is a gung ho medical entrepreneur called Harry Mainchance who's already set up Computa-Baby Pty Ltd, in order to market this sex selection chemical. Any objections?

JANSEN

Oh no, not especially. But he's not acting as a doctor in that capacity. He's acting as a businessman.

MODERATOR

He's giving people what they want.

JANSEN

Yes, he's acting as a businessman. This is not medical research, it's industrial research, and the difference is important.

MODERATOR

Professor Singer, you're a member of the Royal Commission; would you support the right to choose the sex of one's child through this development?

SINGER

Since we have the funds, I would. The arguments about being cosmetic or medical don't really apply. The other thing that perhaps is relevant here is we've only been considering the Australian benefits. In terms of the Third World and the population problems in some countries where people may have large families because of cultural preferences for one or two sons, this gel could actually do an immense amount to reduce population problems.

MODERATOR

In India, girl children may be killed. The gel could save lives?

SINGER

It could do that, certainly.

MODERATOR

Eva Learner, does that argument appeal to you?

EVA LEARNER

No, no. I have great caution about the whole thing. Male and female babies are equal in their status and therefore I wouldn't support this kind of development.

MODERATOR

You're worried about men not being able to change their rather self-regarding desire for boy children?

LEARNER

Yes, exactly so.

MODERATOR

Well by a narrow majority the Royal Commission turns down Dr Jekyll's project. Let's look at the second application, which comes from the Leichhardt Gender Workshop. They're interested in developing male pregnancy, Dr Trounson. You can grow an embryo outside the body in a test tube?

ALAN TROUNSON

Yes, it can be done.

MODERATOR

You could perhaps grow it for a little time in a test tube, then implant it in the male abdominal cavity, where it would generate its own placenta and grow into a baby you could deliver by caesarian section.

TROUNSON

Yes, that's certainly possible. It could happen in Australia within the next few years.

MODERATOR

Bettina Arndt, the male pregnancy—a consummation devoutly to be wished?

ARNDT

It would be very good for men.

MODERATOR

You'd like to give up your seat to a pregnant man in the bus?
(laughter)

ARNDT

Yes, certainly I'd give up my seat to a pregnant man. But I
think about it in terms of being aware of some aspects of the
experience and in terms of learning more about the whole
process of becoming fathers in a more active way; and
particularly in respect to the case of the trans-sexual who feels
himself to be a woman.

MODERATOR

It might make men more gentle, more in touch with life?

ARNDT

More involved, yes.

MODERATOR

Freda Whitlam, if women could be priests, why can't men be
mothers?

FREDA WHITLAM

It would be very good for them to have the experience of the
other side of life. I'm not happy, though, about the moral
question of the engineering. Where is it heading; does it help
the nation, this enormous amount of money being spent just to
gratify the desire of a very few men to have babies?

MODERATOR

But if a man is happily married, his wife's career is taking off
while his is static, wouldn't it be more sensible for the man to
bear the baby?

WHITLAM

I wonder if the child-bearing process is as important as all that
for the fulfilment of people. There are other ways of being
fulfilled.

MODERATOR

A bit of support for the male pregnancy, Dean Shilton, on the
Royal Commission. What's your view?

SHILTON

I believe it would be a confusion in the roles of male and female that could lead to all kinds of complicated problems. We know the confusions in the minds of trans-sexuals for instance, and I don't think that child-bearing would solve their particular problems of identity. I don't believe that male pregnancy would contribute in any way to the needs of males or females.

MODERATOR

Some men would like to have babies.

SHILTON

I haven't met any men yet who would like to have babies.

MODERATOR

Have you met men who would like to have babies, Dr Trounson?

TROUNSON

Yes, we've had dozens of trans-sexuals ask us already.

SHILTON

Well I think that maybe they would need to see whether they could find other ways by which they could be fulfilled, rather than entering into a role which is not a man's role. As far as the Bible is concerned, its teaching is very clear about male and female roles.

MODERATOR

Does the Bible say anything about who should bear the children?

SHILTON

Well it does have many accounts of children being born by women, but certainly none by a man.

MODERATOR

Dr Trounson wasn't alive in those days. (laughter)

SHILTON

I think that we need to take heed of the principles which are there. There's a certain role for men and a certain role for women and if we're going to confuse those roles, we need to have some biblical evidence for doing that and I don't believe such evidence exists.

MODERATOR

Professor Singer, is there a logical objection to male pregnancy?

SINGER

I don't think there is a logical objection. I mean so far as what's not in the Bible, you could point out that the pop-up toaster is also not mentioned but I don't think that means that we shouldn't have them. The only objection is whether the men going into it fully understand the risk that they're incurring, and whether there is a possibility that the child that's born will be damaged through not having had the usual prenatal environment. If one could be assured on those points I don't really see a logical objection.

MODERATOR

Very narrowly, the Leichhardt Gender Workshop project is turned down by the Royal Commission. But maybe it will be third time lucky for Bill Bunsen, the distinguished geneticist. He's a professor, working within all the ethical constraints of this great university, and he wants Royal Commission funding for his project on genetic predispositions. He wants to try to unravel the DNA in our bodies, to see whether its twists and turns *predispose* us to certain forms of behaviour. A perfectly proper project, Professor Kerr?

CHARLES KERR

Perfectly proper, but one which people have been trying to tackle for nearly a hundred years.

MODERATOR

Bill is the most brilliant product of Sydney University, and there's a chance that he could get somewhere with it. No objections, Dr Jansen?

JANSEN

In principle no. He's seeking knowledge . . .

MODERATOR

Knowledge is a good in itself?

JANSEN

It is a good in itself.

MODERATOR

Bill Bunsen has already won international acclaim for proving that the wombat, like the guinea pig, is genetically predisposed against elaborate sexual foreplay. (laughter) No objections?

JANSEN

No objections.

MODERATOR

Bill's project is approved. He's overjoyed. His joy makes him forget for a moment the great sadness in his life. His wife, Wendy, can't conceive by normal methods because she has a blockage in her Fallopian tubes that doesn't respond to tubal surgery. Could you help her, Dr Trounson?

TROUNSON

Yes, if she has functioning ovaries we would use the IVF procedures to create test-tube babies. We treat the women with fertility drugs so that we get a number of eggs, we fertilise those eggs with the husband's sperm in a dish in the laboratory, and then transfer the early developing embryo back to the womb.

MODERATOR

So you get a number of eggs—perhaps seven—from Wendy; you'll put them in test tubes and put a little bit of Bill's sperm into each tube, and hope an embryo will grow. Then two or three days later you'll put the embryo back into Wendy, bypassing the obstruction in her tubes and creating a baby where none could grow before?

TROUNSON

That's right.

MODERATOR

Wendy is a Catholic, Father Lucas: Bill isn't. She comes to you and says, "Father, I'm thinking of going on the program. This is the only way I can have a baby."

BRIAN LUCAS

The advice that I would give her would firstly be to help her understand the implication of this program. The program as described sounds very simple. But there are certain other ethical considerations that one has to take into account.

MODERATOR

What are they?

LUCAS

What becomes of the embryos that are not implanted? Because

the creation of those excess embryos is the point of the overall
program, one would have to be very careful that one is fully
aware of the entire range of ethical implications.

MODERATOR

But if you could satisfy the problem of what happens to
the embryos that aren't implanted, you would say "go
ahead"?

LUCAS

I wouldn't necessarily say "go ahead".

MODERATOR

Why not?

LUCAS

Because she has to decide whether to go ahead, and I'm not
going to tell her yea or nay. She makes her own moral decision.
She's only come to me for advice.

MODERATOR

Right: "Is it amoral to go on this program? Am I being
immoral if I want a baby?"

LUCAS

I'm going to suggest to her that she has to consider the meaning
of human sexuality as her faith presents it to her; that important
unity between sexual relationship and procreation.

MODERATOR

"I know all that Father. Should I go on the program?"

LUCAS

She has to make that decision for herself. Ultimately she is the
one who makes the moral decision, not me.

MODERATOR

"So it's all right for me to go on it? I'm not going to *sin* by
going on this program?"

LUCAS

I have not said that to her.

MODERATOR

She asks you the direct question: "Is it a sin to go on Dr
Trounson's program?"

LUCAS

Well, she can ask me that question, but the point is that . . .

MODERATOR

The point is, what are you going to reply?

LUCAS

I am going to say to her whether or not she sins depends on her perception of the morality of what is involved. I have given her advice as to what her faith suggests to her are the relevant moral principles and then she has to take the responsibility for that.

MODERATOR

"There seems to be nothing immoral in wanting to have a baby in the only way I can. Surely it's not sinful for me to have a test-tube baby?"

LUCAS

Well then, she has to come to terms with the fact that acting in that way will perhaps be contrary to the faith that she possesses.

MODERATOR

But *is* it contrary to the faith? Can't you give me a simple "yes" or "no" answer?

LUCAS

You can give a simple "yes" or "no" answer, but that's not going to be the correct answer. It may be, however, that all of the principles and all of the evidence points to the fact that what she is going to do is not in accordance with her faith. Now that obviously is the position we arrive at, whether or not . . .

MODERATOR

You're going to make her feel just a little bit guilty.

LUCAS

I'm not going to set out to make anyone feel guilty. If she comes to a point where she feels this is not the right thing to do, then she's got to make her choice in accordance with that.

MODERATOR

Dr Trounson, can you take away her guilt a little?

TROUNSON

Yes, we can offer her the possibility of only fertilising the exact number of eggs we're going to replace on that cycle. So if the problem is to do with the excess embryos, they won't in fact exist.

MODERATOR

"I no longer feel guilty. Can I have my baby?" (laughter)

LUCAS

What do you think?

MODERATOR

"I think it's fine. I always wanted a baby and this is the only way I can have a child. There are a thousand children born so far by in-vitro fertilisation—they wouldn't have existed, otherwise. You wouldn't wish all the babies never to have existed?"

LUCAS

Whether or not they exist is not relevant, at all, to the question of whether or not they ought to have existed.

MODERATOR

Wendy's going to try to have a child with Bill; they're happily married; will you take them on the program?

TROUNSON

Yes, if they're married.

MODERATOR

If they're married? What about George and Robyn who have the same problem, but who've been happily unmarried for the same length of time.

TROUNSON

Unfortunately the law has intervened between us. The law in Victoria insists that they be married. It's the only State that prohibits people who are unmarried from having test-tube children.

MODERATOR

They say, "Look, if we succeed in having a baby, then we'll get married."

TROUNSON

But the option is that we go to gaol without passing go if we treat you knowing that you're not married.

MODERATOR

You can actually go to gaol for creating a baby for a happily unmarried couple!

TROUNSON

Unfortunately that's the case in the State of Victoria. I would suggest to George and Robyn that they move to New South Wales to have their baby.

MODERATOR

Well, that's precisely what they do; they move, though in fact to South Australia. John Kerin, would you treat George and Robyn?

JOHN KERIN

In special circumstances, with stable de facto relationships, we will admit them to the program.

MODERATOR

It's a very stable relationship, but as you're investigating Robyn's condition you find that the blockage in her Fallopian tubes is caused by a venereal infection which she picked up during her work as a prostitute.

KERIN

That is past tense now. If she has a stable relationship I don't think the fact that she once worked as a prostitute would significantly alter my appreciation.

MODERATOR

You're not going to make a moral judgement? You're not going to say, "You deserve everything you get for that self-inflicted injury"?

KERIN

No, I wouldn't.

MODERATOR

Well, Robyn is very grateful to you. She's particularly keen to have a child now, because her long-time stable relatee, George, is on bail on a charge of armed robbery. His trial will come in a few weeks' time—prosecuted by Mr Temby, so he'll probably go to prison for ten years. (laughter) Is that not going to affect your decision to take them on the program?

KERIN

You cannot look into the future. This is one of the dangers of making moral judgements about people.

MODERATOR

You won't make moral judgements? You would create a baby

for a prostitute and an armed robber? Mind you, with that
genetic inheritance, it will probably grow up to be a top Q.C.
(laughter) What about Trish? She's thirty-five, a successful
commercial lawyer, who has the same problem as Wendy and
Robyn. She's despaired of ever finding a man worthy of her
hand in marriage, but she wants to be a single parent. She can
obtain some sperm from an anonymous articled clerk in the
DPP's office. Would you treat her?

KERIN
In the current climate in our society, no, I wouldn't.

MODERATOR
Why not?

KERIN
I think the credibility of our programs are under clear scrutiny
by the public community, and I don't think that test-tube babies
for single parents would be acceptable to the majority of people
in the community.

MODERATOR
How do you know?

KERIN
Well, I don't know. It's just a feeling that I would have. I
mean a Gallup poll could be undertaken to determine whether it
is true or not.

MODERATOR
Dean Shilton, why shouldn't Trish have her child?

SHILTON
First of all, I believe it would be morally wrong on Christian
principles.

MODERATOR
But she's not a Christian.

SHILTON
Yes, but the principles are pragmatic in the sense that the whole
community benefits from the application of those Christian
principles. For a single person to have a child creates a whole lot
of problems. Obviously there has to be compassion when it
actually happens, but to voluntarily enter into that kind of

situation through test-tube programs is exacerbating problems that already exist in the community.

MODERATOR

Is there any rational reason why a successful thirty-five-year-old woman should not choose to have children?

SHILTON

The Christian concept is that children are a fruit of marriage and not of any other kind of relationship. Once you start moving from that I believe the whole structure of society is at risk.

MODERATOR

Because children need fathers?

SHILTON

Yes, because they need fathers, and because the whole security of that child is in jeopardy if they don't have them.

MODERATOR

But you've read the latest Youth and Community Services report; sixteen thousand children in New South Wales alone are beaten and abused by their drunken fathers. How can you say that children necessarily need fathers like that?

SHILTON

The whole community I think has something to answer for in that regard, because it is creating an atmosphere in which it is difficult for parents to bring up their children, and tensions arise.

MODERATOR

Trish lives with Georgina, an up-and-coming architect, in a stable lesbian relationship. Would you treat her then, John Kerin? She won't be a single mother; she'll have all the love and support of Georgina.

KERIN

Again I wouldn't, in that situation. I'm not reflecting against a stable lesbian relationship, but again the use of this high technology fertility treatment for that sort of relationship would be controversial and unacceptable.

MODERATOR

"Controversial and unacceptable." Who decides? Who is sitting over you, Alan Trounson, to say, "This is controversial: this is unacceptable; thou shalt not"?

TROUNSON

Nobody's sitting over you. You can make that decision. My only problem about treating those patients is that it would be against the law in Victoria. If I was in another State, I wouldn't have a problem.

MODERATOR

Is there anything, other than law, that's stopping you?

TROUNSON

No, I don't think there's anything but the law stopping me.

MODERATOR

What about ethics committees?

TROUNSON

Yes, there are ethics committees. An ethics committee rules on new procedures and new techniques that you wish to use. If this was considered to be a new procedure, then you would have to have it passed by the ethics committee.

MODERATOR

What's the qualifications for being on an ethics committee? Knowing the difference between right and wrong?

TROUNSON

No particular qualification. People learn ethics by being on ethics committees. (laughter)

MODERATOR

Russell Scott, you're on the federal ethics committee. What are the ethics of discriminating against single women and lesbian couples?

RUSSELL SCOTT

The question of eligibility for treatment is very important. Nobody has yet mentioned the integral question of the welfare of the child. One would have thought that the question of the welfare of the child, the kind of household that it might be going into, the stability of that household, would be considerations that would be at the forefront of the decision.

MODERATOR

We have a very stable lesbian relationship — middle-class, well-off, dedicated. They desperately want a child to love and cherish. It's going to be much better off than having a father who drinks and beats it up. Where are the *ethics* in discriminating against that sort of relationship?

SCOTT

We have a balancing act, because we have in fact conducted an investigation into the attitudes of the Australian community to this very question. The Australian community is conservative, and some seventy per cent indicated approval of this kind of insemination only for married couples.

MODERATOR

I wonder whether, if the people in that study had actually met Trish and Georgina, they would have the same opinion. Trish meets Helen Coonan at a women lawyers' conference. She says, "I'd really love to have a child like yours, but these ethics committees won't help me. Dr Trounson would love to help me, but his hands are tied by the law. Is there anything we can do?"

COONAN

My personal view is that if a medical treatment is available to a class of people in the community it ought to be available to all people, so long as they are able to nurture the child and bring it up in a loving environment. There might be a legal basis for an action.

MODERATOR

As it happens there *is* now a legal basis; the Australian Bill of Rights has just been passed, and it says, "Every person has a right to found a family." "I'm a person," says Trish. "Doesn't this give me the *right* to have access to test-tube technology?"

COONAN

Arguably, yes.

MODERATOR

Mr Temby, you've been so successful as DPP that the surviving politicians have appointed you to the bench. Argue the case on the Australian Bill of Rights before him.

COONAN

Judge, it would be my submission on behalf of Georgina and Trish that they certainly come within the accepted category of

having the right to found a family. They can provide a family
environment, they've been living in a stable relationship and
there doesn't seem to be any reason medically why there can't be
a successful baby resulting from the IVF procedure. Certainly my
clients' rights appear to be guaranteed under the Bill of Rights,
which provides that every person has the right to found a
family.

TEMBY

I grant you the order that you seek.

MODERATOR

So Trish has her child and the discriminatory ethics committee
ruling is struck down as infringing the new Australian Bill of
Rights. What about Sir Boden and Lady Budapest, Dr Kerin?
Sir Boden is a well-known Sydney business identity, blessed with
many millions of dollars and a new Filipino wife, but cursed
with a low sperm count. Would you help him? He's sixty-five
years old, and his wife is thirty.

KERIN

Yes, I think men with low sperm counts can now be helped by
IVF. We can separate the most motile sperm that they have,
and fertilise the egg in a test tube.

MODERATOR

Even though he's sixty-five and could die at any minute. He
wants an heir for his two hundred million dollars.

KERIN

I think they'd need careful counselling about their desire to be
parents, but we could help them obtain a child.

MODERATOR

Sir Boden and Lady Budapest are accepted on the program along
with Robyn and George and Bill and Wendy. What about me?
I'm thirty-eight, a busy barrister—far too busy to soothe
children every evening. But in ten years or so, when I'm a
judge, I'll have plenty of time on my hands and I'd like to have
my children then. My wife is thirty, she's a television presenter
who doesn't want to lose her figure and her job by having a
child now. Professor Glover, we'd like to lay down a few
embryos now, and then in ten years' time, have our children
with the help of a surrogate.

GLOVER

There's nothing that intrinsically worries me about that.

MODERATOR

It's a matter of our convenience?

GLOVER

Yes, in my own particular judgement that would be acceptable.
I have some reservations about surrogacy, but the storing of an
embryo for use at a convenient time doesn't worry me at all.

MODERATOR

Does it worry you, Russell Scott?

SCOTT

From the point of view of present technology, one would have
to think in terms of some time limit. There is a neat solution
that has already been suggested; an absolute time limit of say ten
years, or whatever remains of the reproductive competence of the
wife. The embryos could be stored until her menopause.

MODERATOR

But with test-tube technology, my wife doesn't have to bend to
the tyranny of the biological clock. We can lay down some
embryos and then have our children when it suits us, later in
life. Even, with the help of a surrogate, after her menopause.
Professor Glover, what about our last couple—Daniel and Sarah
Woebegone. They want to have a baby and they're perfectly
fertile, but they just don't want to have sex. Sarah can't bear the
idea of intercourse. She can't ever lie back and think of
Queensland. (laughter) Would you take them on your program?

GLOVER

Oh, yes.

MODERATOR

They are members of a religious sect, the Kingaroy Brethren,
who believe that all sex is wrong, even sex within marriage, and
that test-tube babies are particularly blessed because they're
created outside the body. It's a crackpot idea but they sincerely
believe it. Would you provide children for them?

GLOVER

Oh yes. I'm looking at this perhaps from a biological standpoint,
but their attitudes would not influence that situation at all.

MODERATOR

Professor Singer, do you see any difficulties in providing children for these people?

SINGER

I do see some difficulties here because I can't really imagine a situation in which there are no limits whatsoever on our facilities, and this seems to me to be really a waste of resources to go ahead with such complicated technology for people simply because of their crackpot ideas.

MODERATOR

But you've seen how test-tube technology is developing. It began as a boon for barren marriages. We have now moved from cases of necessity to cases of convenience—even to cases of whim.

SINGER

Someone, at least so far as State support for this is concerned, will have to draw a line.

MODERATOR

But if the State draws a line, Dr Farrell, doctors will always be found who will give people what they want, if it's not immoral?

FARRELL

That's true, but I would suggest to Alan Trounson that he put these people on the end of a very long waiting list.

MODERATOR

But cosmetic surgery, for example, came from the backblocks of Hong Kong to the brass plates of Macquarie Street very quickly indeed.

FARRELL

True.

MODERATOR

And a medical technology which was originated to treat cases of necessity was seized upon by private enterprise to operate in cases of convenience. Does that worry you, Dr Trounson?

TROUNSON

In the current Australian climate I'm not sure that it really should worry us because if people really desire this type of cosmetic medicine, then they can always procure it.

MODERATOR

Dr Kerin, let me congratulate you on your great success the other day in being the first person in the world to freeze the human female egg. How long would an egg or an embryo last in liquid nitrogen?

KERIN

There's no theoretical or practical reason why the human egg or embryo couldn't last for two thousand years.

MODERATOR

It would certainly last four hundred years.

KERIN

At least.

MODERATOR

That's very interesting, because you get a call this morning from the Australian Bicentennial Authority: "We've got a great new idea. We're going to have a Bicentennial Time Capsule, sealed for four hundred years. It will show future generations how Australians live now. We have a video of our America's Cup victory, the unpublished volumes of the Costigan Report, and we want you to freeze us an embryo, so that when the time capsule opens in 2388 A.D., our successors will be able to give birth to an embryo of a typical Australian family circa 1988. Tim and Debbie from the ABC will donate the embryo; would you freeze it for us?

KERIN

I don't think I would.

MODERATOR

Why not?

KERIN

Well, I think you're really dealing with the beginning of a human life once you've fertilised the egg, and you've got to think of the outcome for that child if it survives the freezing process.

MODERATOR

But it's just conceivable that Australia may be a better place to live in four hundred years' time.

KERIN

I think the way it's going it might not be.

MODERATOR

Wouldn't it be fascinating if your technology had been available four hundred years ago, and today we were giving birth to a child of Shakespeare's age? Fascinating, Professor Kerr, for those in four hundred years' time to see our rather primitive genetic structure?

KERR

Fascinating, but little else, I would think.

MODERATOR

Bettina Arndt, you're approach by the Bicentennial Authority. "We'd like to celebrate Dr Kerin's achievement by freezing some of your eggs in our time capsule." In four hundred years' time, it will be the Australian sexcentenary and what could be more appropriate to Australia's sexcentenary than the birth of a child of Bettina Arndt. Indeed, in four hundred years' time they will have perfected the technique of parthenogenesis, whereby a child can be created from a female egg without the need for a male sperm, so they'll probably be able to produce a clone of Bettina Arndt.

ARNDT

How appalling.

MODERATOR

Wouldn't you do that for history?

ARNDT

No. Because I'm a product of my upbringing rather than my genes, and I don't have enough faith in my genes. It would be an arrogant assumption that my genes are so important.

MODERATOR

Peter Singer, can you see any objection to the Bicentennial Time Capsule?

SINGER

Not any really strong objection. I don't believe that the embryo we're freezing is a person. It's a mistake to think of it that way. It's a cell or a couple of cells. I have some worries, I suppose, about whether it's going to be regarded as some kind of freak when it's thawed out in four hundred years' time.

MODERATOR

Why not leave it to ethics committees in four hundred years' time?

SINGER

Well indeed; I don't suppose they'd do any worse than ethics committees today.

MODERATOR

Alan Trounson, let's move back to the clinic where Bill and Wendy are going through the IVF procedures. You take a number of eggs from Wendy, you put them in test tubes, drop a little of Bill's sperm in each and five eggs fertilise. Can you see the embryo?

TROUNSON

No. Only through a microscope.

MODERATOR

You've fertilised five of those eggs; how many are you going to implant?

TROUNSON

I don't like to implant any more than three, because the chances if you implant more are higher that you're going to have triplets and quadruplets.

MODERATOR

So you implant three; what are you going to do with the remaining two?

TROUNSON

If the patients have agreed, we'll freeze those remaining embryos.

MODERATOR

In fact you have three choices, haven't you? You could flush them down the sink; you could freeze them for future implantation; or you could give them to your colleague, Dr Kerin, for his work in researching the cause of Down's syndrome.

TROUNSON

Yes.

MODERATOR

As far as embryo research is concerned, do you have any difficulties with that?

TROUNSON

No, providing the embryo research is aimed towards either improving the procedure or to discovering information of benefit to mankind.

MODERATOR

Would any of those one thousand test-tube babies now in existence have been born at all, without embryo research?

TROUNSON

Absolutely not.

MODERATOR

So embryo research created all those children, Senator Harradine, and it's that very research which you want to prohibit. Why?

BRIAN HARRADINE

Because the role of law is to protect the individual and in this case you're dealing with a human subject, you're dealing with a human embryo. Quite frankly, the building blocks of any society would soon crumble were we to agree to the proposition that one can experiment on one subject for the benefit of others to the detriment of that human subject.

MODERATOR

Let's consider the embryo as a human subject. We're talking about an embryo at, say, fourteen days. Is it visible?

TROUNSON

At about fourteen days, if you were told where in the test tube it was, you might see it as a speck of dust.

MODERATOR

And before fourteen days it's an invisible collection of cells?

TROUNSON

Yes.

MODERATOR

Does it have any brain function?

TROUNSON

No.

MODERATOR

Does it have any heart or mind?

TROUNSON
   No.

MODERATOR
   When does the embryo begin to feel?

TROUNSON
   I can't be sure of that, but it's somewhere beyond day thirty.

MODERATOR
   Father Lucas, when for you does life begin?

LUCAS
   What we've got here is certainly a human being. The only
   difference between the embryo and you and I is that we had the
   right nourishment in the right environment for the right amount
   of time.

MODERATOR
   What about sperm? Is that potential human being?

LUCAS
   No. Sperm is a part of a human being in the sense that it's a cell—a
   product of a human being—but it itself is not a human being.

MODERATOR
   So . . . masturbation isn't an act of cruelty to sperm?

LUCAS
   Whatever it might be, it's certainly not an act of cruelty to the
   sperm.

MODERATOR
   What sort of research can be done on this invisible collection of
   cells, Dr Kerin?

KERIN
   The potential is high. There are techniques where you may be
   able to take one or two cells out of the embryo to do special
   diagnostic tests if you suspect that embryo could be genetically
   abnormal because the parents have a genetic disease.

MODERATOR
   So you could look at an embryo before you implant it, see what
   sort of child it will be—whether it suffers from Mongolism or
   whether it's going to having Huntington's disease, or some

genetic predisposition that Bill Bunsen might discover. What other good could come from embryo experimentation?

TROUNSON

The reduction of genetic abnormalities, as John Kerin says, is indeed of great value, because you can do away with therapeutic abortion. It is known that around about day fourteen the so-called early-stem cells, which go to form the blood system, are developed. Their potential is that they can colonise when injected into an adult, and the experiments have shown they can colonise a mouse that has a blood defect—a thalassemia or a leukemia.

MODERATOR

So where you have some dreadful disease like leukemia, by working on early human embryos you may actually find the cure for leukemia?

TROUNSON

Yes. Absolutely.

MODERATOR

How does it come down for you, Professor Singer? Should the benefits from the research—the prospects of unravelling the causes of leukemia or Mongolism—override the concern that's been expressed about experimentations on early human embryos?

SINGER

They certainly should. The concern that has been expressed is really misplaced. The embryo is not capable of feeling anything, and in that sense it's not a being that has interests like you or I do. You can't talk of it suffering. Really the ethical objections that have been made to this use of early embryos are misguided. They're thinking that there is some moral principle that prevents us working with this being, simply because it happens, biologically, to be *Homo sapiens*. That's not what counts. What really counts is: "Can it feel anything, can it suffer, does it have interests?"

MODERATOR

What about the soul? When does the soul enter the embryo? Aristotle said the soul entered after forty days in the case of the male and eighty in the case of the female. He was a bit of a sexist, old Aristotle (laughter) . . . but you couldn't prove him wrong, Dr Trounson?

TROUNSON

I'm not an expert on souls, I'm sorry.

MODERATOR

Are you, Father Lucas?

LUCAS

I'm not sure about when the soul might enter the human being. I'd take issue with Dr Singer. You wouldn't like to be experimented on even if you couldn't feel it, and I wouldn't like to be experimented on even if I wasn't conscious of it. We have a human being, and we have to respect what that human being represents.

MODERATOR

Dr Jansen, do you see the human being?

JANSEN

I think this is a question of belief, and I can understand the depth of the belief that conception is a magic moment, and that from then on a human being exists. But most doctors and scientists would take the view that while conception is a very important event in the creation of the human being, it's not the only important event. It's followed by implantation, it's followed by the development of awareness and sensitivity, it's eventually followed by the ability to survive outside the mother. These are all important events, and they all increase the importance of that human being very quickly. But nevertheless it is a graded procedure, and if you take any opposite view then you should live with the consequences of that opposite view, namely that if it is a human being with all the interests of an adult, then you really should see the death of an embryo or a spontaneous miscarriage as being as tragic as the death of a child or a teenager, and this is nonsense. We don't. It's just not commonsense.

MODERATOR

These philosophical and theological speculations are endlessly fascinating, but laws are written in black letters, and Senator Harradine's Bill banning all embryo research becomes law, just at the time, Dr Kerin, when your embryo research is a few weeks away, you think, from a dramatic breakthrough in the understanding of Mongolism. All you need is a few more embryos and a few more weeks. Will you continue your experiments?

KERIN

That's a very difficult one. The enormity of the breakthrough for many couples and prospective children is very high.

MODERATOR

Bill and Wendy come to you. Bill says, "We know you're right, you know you're right. These are our embryos—my sperm, Wendy's egg. Use them. Use them in your great work of relieving human suffering." Will you do that? Will you break the law?

KERIN

Well . . . if . . . if I was in this situation I would have already been doing this research, and now so close to it . . . I think I would take counsel from my colleagues . . .

MODERATOR

You've got to make the decision fairly rapidly, Dr Kerin. Your colleagues say it's a matter for your conscience. You're so close to it. Would you go ahead?

KERIN

I think there's a . . . a personal commitment which is against the law of the land, but we've already committed ourselves to this work, and the breakthrough's very close. Now if the law of the land is absolutely against it . . .

MODERATOR

And it is. But the breakthrough is two weeks away, you have the embryos . . .

KERIN

They're there?

MODERATOR

Yes, Bill and Wendy's embryos are there.

KERIN

Yes, I will.

MODERATOR

You break the law. One of your postgraduate students, Bob Quisling, whom you failed recently in bio-ethics, goes to the Director of Public Prosecutions. Mr Temby, you have an eyewitness account of this breach of the new law. Do you prosecute?

TEMBY

Oh certainly. I have no option but to do so.

MODERATOR

No option? What about your public interest discretion?

TEMBY

If the law is a recent law, then the will of the parliament, which is supposed in theory at least to reflect the will of the people, must prevail. One cannot permit the individual views of somebody such as Dr Kerin to prevail. If he chooses to break the law, he must accept the consequences. Certainly there must be a prosecution in those circumstances.

MODERATOR

In Stockholm, the Nobel Prize Committee has recommended Dr Kerin for a prize for his breakthrough. Is it in the public interest to prosecute a great Australian scientist?

TEMBY

Yes, the law must prevail.

MODERATOR

Well, he won't be the first Nobel Prizewinner to receive his prize in prison. How will you present the prosecution to the jury?

TEMBY

I'd simply say, "Here is the law of the land. Here are the proofs that are available to establish that there has been a breach of that law. It is not for you, as jurors, to bring your own personal views into the consideration. You simply decide whether or not the offence has been established beyond reasonable doubt."

MODERATOR

Helen Coonan, you're defending Dr Kerin. How will you address the jury?

COONAN

I'd defend him with great pleasure, and I would make an impassioned plea to the jury to take cognisance of the fact that we have an eminent man who has done some experiments and a breakthrough has been achieved, and it means benefit to many, many lives, both adults and future children . . .

MODERATOR

Well, the matter is before the jury. Russell Scott, old Law Reform Commissioners never die, they simply get appointed to the bench. You are now Mr Justice Scott. Are you going to direct the jury to convict?

SCOTT

I suppose there could be circumstances where that would have to take place.

MODERATOR

Isn't the very reason we have juries, that they can find a verdict according to their conscience?

SCOTT

In historic reason and origin, yes.

MODERATOR

Would you remind the jury of their historic function to find the verdict according to their conscience?

SCOTT

I would.

MODERATOR

Bettina Arndt, you're the jury. Do you vote to convict?

ARNDT

No.

MODERATOR

Why not?

ARNDT

For . . . for the same reasons as Dr Kerin decided to go ahead with the experiment. I think there are a lot of circumstances where doctors have to make decisions and scientists have to make decisions on the basis of a real assessment of the value of this work to the community, rather than on the letter of the law.

MODERATOR

Eva Learner, you're on the jury. Do you vote to convict?

LEARNER

I would take the urgency of the whole thing into consideration, and I would be in favour of not convicting.

MODERATOR
Freda Whitlam, do you vote to convict?

WHITLAM
Yes.

MODERATOR
Why?

WHITLAM
Because we can't break the law. We can change it.

MODERATOR
Charles Kerr, you're on the jury. Do you vote to convict?

KERR
No, I wouldn't. The law is not a law which properly expresses the opinion of the public, or the value which we've got out of this particular scientific procedure.

MODERATOR
The jury acquits Dr Kerin. Rosemary Crowley, was it a wise decision of the parliament to pass this law banning embryo experiments?

ROSEMARY CROWLEY
I think what has emerged from the case, and from the jury's decision, is that it's very necessary for us to go back to that law and try to re-define it.

MODERATOR
Senator Harradine, are you worried that if you pass laws which scientists will break, then juries will fail to convict and discredit the law?

HARRADINE
It is . . . an entirely hypothetical question.

MODERATOR
Parliament decides to reverse the law, and Australia relies upon its interlocking hierarchies of ethics committees to keep our scientists on the rails. But not all countries are fortunate enough to have ethics committees. Over in Paraguay, at the IVF clinic in Concepción, Professor Mengele is doing some interesting experiments. He is experimenting on embryos for long after fourteen days. He's growing a human embryo in a sheep's

uterus. His methods are scientifically sound if ethically intolerable, and he's discovered some very interesting data about the causes and cures of infertility. Robert Jansen, you're editor of the *Australian Fertility Journal*. If Professor Mengele sends his paper to you, will you publish it?

JANSEN

If his paper is scientifically sound, if he has not contradicted any laws of Paraguay, and if, in my view what he has done would not be abhorrent to the readers of my journal, then yes, I would publish it.

MODERATOR

It is abhorrent, but the interest in it is considerable. Would you publish data from concentration camp experiments, which were approved by the laws of Germany at that time?

JANSEN

There is indeed a move at the moment to re-examine some of the data that was accumulated during the war in concentration camps. It is not to be buried and forgotten. It is to be looked at. It's to be looked at with distaste, no doubt, but items that are scientifically correct probably should be published. They can be published in such a way that any reader is in no doubt whatsoever how the data was gained, that the manner in which it was gained is completely unacceptable; but if that information can be of use to people, then it ought to be made available.

MODERATOR

Is it right, Father Lucas, to try to build a better world on the backs of embryos whose very fate proclaims the way medical research ought *not* to be done?

LUCAS

The fact is of course that this has been done, but the real question is whether it ought to have been done in the first place.

MODERATOR

It shouldn't have been, but there it is. It's scientific knowledge.

LUCAS

I think that scientific knowledge does not have a value in itself just for the sake of being scientific knowledge, and if publishing that sort of material is going to be abhorrent to people, it is not really going to further the knowledge of things that we ought to have knowledge about, and there's no point in publishing it.

MODERATOR

Charles Kerr, would you publish it?

KERR

There are difficulties with a lot of the Nazi studies of which I'm aware, because the subjects were treated in a particularly barbarous manner. Objectively the information might be of interest scientifically, but taking the whole thing in context, it may cause such distress, particularly in surviving relatives, that it may not be wise to publish it.

MODERATOR

Is it right for science, Professor Singer, to use data from concentration camp experiments, or from thoroughly unethical behaviour towards embryos and foetuses?

SINGER

I think it's very difficult because what you want to avoid doing is encouraging people to do that kind of research in order to get it published. That's why I'd be worried about publishing the ongoing research of Dr Mengele in Paraguay. On the other hand, one could say that in the case of the concentration camp experiments, even though they may be even worse, the people who carried them out have as far as possible been punished for it. It's not ongoing research. I think one could agree with Dr Jansen that to simply allow possibly valuable data to be lost does no-one any good; certainly not the victims of the experiments.

MODERATOR

Doesn't publication give the experiments a retrospective legitimacy, Freda Whitlam?

WHITLAM

Yes, but I think perhaps we owe it to the victims of the research. At least their deaths will mean something.

MODERATOR

Let's move to another topic. Alan Trounson, have you had difficulty raising money at times for your test-tube baby program?

TROUNSON
Oh yes. We've had to sell raffle tickets, lamingtons, chooks. (laughter)

MODERATOR
Of course now, you've made Melbourne the test-tube baby capital of the world. Your clinic's fame has spread far and wide. It's even reached the little town of Mafia in the Sicilian hills where Australia's most wanted man, Robert Trimbole, lies on his deathbed. He leaves your clinic in his will a million dollars; all you have to do is to name a ward after him. Do you accept the money?

TROUNSON
I'll accept the money, but not the conditions. (laughter)

MODERATOR
Well then, according to his will, the money goes to the Irish Barristers' Benevolent Society. (laughter)

TROUNSON
So be it.

MODERATOR
The Irish barristers get it. Professor Glover, have you had trouble raising funds?

GLOVER
Yes.

MODERATOR
The well-known cigarette manufacturers, Koffmans, approach you, offering you a million dollars. Would you take the money? They're sick of sponsoring cricket. They want to sponsor some babies instead.

GLOVER
I think in the current climate, yes, I think I would do it. You can argue yourself into this kind of thing because the benefits of that money would outweigh the moral dilemma. So I think I would accept that money.

MODERATOR
Koffmans gives you the million dollars, and they start advertising: "Koffmans breathes life", "Babies — a Sterling idea". (laughter) Are you worried about the use of your name and your science in promoting death?

GLOVER

Yes, I would be. But then I think that the same argument could apply to people who accept money of that nature from sport, so I don't think that it's the cigarette issue that really is the main consideration there. The main consideration is the money.

MODERATOR

Professor Kerr, you're Vice-Chancellor of Professor Glover's university. Is the main consideration the money?

KERR

No. It's a much deeper issue than that. If you take their money you are conforming with a carefully worked out promotional policy of the tobacco industry—a new strategy to complement sport. As a matter of policy I would have nothing to do with it. The priority is to try and reduce an extremely harmful, dangerous habit in the community.

MODERATOR

You're on the senate, Freda Whitlam. How does it come down for you? Should the million dollars be accepted?

WHITLAM

No. It's tainted.

MODERATOR

Dean Shilton. Should the university accept the money?

SHILTON

I don't believe it should, particularly if the funds come from things which are harmful in themselves. Obviously many people die each year in Australia because of smoking . . .

MODERATOR

Yes, but many people are going to be born because of this donation. Koffmans is replacing some of the people it kills. (laughter)

SHILTON

Yes, but I don't think that the whole program of bearing children is necessarily going to fail because they don't get money from a certain source. In fact if they get it from a source which compromises the whole moral issue, then they may not get it from other sources where they should rightfully get it from.

MODERATOR
Are we, Dr Trounson, being a little bit precious about this?

TROUNSON
Yes. I mean in the past we've accepted money from the Ford Foundation, and you could argue that the motor car is a considerably larger killer of mankind than cigarettes.

MODERATOR
You've now set up a private company to market your test-tube technology. How would you feel if it were taken over by a brewery? You could become Elders IVF. (laughter)

TROUNSON
Personally, I'd be delighted. It means more funds, more babies.

MODERATOR
It's midnight at the clinic, and all is well. Those precious embryos await implantation, in test tubes tagged "Bill and Wendy", "George and Robyn", "Sir Boden: potential heirs". Suddenly, there's a lightning strike. The university maintenance staff go on strike against the withdrawal of their campus car-parking facilities, and all those embryos die in their dishes. Sir Boden is furious. He wants to sue the union for negligence. What's his embryo worth? What damages can he get?

SCOTT
I wouldn't have thought, on present principles, he would be able to get damages.

MODERATOR
Really? But they're potential life, potential children, potential heirs.

SCOTT
That's right, but we haven't decided whether we have a human being or not on our hands.

MODERATOR
By "we" you mean the law?

SCOTT
Yes, and how it determines the question might well be critical.

MODERATOR

"But my wife has gone through months of agony producing the eggs; I've had to masturbate which isn't easy for a man of my age and heart condition. Surely we deserve some recompense from this wretched union for killing our potential children."

SCOTT

If the law decides to classify them in that way, there are legal principles that would enable you to recover damages. I really couldn't estimate how much, though. We could go from zero to infinity; the latter if Professor Kerr was able to genetically predict the production of an Einstein, or a Robertson.

TEMBY

I disagree with Russell Scott's legal analysis. Whether or not you can recover damages does depend on whether the embryo is human life. But if it is, then I think that in the same way that you can't have property in a dead body, you can't have property in the embryo if it is human life. The law is remarkably ill-suited to decide these novel questions. There's a clear need for legislation.

MODERATOR

So, oddly enough, if the embryo, as Father Lucas contends, is human life, then in your view it has no protection in law?

TEMBY

That's right. Because if it is human life it is not property. You cannot trade in human life. You cannot buy and sell people.

MODERATOR

But if it's not human life, then Sir Boden can recover a large sum of damages?

TEMBY

That's right, he has property in his sperm and if it has been obtained by him for a purpose then it accordingly has a value.

MODERATOR

But it's obtained fairly naturally. I mean as I walk around here I'm producing five hundred sperm a second. That's a lot of property.

TEMBY

My point is that abandoned property cannot be stolen so the by-products of a merely casual act of masturbation do not have value and cannot be stolen. But if one masturbates to produce sperm for reproductive purposes, then that has value, and can be stolen.

MODERATOR

Suppose that a protestor against IVF had smashed into the laboratory and deliberately destroyed those embryos. As DPP, is there anything you can prosecute him for? Is there a crime of embryo slaughter?

TEMBY

No, there's not. He could only be prosecuted for something very minor, like wilful damage to a test tube. That simply reflects the obvious fact that the law is presently languishing behind scientific developments.

MODERATOR

Of course Bill and Wendy can create more embryos, and so can Sir Boden and Lady Budapest. But it's not going to be easy for George and Robyn, because yesterday George was sentenced to fifteen years' imprisonment for armed robbery. He's in prison at Long Bay and the warders are a bit concerned about letting his sperm go on an early release scheme. (laughter)

TEMBY

I see no reason why not. Once you've decided the proper limits and constraints of an IVF program then I don't see why it has to be the case that anybody, even a criminal, is precluded from it.

MODERATOR

So there's no problem with prisoners being able to send their sperm out of gaol to impregnate their wives and girlfriends?

SCOTT

I wouldn't have thought so.

MODERATOR

Would you think so, Dean Shilton?

SHILTON

You say girlfriends . . . I don't believe that should be allowed because one of the reasons for imprisonment is to restrict that person's freedom to certain areas and that's part of the punishment. To suggest that the sperm could be produced for a girlfriend, would be against the moral principles about sexual relationships within marriage.

MODERATOR

That's the view that the government takes at present, so George's sperm isn't able to go over the wall. But Bill Bunsen is concerned about another matter. Bill's research into genetic predispositions has had a dramatic development: he thinks he's discovered the genetic coding that produces a predisposition to homosexuality. Dr Jansen, ought he to continue his work?

JANSEN

Of course.

MODERATOR

Charles Kerr?

KERR

Yes, I think so.

MODERATOR

No-one knows about his breakthrough yet, but people will soon realise that he's breeding a lot of gay bandicoots and muddle-headed wombats. Bill goes back to the Royal Commission and says, "I'm very worried that with early amniocentesis and with genetic diagnosis, we'll soon be able to tell at a very early stage whether the baby has Down's syndrome or Huntington's disease . . . or homosexual predispositions." Do you see any dangers?

SINGER

Yes, I see some dangers. I think that we need to have some controls over this, and I do think it's time for us to make this Royal Commission permanent, and allow it to review case by case the various techniques for detecting abnormalities in vitro or beforehand.

MODERATOR

If you now have a government that can bar homosexuals from pubs, might you not one day have a government that allows therapeutic abortions for a foetus with homosexual predispositions?

SINGER

Yes, conceivably you might, but I don't think you can guard

against that by saying that the research ought not to go ahead. You can't guard against bad governments forever. You just have to try and get your government to be as sound as possible on each issue.

MODERATOR

While he's pondering these implications of his work, Bill gets a job offer from the University of the Deep North—a private university whose campus is situated in luxurious surroundings on Hamilton Island. Any problems with him taking the Bjelke-Petersen Chair of Eugenics?

KERR

None at all. It's what happens to the results of his research in social terms that concerns me.

MODERATOR

Bill takes a Sunset Airlines champagne flight to Hamilton Island to discuss the job offer. Sir Boden and his wife are on board— he's going to receive an honorary degree in law for his contributions to the jurisprudence of property development—but unfortunately the pilot has a genetic predisposition for alcohol and there's a tragic crash. Sir Boden and his wife are killed, Bill is crippled from the waist down. Helen Coonan, there are five frozen embryos left in the clinic. What should happen to them? Sir Boden's made a will leaving all his money—two hundred million dollars—to these potential children.

COONAN

I think that in the absence of there being any real property in the embryos—since they're not property—they ought to be destroyed.

MODERATOR

The embryos ought to be destroyed, Father Lucas? Do you agree?

LUCAS

The embryos ought not to be there in the first place. (laughter)

MODERATOR

It's too late for that; the embryos are there. What should be done with them?

LUCAS

I don't know that there is any solution other than that let nature take its course.

MODERATOR
Destroy them?

LUCAS
They will inevitably die.

MODERATOR
If the embryos are not allowed to become children, all the Budapest fortune will go to Sir Boden's next of kin. He has only one kinsperson—his brother, Vlad. Boden and Vlad were boys in Eastern Europe, separated in the chaos just after the war. Boden found his way to Australia, but Vlad was trapped behind the Iron Curtain. He's now a devout communist and Director of the Stalin Institute for Peace through Weapons Research. He's come to Australia claiming that money. It will all go to him if you don't succeed in getting those embryos implanted.

COONAN
These embryos are going to be totally separated from their genetic parents. Now it would be difficult to find host parents.

MODERATOR
No difficulty at all. Harry Mainchance has just opened a surrogate agency, Rent-a-Womb Pty Ltd.

COONAN
Yes, but that's not necessarily going to be in the ultimate interests of these potential lives.

MODERATOR
The ultimate interests of those potential lives is to inherit two hundred million dollars.

COONAN
I think that's a value judgement and in the absence of there being any specific instructions from the biological parents as to what's to happen . . .

MODERATOR
There are specific instructions in Sir Boden's will that if anything happens to himself and Lady Budapest their embryos are to be implanted in a surrogate. Russell Scott, you're his executor; how can you get these children born alive?

SCOTT

Sir Boden has left his property to his embryonic children. If that's the case there would be a most extraordinary result under our recently enacted Australian law, because that law says where donor sperm is used to create an embryo, the donor of the sperm is deemed not to be the father of the child. So you have the likely result that under our specially enacted law, Sir Boden's genetic children, when born through a surrogate, will be deemed in law not to be his children, but the surrogate's! They could not inherit his fortune. It would all go to Vlad.

MODERATOR

Wendy and Robyn are now both in the same difficulty. Robyn's George is in prison, and the government won't allow him to inseminate her. Bill's injury in the plane crash prevents him from producing sperm to fertilise Wendy's eggs. But Bill remembers that when he was a medical student, they all used to go off and donate to your sperm bank, Professor Glover. He asks whether you would supply some donated sperm to help Wendy have a child.

GLOVER

Oh, yes indeed.

MODERATOR

How does one donate sperm to your sperm bank? Do you take anyone off the street?

GLOVER

Oh no. Oh no.

MODERATOR

You mainly use medical students?

GLOVER

It happens that there is quite a predominance of medical students among the donors.

MODERATOR

Why not law students, or young builders' labourers?
(laughter)

GLOVER

We have law students too.

MODERATOR

Well, I'm a law student and I want to make a donation. What do I do?

GLOVER

You make the offer and then you undertake a medical examination and have a medical history taken. If the results are acceptable to our team, then you are put on the list of donors and called up to make a deposit.

MODERATOR

How do I do that? Do you give me a test tube and a pornographic magazine and show me into a cubicle . . .?

GLOVER

Yes, well that depends on your imagination.

MODERATOR

What do you do for pornography in Queensland? (laughter)

GLOVER

In Queensland our donors have a lot of imagination and we don't bother. (laughter)

MODERATOR

Well I go into the cubicle with my test tube and *Farmers' Weekly* (laughter) . . . but before I make this deposit I want to make sure that in twenty years' time some badly brought up delinquent won't knock on my door and call me father. Can you guarantee me confidentiality?

GLOVER

Oh yes.

MODERATOR

Oh yes, Dr Kerin?

KERIN

As the conditions stand in South Australia at the moment, yes we can.

MODERATOR

Wendy agrees to accept some of your donated sperm, but she's a bit worried. She'd like sperm from a donor who's a reasonable match to her crippled husband, Bill. Can you arrange that? Bill's got red hair, he's about six feet tall; would you get a donor matching those physical capacities as closely as possible?

GLOVER

If there's a specific request then one could do one's best.

KERIN

Our aim is to get the closest match possible to the infertile husband.

MODERATOR

Bill, before his accident, was very athletic. He was a keen golfer. Any chance of getting an athletic, red-haired donor who is six feet tall?

KERIN

We try and match the body shape and height, but not the particular social attributes of the infertile husband.

MODERATOR

Do you try to match his brain?

KERIN

As a principle, no, we don't.

MODERATOR

Why not? If I can inherit my father's big nose and bad teeth, why can't I inherit his brain, Professor Kerr?

KERR

Inheritance of parental intelligence is complicated, and it doesn't get transmitted to the next generation in a simple manner.

MODERATOR

I see. Wendy says, "Dr Kerin, Bill and I are politically quite orthodox, and we hear there are a lot of lefties at your university. I'm rather worried about getting the semen of some communist medical student. Any chance of finding us a Young Liberal?" (laughter)

KERIN

I guess there is a chance, but we would be reluctant to involve ourselves in that sort of selection.

MODERATOR

In fact, you actually come up with a six-feet-tall, red-haired medical student who's quite athletic and a member of the Young

Liberals. He's a good match, Dr Kerin, but he is Jewish. Would you tell Wendy that?

KERIN

We don't normally divulge that information unless they specifically ask.

MODERATOR

Bill's a member of the Royal Sydney Golf Club, which has never been keen on Jewish members. Suppose Wendy says, "We don't want Jewish genes in the family." Would you make a point of not providing semen from a Jewish donor?

KERIN

Yes, I think we would. That might limit the selection of donors available.

MODERATOR

Would you, Professor Glover, apply that racist test if you were specifically asked?

GLOVER

I have to confess it's something I haven't thought about, but probably not. I wouldn't have thought it was significant.

MODERATOR

Wendy is provided with sperm from an anonymous donor to Professor Glover's fertility clinic. But Robyn, whose boyfriend George is in prison, prefers to shop around for some more prestigious spermatozoa. As it happens Australia's first celebrity sperm bank, The Gene Machine, has just been opened in Macquarie Street by our old friend Harry Mainchance, and he offers a wide range of selections to Robyn. She can purchase Rhodes Scholar sperm for a thousand dollars a millilitre, Olympic medallist for two thousand, television personality for five thousand—unless he's ABC, which Harry gives away free. (laughter) He's trying for an Australian Nobel Prizewinner, but Patrick White is proving uncooperative and he might have to import some from America. Should there be a law against this, Ian Temby?

TEMBY

Yes. What these people are doing is seeking to create some sort of a super race, and in the long term that terrifies me. We live in a society in which there's a wide diversity of individuals. There is no particular reason to think that society would be improved by having more remarkably clever people within its ranks. It's contrary to basic human nature not to let biology take its course, except perhaps in the special circumstances we've been talking about today. In ordinary circumstances one should shy right away from notions of creating a super race.

MODERATOR

Bettina Arndt, does it worry you?

ARNDT

Yes, it worries me because it de-emphasises the importance of looking after children and nurturing them in the ordinary environment. If parents think they can do their job simply through selection of genes, they're wrong. They need to be directed towards creating a better environment for children.

SINGER

I think it's a stupid idea. Anyone who took part in it would be stupid because they probably aren't going to get what they want and the pressures on the child could very well be disturbing. But I don't know that I'd go so far as to make it illegal.

MODERATOR

Celebrity sperm banks have done well in the United States. They seem to believe that intelligence is inherited.

KERR

It is a ridiculous idea because it's perpetrating a deception on the public. The inheritance of intelligence is not such that you can guarantee with any degree of probability at all that sperm from a high intelligence donor will end up creating a high intelligence child. It just doesn't work like that.

MODERATOR

Senator Crowley, would you ban it? Something that people want, but for no rational reason?

CROWLEY

To the extent that I'm going to have to do that by law, yes I'd want to ban it.

MODERATOR

Of course if you ban it, Helen Coonan, people will go to America to get celebrity sperm.

COONAN

Yes, but in America everything is merchandised, even sperm.
The sperm of celebrities is just another piece of property they
can merchandise. It's a concept that I find quite abhorrent, and
really it ought only to be allowed under very stringent and
specific conditions.

MODERATOR

Well, Robyn falls for Harry Mainchance's sales pitch. She
chooses the "television personality" category and he hints that
it's from Channel 9, so she hopes that it's George Negus not
Kerry Packer. She brings it to you Alan Trounson for the
implantation. You successfully produce six embryos — three male,
three female. Since you're going to implant three, will you ask
Robyn whether she wants the males or the females?

TROUNSON

Yes, I would do. If I had the technology to sex an embryo I
presume that information should be made available to the
patient.

MODERATOR

You would give the patient the choice. Would you give the
patient the choice, John Kerin?

KERIN

Yes, I would.

MODERATOR

You were worried earlier about the sex selection chemical for the
general population, Dean Shilton. Do you object to IVF doctors
giving patients the choice of sex for their children?

SHILTON

Yes. In fact I object to the idea of a sperm bank anyway,
because I believe that anonymous donation of sperm creates all
kinds of problems in respect to relationship within a marriage
and the identity of the child. It could be considered a kind of
clinical adultery by remote control and that worries me
morally.

MODERATOR

Eva Learner, should Dr Trounson implant the three male
embryos? That's what Robyn wants him to do.

LEARNER

I think that I'd pop one of each sex in. (laughter)

MODERATOR

Sneaky. You wouldn't tell her. But doesn't the patient have the right to decide what goes into her body?

LEARNER

She does indeed, but we hopefully do good counselling, which would make her want one of either—or either one.

MODERATOR

She's going to get three. Two of which sex?

LEARNER

Two female. (laughter)

MODERATOR

Dr Kerin is doing some tests on these embryos. You take one cell and examine it, and you find, unfortunately, that the donor semen hasn't been checked properly and the embryos have a gene associated with Huntington's disease—a disease that stays latent in the body till about the age of forty-five and then strikes, causing senile dementia and death. What should be done with these defective embryos?

KERIN

That technology is not yet available but it probably will become available in the future. I think we're duty-bound, knowing that fact, to inform the woman about it and it may be up to her to make the decision about implantation because of the potential implications for her child. She has a right to know.

MODERATOR

So if you discover through the technique of cell biopsy, which will be available within a few years, that those embryos have Huntington's disease, you would inform the patient and let her choose whether or not to have them implanted?

KERIN

It's a difficult one. I think you're at least duty-bound to inform the patient about the defects in those embryos.

MODERATOR

You do, and Robyn says, "I want nothing to do with them."

What do you do with the defective embryos?

KERIN

If they're defective, then depending on the law of the land at that time, I think you just let them demise.

MODERATOR

Father Lucas, an embryo which you contend is a human being is a potential sufferer from Huntington's disease. He could win Wimbledon at seventeen, become Treasurer at thirty-nine, Prime Minister at forty-four, and then go mad. Let him "demise" now?

LUCAS

I think that human beings who suffer from an illness or potential for illness require care.

MODERATOR

So they should be implanted in a surrogate?

LUCAS

I would say that irrespective of whether there was a defect or not they should not have come into existence and probably the prudent thing to do would be to allow them to demise.

SINGER

"Let it demise" is a nice way of saying you can kill it. I don't think it will make any difference whether you let it demise or kill it. At this stage we're simply saying that the embryo ought not to be implanted in Robyn or anybody else.

MODERATOR

But if there were women who were prepared to act as surrogate mothers for defective embryos . . .?

SINGER

No, I don't think you should do that. You should point out the suffering that the children will have and if they want to be surrogate mothers no doubt there are embryos without defects that would give rise to a longer, more fruitful and presumably, on balance, a happier life.

MODERATOR

Ladies and gentlemen, time passes, as time is wont to do, and the Royal Commission continues its deliberations under new Royal patronage. The coronation of King Charles and Duchess

Diana takes place on the very day that Bill and Wendy's test-tube baby, Amanda, is born. But the more some things change, the more others remain the same. South Africa has still not satisfied the international community, and the Commonwealth Commission, led by Sir Malcolm Fraser, has recommended its exclusion from the civilised community. Dr Trounson, you're invited to captain an Australian Test-Tube Baby Team to go to South Africa and demonstrate your new test-tube techniques. Would you go?

TROUNSON

No, I wouldn't go. I have been in the past, so I do have an understanding of what the situation is there and I disagree with the provision of infertility services in that community primarily to the white population. I would not lead an IVF team to South Africa. The medical resources there are firmly in favour of the white population, and very little are made available to the black people. It's much more costly to produce an IVF baby than it is to provide family planning or some other protective medical procedure to the black population. It's a personal decision, and I wouldn't have any problem making it.

MODERATOR

Even though it would mean sharing knowledge among the scientific community, among your scientific colleagues in South Africa?

TROUNSON

I don't have any objection to South African doctors coming to Australia, or to sharing information with them. I would not lead a group to South Africa to positively promote a technique which would only be made available on a discriminatory basis.

MODERATOR

Dr Kerin, you're offered a quarter of a million dollars to captain the team—American dollars, so you don't have to worry about devaluation.

KERIN

I won't be bribed that way. Dr Trounson's principle is sound. In South Africa there is discrimination against the black community in provision of medical resources.

MODERATOR

Ladies and gentlemen, more time passes. The Bicentennial comes and goes. King Charles, despairing of Britain's inner-city problems, abdicates the throne to make natural ice-cream in a Welsh commune, Duchess Diana opens a fashion boutique on Madison Avenue, and the new King Andrew anxiously awaits the report of his Royal Commission on human relationships, of which he has had more than most. (laughter) Amanda, Bill and Wendy's test-tube baby, is now growing into delicate womanhood. Should she be told that Bill is not her real father?

LEARNER

Very definitely she should be made aware of it as she's growing up.

MODERATOR

But Dr Glover has done his work well, and there has been a reasonable match. Amanda is tall with red hair and an aptitude for science. She need never know that Bill is not her real father.

LEARNER

The chances are that she might find out anyway. Lots of children, whether or not they're adopted or artificially conceived, have concerns about their origins and there is a chance that somebody else in or around the family may know about it and let it out.

ARNDT

I think children should be told. It's part of accepting that artificial insemination is a reasonable thing to do and that we're not ashamed of the fact that we choose to create a child in this way.

SHILTON

I believe there should be complete honesty and openness between parents and members of the family and that that's the only way by which you build up sustaining relationships. There ought to be means by which any child could find out the information if they wanted to do so. Perhaps there should be a record of the name of the father kept with the Health Commission, or something like that.

MODERATOR

Time has wrought its changes in Dr Peter Jekyll, the doctor who discovered the sex selection chemical all those years ago. He's now a lonely, childless, medical multimillionaire, dying of an early cancer. But he remembers that when he was a young medical student, he made a donation, Professor Glover, to your sperm bank. He wonders desperately if his sperm was used to produce any children, and if so whether you'd give him the parent's name so that he can contact his children before he dies, and leave them his money. Would you do that?

GLOVER

No.

MODERATOR

Why not?

GLOVER

As soon as an artificial insemination donor has deposited semen it is no longer his property, and so I don't think that he can have any claim on it whatsoever.

MODERATOR

It's one thing for a father to be berated in later life by a badly brought up child who is genetically his, but it's quite another thing for a child to receive a visit from a Father Christmas wanting to leave it a lot of money. Is it really in the child's interests not to tell Dr Jekyll the whereabouts of his children?

GLOVER

Well, it may not be in the mother's interests and I still maintain that once somebody has donated semen for purposes of artificial insemination he has absolutely no proprietary rights over that semen sample at all.

MODERATOR

Is that right, Mr Temby? Surely when you're promised confidentiality it's your privilege and you can later waive it. You can say, "I want to find out if I fathered any children, and who they are"?

TEMBY

I take the view that once you've donated sperm then you've lost all right with respect to it and that should be made perfectly clear at the time of the donation.

MODERATOR

Eva Learner, you favour children being told their real parents. What about parents being told their real children?

LEARNER

Yes, and I would in the future ensure that records are kept, and if there was an inheritance there for a potential child of the donor, I would certainly support the child receiving it.

MODERATOR

Dr Jekyll's tragic story, involving as it does death and children, is of course featured on *Willesee*. (laughter) The Bunsen family, sitting around watching it, get to talking and Bill tells Amanda that he isn't her real father. Her father was a donor at some stage to Professor Glover's clinic—probably in those days, a young medical student. Amanda is now nineteen, highly strung, and over the next few months she becomes obsessed with finding out the name of her real father. Would you, Dr Kerin, go back in your files and find the name of the student who donated the semen so long ago?

KERIN

The way our programs are structured we do promise anonymity to both the donor and the recipient and I don't think I would break my promise, even under those circumstances.

MODERATOR

Bill and Wendy want you to break your promise. They support Amanda in her search.

KERIN

I think I'd have to explain the circumstances and I'd have to uphold a fairly hard line on this issue.

MODERATOR

Why?

KERIN

Because when the donors in the program are selected, we inform them that they will have no knowledge of prospective children that they may father.

MODERATOR

But what would be the social consequence of allowing Amanda to find her real father? Would sperm donors really dry up?

KERIN

I think in the present climate within our community, donors literally would dry up because they'd be under threat of being

identified and they've got no idea of who the prospective
children will be or what the demands of those children upon
them could be. They'd be quite threatened.

MODERATOR

Amanda is suffering from what psychiatrists call "genealogical
bewilderment syndrome", which means all she wants to do is
find her real dad. Eva Learner, do you support her?

LEARNER

Absolutely. My view is that the child's rights are dominant in
the situation. Without question she has a right to know who
her father is. And the knowledge will ease her anxiety and help
her discover an identity that she's been searching for. It would
not necessarily in any way affect her relationship with her social
parents.

MODERATOR

Are you going to get any donors, Professor Glover, if this case
is publicised and they learn that their children can come back to
haunt them?

GLOVER

If donors felt that was a possibility, we'd get no donors.

MODERATOR

Amanda comes to your law firm, Helen Coonan. Will you take
action against the sperm bank, to force them to reveal her real
father? There are children's rights in the new Bill of Rights, and
it's arguable that the basic right of a child is to find its true
parents. Argue it before Mr Justice Temby.

COONAN

Under the Bill of Rights my client has a right to know her real
parentage, to know her biological parents. She has in fact been
born as a result of in vitro fertilisation by donor father. We
have been able to identify the sperm bank and we know the
doctor who carried out the procedure. There's no doubt that
those records are available and the biological father of my client
can be identified. She is now nineteen years of age, she is legally
an adult and the applications we've made to the sperm bank and
the doctor have been fruitless. It would be my submission that
it's my client's right to have this information and I would seek
an order that the information be released to her.

MODERATOR

Russell Scott, you are representing the sperm bank and its claim of confidentiality.

SCOTT

There's an extraordinarily difficult social question to be answered in this contest between on the one hand the child's right to know, and on the other hand the claim of the individual to privacy and confidentiality. It is a very difficult balancing act, but the dilemma should be solved in favour of the individual claiming the privacy.

MODERATOR

While Mr Justice Temby retires to consider his verdict, Wendy, sitting behind Amanda in the courtroom, thinks of all the changes in the world since she first tried to bring a child into it: how Robyn, the prostitute who attended the clinic with her, met and married the wealthy Vlad Budapest, and persuaded him to stay in Australia and donate the Budapest fortune to endowing a Chair in Peace Studies at Sydney University; how Bill, who mistakenly thought he had discovered the genetic key to homosexuality, won a Nobel Prize last year for isolating the rogue gene which causes the disease of homophobia — the excessive hatred of homosexuals; how the Gene Machine went into liquidation and Harry Mainchance went to gaol for fraud when semen he certified as "Nobel Prizewinner" was discovered to have been collected at a stag night for his Australian Rules Football team; and how we don't even have Royal Commissions any longer — the future of King Andrew's human relationships having hastened the declaration of a Republic. (laughter) Mr Justice Temby, how do you rule? Will Amanda discover her true father?

TEMBY

Well, firstly I have no doubt that the claim which is made is a genuine one, and that's accepted without reservation. The problem is difficult and the court has every sympathy for the plaintiff but the Bill of Rights does not make clear that in circumstances such as these there is entitlement to the information you seek, and which would have to be provided contrary to assurances given to the donor of the sperm. Accordingly, the court finds in favour of the defendant, the sperm bank, and dismisses the application.

MODERATOR

Amanda appeals to the Court of Appeal where the Chief Justice, Sir Neville Wran, does something he's wanted to do for a very long time, namely quash Mr Justice Temby. (laughter) He orders the name of Amanda's father to be handed over. The envelope is given to Amanda—she tears it open with trembling hands—and then turns, streaming tears of joy, to embrace William Bunsen, her one and only father, who once when a young medical student, dropped his genes in Professor Glover's fertility clinic, before going on to his celebrated scientific career.

SHOULD YOU TELL THE PRESIDENT?

What happens when a Duntroon-trained military dictator emerges in a country to our near north, diverts Australian uranium to make an Islamic Bomb, and engages in international terrorism to a degree which provokes American reprisals? Under the impending shadow of a nuclear winter politicians make plans to evacuate the cities and protesters contemplate dying for peace, while in a Balmain basement the secrets of Pine Gap code-breakers are offered for publication to the *National Times*. The Prime Minister agonises in his Canberra bunker over information that could start World War III: should he give the order to cancel the Bicentennial?

The current direction of Australian foreign policy — support for ANZUS, American spy bases and visits by nuclear-armed warships — is challenged by a developing international crisis, handled by the very Ministers and public servants who would have to decide how to react to such a crisis if it really occurred. Conducted to mark the International Year of Peace, this prophetical hypothetical explores Australia's present and future role in international affairs and disarmament.

SHOULD YOU TELL THE PRESIDENT?
Participants

KIM BEAZLEY
  Minister for Defence

PETER BOWERS
  National Correspondent, *Sydney Morning Herald*

DEBORAH BROOKS
  Coordinator, People for Nuclear Disarmament

RICHARD BUTLER
  Ambassador for Disarmament

DR DAVID DENHAM
  Seismologist, Bureau of Mineral Resources

DR ANNE-MARIE GRISOGONO
  Scientists Against Nuclear Arms

BILL HAYDEN
  Minister for Foreign Affairs

SIR WILLIAM KEYS
  National President, Returned Services League

ANDREW MACK
  Head of Peace Research Centre, Australian National University

MICHAEL MACKELLAR
  Former Minister for Immigration

MAJOR GENERAL KEVIN MURRAY Q.C. (retired)
  Former Senior Officer, Army Reserves

PAT O'SHANE
  Secretary, New South Wales Ministry for Aboriginal Affairs

JOHN PILGER
  International Journalist

BILL PRITCHETT
  Former Secretary, Department of Defence

DAVID SADLEIR
First Assistant Secretary, Department of Foreign Affairs

KEITH SUTER
Former Federal President, United Nations Association of
Australia

PROFESSOR SIR ERNEST TITTERTON
Nuclear Physicist, Australian National University

*Recorded at Film Australia,
Lindfield,
January 1986.*

SHOULD YOU TELL THE PRESIDENT?

MODERATOR

Let us imagine, ladies and gentlemen, a small boy playing on a Sydney street in this, the International Year of Peace. He's been playing a game that small boys in Australia traditionally play, not doctors and nurses, but the sort of game that ends "Bang, you're dead", as make-believe bullets speed from clenched fingers. He's happy because it is his birthday next week and he wants a new toy—a realistic submachine gun, with caps that smell of cordite and a vaporiser to zap the enemy. He's your son, Kim Beazley; does he get the gun?

KIM BEAZLEY

I have two daughters.

MODERATOR

She's your daughter. (laughter) Does she get the gun? It's only twenty dollars; your ministerial salary will stretch to that. Little Thomasina next-door got a bazooka for Christmas. The honour of the Beazley family is at stake. (laughter)

BEAZLEY

Yes, I think she would probably get it.

MODERATOR

She's your daughter, Deborah Brooks; will she get the gun?

DEBORAH BROOKS

No.

MODERATOR

Why not?

BROOKS

I believe that we have to encourage our children from a very early age not to be aggressive and I think that guns, more than knives, perpetuate aggressive feelings that could lead to war.

MODERATOR

"Aw gee, Mum, all the other kids in the street get a gun—I get a lecture. (laughter) What do I do when they start shooting at me? Pretend I'm a New Zealander? Then no-one will play with me."

BROOKS

Possibly you could change friends.

MODERATOR

John Pilger, does your son get the gun or the lecture?

JOHN PILGER

He would get some token resistance, but he would then get the gun.

MODERATOR

You put your hands up; you surrender.

PILGER

That is right.

MODERATOR

What about your son, Pat O'Shane?

PAT O'SHANE

Definitely not. I share the views of Deborah Brooks. My daughter wouldn't get a lecture either. She'd get another present—a book.

MODERATOR

She wants a book *Biggles Flies through the Black Cloud*. (laughter) She's very keen on Biggles books. Would you buy her that?

O'SHANE

No. Once again, I don't believe in censorship, but I do believe in discussing issues. Books like *Biggles*, I think, present an uncritical picture.

MODERATOR

All the men are buying their children guns and all the women are buying their children books. Anne-Marie Grisogono?

ANNE-MARIE GRISOGONO

I have two sons and I have always had a policy of not giving them war toys. They know that, they respect that, and they do not ask for them . . . but they do make guns out of Lego. (laughter)

MODERATOR

It is difficult, isn't it? Kim Beazley, what is the best form of defence when you are defenceless?

BEAZLEY

We are not defenceless.

MODERATOR

But if you had met the school bully in the playground . . . I suppose you were the school bully? (laughter) Master MacKellar, what do you do when you meet Bully Beazley in the school playground?

MICHAEL MACKELLAR

I beat a strategic retreat . . . or I could form my own gang. (laughter)

MODERATOR

His gang has got more members than your gang.

MACKELLAR

Then you have to go on a recruiting campaign.

MODERATOR

You could always call the teacher to give him the cane—the child's first taste of conventional weapons. Is that the way it works, Keith Suter: we allow our kids to play with war toys, because they know at the end of the day there is punishment if they go too far?

KEITH SUTER

Children should not be given war toys. They should instead be given lectures and they should be introduced to the real problems of the world. By giving them a lecture or a book you can introduce them to the real world which awaits them.

MODERATOR

You said you were not in favour of censorship, Pat O'Shane. There are some new toys on the market—video games like "Rambo Raygun versus the Space Invaders" and "Nuke the Gook", a tasteless game inviting children to re-fight the Vietnam War with nuclear weapons. Sweden bans them; should we do likewise?

O'SHANE

I think so. My reason for saying that is that presently we

uncritically churn out this sort of material. Until we have a much broader approach to education about peace and war issues, then I am certainly in favour of banning those kinds of videos.

MODERATOR
They are exactly the sort of games that your grandchildren, Sir Ernest, want you to buy for their birthday.

SIR ERNEST TITTERTON
Yes, and why not. This *is* the real world. The world is armed to the teeth with real weapons. We must not be afraid of weapons. The thing we have to be afraid of is people, because a weapon is completely inert until it is animated by people, be it a woman or a man.

MODERATOR
You don't think there is a danger of kids growing up thinking that war is a game?

TITTERTON
Not at all. If we worry about that, you had better consider controlling the media.

MODERATOR
We will consider that a little later on. (laughter)

MODERATOR
If, ladies and gentlemen, you were to board Qantas flight QF007, the new fast track to New York via Seoul and Anchorage, you'd fly not far from the rickety democracy of Malaria. Malaria; a country teeming with people, corruption and tropical rain; a country with a vote at the United Nations and an overdraft at the World Bank; a country, nonetheless, that is closer to Darwin than Darwin is to Sydney. The regime of President Buldoza is something of a human rights black spot. Priests and communists are locked up without trial, political opponents disappear, the people suffer poverty while the President's wife pays visits to Swiss beauty salons and bank vaults. But Malaria is staunchly anticommunist, and Australia has for some time supplied it with civil and military aid—Nomad aircraft, field hospitals, and training courses for Malarian officers at Duntroon. Kevin Murray, you are the very model of a modern major general; do you approve of military aid to Malaria? It's a buffer against communism, and against Islamic fundamentalism.

KEVIN MURRAY

The opening of our educational establishments to officers from countries in our region would be difficult to criticise. Irrespective of one's view of the politics of the home government, it would be a means of extending the hands of friendship and cultural exchange and of showing the people who we are and what we are in a real sense.

MODERATOR

What are the advantages of training Malarian army officers at Duntroon?

BILL HAYDEN

It is not in Australia's role to involve itself in assisting any other country to avoid Islam or communism; that is a domestic problem of that country. If it is a country in which there are human rights problems, our policy is quite clear. We would be required to withdraw aid from that country. But if the situation is itself of flux, if there is evidence in Malaria of, say, a junior officer class starting to emerge, which could benefit from the training methods of our armed services and exposure to Western ideals, then . . . I would be prepared to consider it.

MODERATOR

Would there be advantages in the Malarian army officers coming to Duntroon?

HAYDEN

If it means it is going to help that country move towards true liberal values, and pluralism and respect for rights, and is going to start the momentum towards establishing decent military traditions, then yes, it can be used to positive advantage.

MODERATOR

Very well, a group of junior army officers comes to Duntroon to learn Australian army traditions. They are led by Colonel Jekel, known as "Flaky" Jekel because his suntan tends to peel. (laughter) He has a brief from the Malarian government to buy military equipment—Malaria has just had a big loan from the World Bank, most of which it wants to spend on re-equipping their armed forces. He notices some of our fossil-class minesweepers, Kim Beazley; can he buy them?

BEAZLEY

The minesweepers you have in mind would probably guarantee the loss of lives of at least some of the military of Malaria. (laughter)

MODERATOR

What about your pride and joy, the Jindalee Over-the-Horizon Radar?

BEAZLEY

No way does he get the Jindalee.

MODERATOR

Why not?

BEAZLEY

Because the Jindalee is a surveillance system which is excellent in preserving the Australian technological edge in this region.

MODERATOR

It sounds like we should privatise it, Mr MacKellar. (laughter)

MACKELLAR

If you want it to be successful . . . (laughter)

MODERATOR

All right, he gets the minesweepers and not the radar. The problems in Malaria have led to street demonstrations against the Buldoza regime. Colonel Jekel, on behalf of his government, goes to David Sadleir at Foreign Affairs. He explains that the Malarian army does not have any crowd control equipment—no rubber bullets or tear gas for dispersing demonstrators. People are getting shot and killed. They need desperately tear gas and rubber bullets—to help them save lives. Can they buy some of those from Australia?

DAVID SADLEIR

I would have to report his case to my Minister.

HAYDEN

This is a hell of a life. I am getting more bucks on my table now than I have had for the last year. (laughter) They do not go. We have a rule that military equipment or equipment capable of being used for aggressive or offensive purposes will not go to any country.

MODERATOR

But this equipment will prevent loss of life.

HAYDEN

Tear gas and rubber bullets can seriously injure people. I do not think we should get drawn into that level of domestic problem in Malaria. I have rejected proposals like that which have come to me in the past. I do not want to be any part of oppressing people. I suspect they have a justifiable reason for demonstrating.

MODERATOR

There are two Australian drug smugglers on death row in Malaria. The Malarian High Court has rejected their appeal. It is intimated to you that if Australia permits this equipment to go, then President Buldoza will show clemency.

HAYDEN

I do not believe that judicial decisions should be determined by what actually are bribes — hostage money.

MODERATOR

Your attitude is a great disappointment to the Queensland Rubber Company, which manufactures condoms and wants to move into rubber bullets. Would you actually place an embargo on them, David Sadleir? Stop them from exporting rubber bullets from Queensland?

SADLEIR

Certainly. If it was a government decision that they should not be exported, yes.

MODERATOR

If you were a Malarian demonstrator, Pat O'Shane, wouldn't you rather be gassed than shot?

O'SHANE

I would be prepared to die for my cause. If I had a commitment to freedom, liberty, equality and, above all, peace and humanity, I would be prepared to go to the wall for that.

MODERATOR

There is one final request from the Malarians. They are signatories to the Nuclear Non-Proliferation Treaty, and they are rather keen to buy some Australian uranium. Given that they will abide by all the safeguards that we impose — and our safeguards are the toughest in the world—are we obliged to sell it to them?

SADLEIR

If this regime was as unattractive as you have described it, then I think we would have very serious reservations about selling uranium to them.

MODERATOR

Other countries will have no reservations at all about selling them uranium, will they, Andrew Mack?

ANDREW MACK

The President of Niger has said that he will sell it to the devil.

MODERATOR

So he will certainly sell it to President Buldoza. Why then should we worry about where our uranium is going?

MACK

Because two wrongs don't make a right.

MODERATOR

Malaria wants to use this for peaceful purposes. It has a bad track record on human rights, but so do a lot of other countries. If you are satisfied, entirely satisfied, that they are using it, just as Indonesia is, for peaceful purposes, any problem about selling it?

HAYDEN

We would have to look seriously at it because under Article 4 of the treaty, which we regard as the cornerstone of arms control arrangements in the world today, there is an obligation on material source countries to supply materials to signatory countries.

MODERATOR

There is an obligation on Australia in that treaty?

HAYDEN

That is right. We would have to be satisfied that the country would remain stable, that it would adhere to the principle of the safeguards arrangement which had been entered into and that the Non-Proliferation Treaty would continue to be respected. And that means very simply the uranium would not be diverted towards nuclear weaponry. We first enter into safeguard arrangements with a particular country, and the next step is we enter into a contract with them. We have entered into safeguard contracts with quite a large number of countries.

MODERATOR

We are satisfied about all those things, and so the uranium goes north. Ultimately of course whether these treaties are going to stick is a matter that Richard Butler has very much in mind. You are the Australian Ambassador for Disarmament. How long have you been conferring?

RICHARD BUTLER

At that conference, for eight years now.

MODERATOR

And how many treaties have you notched up?

BUTLER

In those eight years, none.

MODERATOR

Ah—it's early days yet. (laughter)

BUTLER

But really the conference has been going since the beginning of this century and the overall history is quite good and one of the treaties is the Nuclear Non-Proliferation Treaty, the most vital nuclear arms control treaty.

MODERATOR

Are all countries members?

BUTLER

No, it is a very exclusive group. There are one hundred and sixty countries in the United Nations and only forty of them are at the conference on disarmament. We are one of them.

MODERATOR

Why were we elected?

BUTLER

We were put there as a result of a decision of the Secretary-General of the United Nations. We are only one of ten Western countries.

MODERATOR
Are we there because we are an American ally?

BUTLER
No, we are there in our own right, and that is a right that has been asserted very very sharply in the last couple of years.

MODERATOR
Do we caucus with the Americans?

BUTLER
No, we caucus with the Western group of which we are a member, and of which America is also a member.

MODERATOR
But we are not seen as neutral; we are seen as being allied with America.

BUTLER
Our home is in the Western group in Geneva, in what is called the Western Association of Nations but we remain in very very good and constant conversation with the other groups, in particular the neutral group.

MODERATOR
Wouldn't we have rather more influence if we were perceived as being amongst neutrals like Sweden and Yugoslavia and Egypt, rather than being perceived as pro-American?

BUTLER
No, because that would be quite false; it would be in a sense a lie. We are a Western country; that is our history, that is our democratic tradition, that is where we come from.

MODERATOR
Mr MacKellar, are you happy with the expenditure on our mission to Geneva, or is it just another drain on the devalued Australian dollar?

MACKELLAR
The essence of our membership I would agree with, and of course it came about when my party was in government.

MODERATOR
So if you were returned to government would you keep Mr Butler in Geneva?

MACKELLAR

Not necessarily Mr Butler, but we would keep a presence there.

MODERATOR

You wouldn't transfer him to be Trade Commissioner in Vancouver?

MACKELLAR

There may well be a vacancy there. (laughter)

MODERATOR

Am I being a bit tough on Mr Butler, John Pilger? You have been making films about disarmament for British television; do his efforts in Geneva come to your attention?

PILGER

I think Mr Butler's efforts have been significant, especially some of the speeches he has made in support of the freeze initiative and a comprehensive test-ban treaty. But he has just mentioned that Australia is with the Western association because that is its tradition. Well, Sweden is also a Western country and it also has a democratic tradition and they don't seem to be troubled by being on their own. I think it is a pity that initiatives that Mr Butler has made in Geneva have been constrained, if you like, by our being a member of the Western group. I question whether Australia is a natural member. I would have thought that Australia could make just a few moves to be perceived around the world as truly independent.

MODERATOR

Andrew Mack, is that the way you see it?

MACK

I agree there is a problem in being part of the Western group. The way our diplomats work is to try and persuade people behind closed doors. Another way is to stand up and make statements which may be extremely embarrassing to your major allies. But I think historically it is interesting to note that the allies of the United States have had an effect on the United States; for example in the fifties; in Asia particularly.

MODERATOR

Richard Butler, would you comment on those two views?

BUTLER

I admire John Pilger's work immensely but I cannot agree with him when he poses the question of our true independence. Everything we have done in disarmament had been on the basis of our utter independence. I agree with him on the Western group being a bit of a constraint, but we are Western: to move us from that position would be immensely difficult.

MODERATOR

Let us hear Australia speak on disarmament. The United Nations General Assembly rolls around again. There is a resolution on the table calling for immediate talks on a comprehensive test-ban treaty; one banning nuclear tests for all time. Bill Hayden, will Australia support that resolution?

HAYDEN

Certainly, and not only will we support that resolution but we have in fact taken the initiative in this area.

MODERATOR

Australia does take the initiative in the area. You come to the UN rostrum yourself. What reasons do you give to the world for promoting this resolution?

HAYDEN

Australia has the right to be heard when it expresses its concern about the nuclear arms race. It's opposed to the nuclear arms race and wants to see a nuclear-free world, but it accepts this is a very imperfect world, with serious instability. So we're involved in deterrence, through the monitoring station at Pine Gap. Because of that we take a risk, and we want to be heard.

MODERATOR

Peter Bowers, you are editor of the *Sydney Morning Bugle*. Are you going to report that speech? I imagine you have a copy of it in advance.

PETER BOWERS

Yes.

MODERATOR

There is a lot of other news today. "Australia beats Ireland in World Series cricket";"Government minister in AIDS corruption scandal";"Homes à Court makes a bid for the Sydney Swans";"George Negus marries—official". (laughter) Where is Bill Hayden going to appear in the paper?

BOWERS

The *Bugle* is a big paper and there is space for all news and, depending on the balance of it, Hayden would be a very small pointer on page one and a story on the inside page.

HAYDEN

Is that page forty-one or forty-two?

BOWERS

(pause) Forty-two. (laughter)

MODERATOR

What does he have to do to get on the front page? Tell better jokes? Take his shoe off and bang it on the table at the United Nations? Break down and cry?

BOWERS

Get a result.

MODERATOR

Get a result. That's a pretty tall order.

HAYDEN

Well, the whole experience is that arms control is itself painfully slow, but the object is so desirable that we cannot forfeit our efforts.

MODERATOR

Sir William, you read that speech on page forty-two of the *Bugle*. Do you agree with calling for immediate talks about a test-ban treaty?

SIR WILLIAM KEYS

Absolutely. Yes, I think so. The recent summit between Gorbachev and Reagan didn't achieve specifics, but it started the process of negotiation with talking. I think that is where the solutions come from.

MODERATOR

You supported the Minister's speech calling for an immediate test-ban treaty?

KEYS

Yes.

MODERATOR

You were challenged by Peter Bowers, Minister, to get a result.

You got a very odd result. America voted against your resolution.

HAYDEN

The United States voted against the proposal because the Americans claim that they have problems with the technical means of verification which would have to be put in place: they are far from confident that any technical means of verification would be effective.

MODERATOR

So, by making that speech you knew it would embarrass America.

HAYDEN

We knew that the United States had a different view to ours. They made that clear—that they would vote against anything that we put up in the comprehensive test-ban treaty area.

MODERATOR

But you knew that you would embarrass an ally, because it is always more embarrassing to be criticised by a friend than an enemy.

HAYDEN

I think the United States would have a thick enough hide.

MODERATOR

Is this where Australia gets any clout it does have in world affairs—from its capacity to embarrass America?

MACKELLAR

No, I don't think that is correct. I think Australia should make up its own mind about any particular issue and then state that clearly.

MODERATOR

Were you in favour of the Minister's speech?

MACKELLAR

Yes. I think that if Australia simply sets out to embarrass America at every opportunity, then obviously the currency of embarrassment will decline very quickly. But if America understands that the speeches that are made on behalf of the Australian people are done with the very best interests of the Australian people in mind, regardless in this instance of the feelings of the Americans, the impact of this speech can be greater.

MODERATOR

Richard Butler, why is verification such a great stumbling block to achieving a test-ban treaty?

BUTLER

What the Americans are saying is that they want to be sure that if the test-ban treaty is put in place, it cannot be cheated on.

MODERATOR

We have got to find a means of ensuring that no country can cheat, can pass a little bit of nuclear wind in some cavern under the ground?

BUTLER

Precisely.

MODERATOR

David Denham, is Australia particularly well positioned for verifying the occurrence of nuclear tests?

DAVID DENHAM

It is very well positioned for monitoring both nuclear explosions and earthquakes in this part of the hemisphere. If one is to have a comprehensive test-ban treaty, then you must be able to monitor worldwide and Australia's geography enables it to monitor a very large part of the hemisphere.

MODERATOR

Suppose you set up your seismic array at Alice Springs. Can you get Mururoa?

DENHAM

Yes.

MODERATOR

China?

DENHAM

Yes.

MODERATOR

Malaria?

DENHAM

Yes, you can really get Malaria. (laughter)

MODERATOR

How does seismic monitoring work?

DENHAM

The seismic array picks up the regular rhythm of the earth and any disturbance of that caused by a bomb test.

MODERATOR

How far down can you go? Down to five kilotons? Or one? Half a kiloton?

DENHAM

At the moment we can be pretty safe in being able to pick up a bomb that goes off that is over ten kilotons. There are difficulties in picking up bomb tests under ten kilotons, and in distinguishing them from small earthquakes.

MODERATOR

That is why America was able to conduct some fifteen or sixteen secret tests last year in Nevada? They were very small bombs?

DENHAM

Yes.

MODERATOR

So, first of all we need the political will to put the technology together, because unless we do we are still going to have difficulties distinguishing between earthquakes and small explosions?

DENHAM

Right.

MODERATOR

That is the problem, and Australian scientists think they have solved it. They have put the technology together and produced SPASM—the Specific Array for Seismic Monitoring. SPASM will enable us for the first time to tell the difference between a small earthquake and a small nuclear test in some underground site thousands of miles away. Can we have the money to develop it?

BEAZLEY

We would have to consider what defence advantage it was to Australia. In my view a successful test-ban treaty would be of enormous benefit.

MODERATOR

Any doubt that SPASM is of enormous benefit, Richard Butler?

BUTLER

No doubt at all. Verification has been the major stumbling

block. The development of SPASM may well break that down, and prove that a test-ban treaty can be verified, can be trusted, and thus end any political obstacles for entering into such a treaty.

MODERATOR

SPASM could break the log jam, and Australia can play a part in that. Dr Denham, what you would like to do really before SPASM goes into operation is have a little test—a controlled half-kiloton nuclear explosion—to check that SPASM works effectively. It would be desirable to have an underground test on an island some thousands of miles away from Alice Springs. Perhaps Lord Howe Island, after Mr Wran gets back from holidays. (laughter) Mr Sadleir, Dr Denham wants to set off a teensy-weensy little nuclear explosion—only half a kiloton—on Lord Howe Island.

SADLEIR

Sorry, it is not possible.

MODERATOR

Why not?

SADLEIR

Because we are a party to the South Pacific Nuclear Free Zone Treaty which prohibits the acquisition, stationing or use of nuclear explosive devices, whether for warlike purposes or for so-called peaceful purposes.

MODERATOR

Lord Howe Island is out because it's in the South Pacific. What about the Cocos Islands? That would be just as good. There is no Indian Ocean nuclear free treaty, is there?

SADLEIR

There isn't as yet any treaty of that kind in relation to the Indian Ocean. But Australia undertook in signing the South Pacific Nuclear Free Zone Treaty a specific obligation to apply its provisions to all Australian territories, including Australian territories in the Indian Ocean. So we can't test there either.

MODERATOR

Professor Titterton, we could have it at Monte Bello Island. It would be like old times. (laughter)

TITTERTON

There is no treaty that precludes us doing what we have already done in Australia.

MODERATOR

Bill Hayden, you have the final decision; a little half-kiloton nuclear test, in the interests of developing our verification device?

HAYDEN

As I understand our obligations, we can't fiddle around in this way even for peaceful purposes.

MODERATOR

You are doing it for disarmament.

HAYDEN

No, we don't need to use a nuclear test. We can simulate that by other means.

MODERATOR

Very well, Dr Denham, you simulate a nuclear test; you don't use the real thing. And SPASM seems to work. For the rest of the world, 1986 is the United Nations International Year of Peace. But for Queensland, which recognises the United Nations only with some difficulty, the Premier has decreed that 1986 is not the Year of Peace, it is the Year of Police. There will be "Police in our time" parades, police boys' clubs boxing exhibitions, "Pin the tail on the pervert" competitions. (laughter) There is really no room in Brisbane, Deborah Brooks, for the sort of peace march that you are planning. You can have your march in the university, you can have it in the parks, but you cannot do it in the streets and frighten the police horses. Are you going ahead with it?

BROOKS

Yes.

MODERATOR

Really?

BROOKS

If there is enough public support through community peace groups, and all the organisations, and the individuals wanted to proceed with it, yes, I would. If local grassroots activists felt that they were not prepared to be imprisoned or receive harassment from the police, then I would not.

MODERATOR

You are expecting a hundred thousand people. Do you really think it helps the cause of peace to have violent demonstrations?

BROOKS

I don't think they would be undoubtedly violent demonstrations. There have been other marches where there have not been permits. There have been strikes in Queensland where there has been police intervention and they do not have to be violent.

O'SHANE

We are also demonstrating against the laws of Queensland. I think wherever there are repressive laws, then we have to say that they are part of the very broad issues that we are concerned about as peace activists. If marches are violent, that's because of the Queensland government and its agents, the police. We impress upon our supporters that we are in fact concerned about peace and not about violence.

MODERATOR

Who are you trying to impress?

BROOKS

The whole world.

MODERATOR

The whole world—including Australian politicians?

BROOKS

Certainly Australian politicians.

MODERATOR

There is a massive demonstration, Bill Hayden: half a million people around Australia demonstrate against nuclear-powered ships in Australian ports. Would you change your policy on that as a result of demonstrations?

HAYDEN

No, because I don't believe any government policy can be made on the basis of street demonstrations.

MODERATOR

What can it be made on the basis of? Opinion polls?

HAYDEN

It has to be made on the basis of what one concludes are in the best interests of this country.

MODERATOR

Michael MacKellar, as a result perhaps of the International Year of Peace, the opinion polls — theirs and yours — are saying seventy per cent of Australians support a ban on nuclear-powered ships. would you change your policy?

MACKELLAR

No.

MODERATOR

And perhaps get a lot of votes?

MACKELLAR

Yes, but I agree with Bill Hayden that governments are elected to govern. If it is in the best interests of the Australian nation to continue a policy of allowing nuclear-powered ships to visit Australia, then that policy should prevail. You go out in the highways and byways and tell the community why.

O'SHANE

But the community is going out on the highways and byways to tell the politicians why not.

MACKELLAR

Politicians are a strange breed of people . . .

O'SHANE

They certainly are. (laughter)

MACKELLAR

. . . because regularly they put themselves forward at elections, which has a very salutary effect.

MODERATOR

You do not change your policy on the basis of public opinion. You might change your leader, but you do not change your policy? (laughter)

MACKELLAR

So far, thank goodness, we do not have government by Gallup poll in Australia. (cynical laughter, led by Peter Bowers)

MODERATOR

Andrew Mack, you have been studying the opinion polls; I
suppose the peace movement has been growing in support?

MACK

Yes, I think that is true. I think the peace movement has been
very successful in mobilising support in its natural constituency.

MODERATOR

I guess that means that support for the ANZUS Treaty, which
is our alliance with America that binds us to the bomb, has
dropped?

MACK

On the contrary, it has gone up by ten per cent in the last year.

MODERATOR

What does that mean?

MACK

I think that really suggests the peace movement has been very
successful in actually *scaring* the Australian electorate into support
for the security blanket called the ANZUS Treaty.

MODERATOR

How do you respond to that, Deborah Brooks? The irony that
the peace movement, by focusing attention on the horrors of the
bomb, has actually made Australians crave even more the
security blanket of the ANZUS alliance?

BROOKS

I think that is true because I do not think at this stage the peace
movement has come up with an alternative policy in the current
situation. We need something we can market successfully to the
populace, to convince them that we are not trying to take away
Australia's defences and that we can in fact replace ANZUS with
something that has Australia's national interests at heart.

MODERATOR

We are afraid of the bomb, so we cling to the Americans.
Logical?

PILGER

There is, perhaps, a logic in craving a security blanket. We now
live in a time when young children ask their parents about the

nuclear war. But craving an American security blanket is like craving a hairshirt on a 32°C Sydney summer day.

MODERATOR

That is the view the New Zealand government takes. It has passed legislation banning nuclear-powered or nuclear-armed ships from its ports. Which is tough luck for the USS *Armageddon,* a battle cruiser of the 13th fleet, which develops rudder problems just north of the Bay of Islands. Can it limp into Sydney for a refit at Garden Island, Kim Beazley?

BEAZLEY

Nuclear warships are entitled to visit this country, and where a United States ship was in trouble off Australia's shores, and requested entry into Sydney, then I think we would give it that permission.

MODERATOR

It is nuclear-powered, like most of the 13th fleet. Would you ask whether it is carrying nuclear arms?

BEAZLEY

No.

MODERATOR

Why not?

BEAZLEY

No problem would arise unless we were informed that one of the problems associated with the ship was a problem with a nuclear weapon.

MODERATOR

We don't know whether there is a problem, because we don't know whether there is a nuclear weapon on it. We suspect there is. We rely on American assurances that there are no nuclear bombs on board the B-52s that land in Australia. If we ask about the B-52s, why don't we ask about the ships?

BEAZLEY

There is a separate agreement on the question of the B-52s. The United States agreed with the previous government that for the purpose of those flights, which are defined as training flights, they would be not armed and carry no bombs. So those B-52s that come over to Australia for training purposes don't carry nuclear weapons. It is a very specific, very limited agreement. The question related to port visits raises different issues. We accept the American policy of non-disclosure.

MODERATOR

The *Armageddon* goes into dry dock in Garden Island. It looks as though it will be stationed there for two or three months for a refit, and we suspect it is nuclear-armed. Is that a breach of the South Pacific Nuclear Free Zone Treaty?

SADLEIR

No, it isn't, because although you use the word "stationed", in fact in the treaty the word "stationed" has a very specific definition. In this case we would simply be extending assistance to a ship in distress.

MODERATOR

It will be stationed here for about three months.

SADLEIR

The weapon wouldn't be deployed.

MODERATOR

If the entire 13th fleet spent the next year travelling around Australia, making goodwill visits to various ports in turn, that wouldn't be a breach of the treaty, because its nuclear weapons wouldn't be "stationed" here?

SADLEIR

It would not be a breach because it wouldn't fit into that definition. But if there was resort to that kind of device to get around the "stationing" clause in the treaty, then it would be open to any other party to the treaty to question Australia on whether or not this really constituted "stationing". It would go to a consultative committee of all parties to the treaty who would have to decide whether or not Australia was evading the terms of the treaty.

MODERATOR

Is this treaty of much use, Pat O'Shane?

O'SHANE

It has some uses but I am inclined to think they are minimal. It has put nuclear-free zones on the agenda for public attention. It certainly doesn't meet the needs of the South Pacific . . .

MODERATOR

We have nuclear-armed ships in the Pacific, nuclear satellites over the Pacific, nuclear submarines under the Pacific. In reality, Andrew Mack, do we have a nuclear-free Pacific or a nuclear-full Pacific?

MACK

I think we have a relatively nuclear-free South Pacific but we have an extremely nuclear-full North Pacific. There are around three thousand nuclear warheads in the Pacific altogether.

MODERATOR

That is almost as many as in Europe.

MACK

Yes, indeed it is.

BUTLER

What we have done in bringing that treaty into existence has been recognised around the world as a very significant achievement. I know what Pat was concerned about, but certainly when I tabled that treaty in Geneva four months ago there was a stunned silence. You know, something had actually happened in disarmament, and it came from our part of the world and it gave the negotiations in Geneva a shot in the arm.

HAYDEN

I honestly beleive that Secretary-General Gorbachev and President Reagan went to Geneva because lots of countries on this side of the communist bloc, like Australia and Canada and Holland, were becoming increasingly concerned about relations between east and west, and countries like Hungary and others within the communist bloc countries were equally concerned. The important thing is that at last, since SALT 2 went into cold storage, both sides are talking very seriously about arms control and disarmament. It may not work but it is quite an achievement to get them there.

MODERATOR

A lot of people believe that only by direct action—emphatic and dramatic action—will politicians be moved. One of those people is Joan Dark, Co-Chairperson of the East Balmain Anti-Appeasement Workshop. She's a friend of yours, Pat O'Shane, and she says: "The *Armageddon* is in port. I've just got back from a sabbatical at Greenham Common. The way to focus attention is to cut the wire and go in and plaster the ship with paint. 'Yanks away', 'Lange Si, Hayden Non.' (laughter) Going to come with me?"

O'SHANE

I would counsel against cutting the wire.

MODERATOR

Didn't you say earlier you were prepared to break the law?

O'SHANE

I think we have to challenge the laws, yes. At the same time, however, we have to be very careful about the way in which we carry out our campaign. I certainly favour flying banners and making known our views. We can sit at Lady Macquarie's Chair, pitch our tents and take our small flotilla out on the harbour and get our message across.

MODERATOR

Will you get the message into the *Sydney Morning Bugle* by doing that? Page forty-two again? (laughter)

BOWERS

Up a bit from page forty-two.

O'SHANE

We would lose our message if we cut the wire.

MODERATOR

"But I want to create an incident. Those guards at Garden Island are armed, aren't they, Major General Murray? Armed guards, guarding the *Armageddon*?"

MURRAY

I am not even sure they are in the navy. We would have to have a hot line to the Labour Council. (laughter)

MODERATOR

Bill Pritchett, who's guarding the *Armageddon*?

BILL PRITCHETT

Probably some American marines are armed. But the *Armageddon*, I think, would probably call upon the Australian police force.

MODERATOR

"Yes, and they are armed as well! I'm game to die for peace, Pat O'Shane."

O'SHANE

I think there is a time and place to die for peace. Earlier I was in Malaria and it was an extremely oppressive regime.

MODERATOR

"And this regime is so open? Michael MacKellar is not going to change his view if the opinion polls are seventy per cent against him. Do you really have a government that's open to argument?"

O'SHANE

Open to argument? Yes, I do. I do not believe that the sort of adventurist action you are trying to take is the best way to get our message across. The only reason that would be on the front page is because we cut wires and managed to get ourselves arrested.

MODERATOR

"If you managed to get yourself shot, you would be the lead story. 'Pat O'Shane shot by Americans.' Bowers would run a special supplement. (laughter) Deborah Brooks, will you come with me?"

BROOKS

I wouldn't be taking part in actions that were likely to antagonise people within my organisation. But I would encourage people to make known their protests and their views.

MODERATOR

"You would encourage me, but you wouldn't come with me?"

BROOKS

If that was what you believed was appropriate for you, that is your choice. It would not be appropriate for me.

MODERATOR

"I do believe I should break the law to get in the front page of the *Sydney Morning Bugle*. Keith Suter, would you give me your blessing?"

SUTER

No. I wouldn't, because you'd be bringing the peace movement into disrepute. What we're trying to do is to appeal to middle-aged, middle-of-the-road, middle classes. When we've got them on our side we will then have the support of Bill Hayden. People like you, who go around causing trouble, will just add to people feeling that we have to have ANZUS. You would then be an agent provocateur—probably paid for by the Pentagon. (laughter)

MODERATOR

"You've convinced me, Keith. (laughter) I'll stay at home. We're having an East Balmain Anti-Appeasement Workshop wine-tasting next week. See you there." (laughter)

SUTER

I'm a Methodist, so I don't drink; but maybe Paul Keating will go. (laughter)

MODERATOR

Bill Hayden, let me see if I can take you away from all this. Do you ever get tired of relentless reporters, smoke-filled rooms, undrinkable TAA coffee? Do you ever want to retire?

HAYDEN

Yes, sometimes.

MODERATOR

Well, the time comes for you to retire. You get a good superannuation deal from the Treasurer—with an element of belated compensation for wrongful dismissal—and you buy a little pub. Not in Queensland—after so long in the ALP you are sick of having to chuck out deviants (laughter) but a little pub in Alice Springs—the Drover's Dingo. As you serve behind the bar, Australians touring the outback, seeing parts of their country they've never seen before, sometimes say to you, "Bill, we flew back from the Rock today and we saw these strange white bubbles rising out of the ground at Pine Gap—a sort of electronic Stonehenge. What are they there for, Bill?"

HAYDEN

Well, there's them that says it's all for the good of this country, but between you and me there's something darker going on out there . . . and it would be my odd sense of humour that would lead me to say that, because someone would repeat it to Peter Bowers and he would give me a front-page story for the first time in my life. (laughter) But I do believe that they make a valuable contribution to a greater level of stability in what otherwise would be a very worrying, unstable nuclear world. It is better that we didn't need these things, but we do need them and there is no alternative. Now, I want to work for peace, but I can't bring it.

MODERATOR

Have another beer, Bill, and tell us; are we a nuclear target as a result of those bases?

HAYDEN

We may be a nuclear target in certain circumstances, yes.

MODERATOR

When you were in government did you ever get anything from them which was really vital to Australia's security?

HAYDEN

Yes. The fact that they bring a level of predictability to the relationship between the superpowers means that the security of this country is greatly enhanced. If it was not for the information from them, we would have nothing but suspicion to go on which would lead to paranoia . . .

MODERATOR

I have got to ring my brother in Malaria tonight. Can they listen in to that call?

HAYDEN

I am not able to discuss what the facilities do, as you well know. All I will say is that the facilities are important for verification measures. I always think this is a dilemma that the peace movement has to face. If we genuinely want arms control in place, then verification measures are absolutely critical.

MODERATOR

Andrew Mack, you are preparing a paper on the role of the American bases. What are they doing for most of the time?

MACK

Pine Gap is essentially a ground station for American spy satellites which are poised some twenty-three thousand miles up above the equator, looking down and listening.

MODERATOR

What are they listening to? What the Americans want them to listen to?

MACK

Indeed. Mostly, what is going on in the Soviet Union and China.

MODERATOR

They could be listening, for all we know, to internal telephone conversations in the Kremlin.

MACK

Indeed, and they have done that in the past apparently.

MODERATOR

Or picking up a short-wave radio discussion between two tank commanders on the East German border.

MACK

That is the sort of information they gather, because we have an interest in knowing what the Soviets are doing constantly.

MODERATOR

If there were a conventional war in Europe and the Soviets needed to stop the allies getting that sort of information, might they decide to take out Pine Gap?

MACK

That is always a possibility.

MODERATOR

If they did want to take out Pine Gap, what would they take it out with?

MACK

They have a number of options. They could use missile-firing submarines, or SS-18 missiles fired from Soviet territories.

MODERATOR

Would they use conventional weapons?

MACK

No, they would have nuclear warheads.

MODERATOR

John Pilger, are we crazy to have these time bombs ticking away on Australian soil?

PILGER

The loudest tick is North West Cape—a relay station through which messages are passed from Washington to United States forces; not only the navy and submarines, but air force and army. North West Cape is there for the United States and the United States only. It is a bait for a particular kind of provocation.

MODERATOR

A bait for a nuclear attack. Are we crazy, Michael MacKellar, to have these baits on our soil?

MACKELLAR

No, I don't think we are and I don't like the use of the term "bait". I believe we have to make an initial decision as to whether we are a US-aligned country. We *are* an aligned country, and we must accept the responsibilities which go along with that alignment. I think we have a quite proper justification for assisting allies in the building of effective monitoring systems and effective anti-war systems.

MODERATOR

Should they be there, Dr Grisogono?

GRISOGONO

It is unfortunate they are American installations and that we do not have much control over their other functions. Obviously Pine Gap has a lot of time to fill in between verifying missile tests, and we do not have any control over what they listen to. The much more preferable situation would be to have a monitoring system under the auspices of the United Nations. Australia would be quite ready, willing and happy to cooperate with such a UN agency and to offer Australian soil for its bases. If the information collected was purely and simply verification of arms agreements and peace stability, I believe we would not be targeted.

MODERATOR

Richard Butler, you are in Geneva seeking to negotiate a test-ban treaty. You get a call from the Russian Disarmament Ambassador, your opposite number, Max Smirnoff. He says, "Comrade Butler, can we have lunch again?"

BUTLER

We have lunch about once a month. I always pay.

MODERATOR

You take him to that charming little French restaurant
overlooking the lake, and over the caviar fondue, he puts to you
an interesting proposition. "We will support the Australian
initiative for an immediate test-ban treaty, and we will accept
SPASM, your verification device, on our soil—on the condition
that Australia closes down the American bases at Pine Gap and
Nurrungar and North West Cape. What do you say?

BUTLER

I would unhesitatingly make clear to Mr Smirnoff straightaway,
that the Australian government, while it is prepared to consider
any Soviet proposal quite seriously and study it deeply, is not
going to be in a position to be traded off or blackmailed.

MODERATOR

"Sure, sure, Richard, I can understand your reluctance to close
down American bases. All right, we will support your
resolution, and accept SPASM on our territory, if you
internationalise them. You tell us they have got these wonderful
verification facilities—fine. Let a United Nations team operate
Pine Gap and Nurrungar."

BUTLER

I think the idea of an international verification agency—which
Dr Grisogono mentioned—is actually extraordinarily interesting.
If the Soviet Union and the United States were prepared to talk
seriously about that, I don't think they would find the
Australian government wanting, because verification is so
important and it could be objectified and made open . . .

MODERATOR

Your Minister, since Bill Hayden has retired, is Kim Beazley,
and he's on a fact-finding tour in Geneva at the moment. He's
finding out some facts about the food at the next table. Have a
chat to him about Smirnoff's trade-off.

BUTLER

Minister, my Russian colleague has put a very interesting
proposal to me. Part of it stinks and I do not think we should
think about it, but the best bit is that we might create an
international verification agency. When it comes to strategic
arms limitation agreements, which are the key to the

preservation of international stability, it is important that the Soviets can be convinced that the Americans are conforming to the treaty and vice versa.

BEAZLEY

We would be prepared to assist in the establishment of an international verification agency. Strategic arms limitation agreements are the key to the preservation of international stability, and it is vital that the Soviets are convinced that the Americans are conforming to the treaty, and vice versa.

MODERATOR

Ladies and gentlemen, the time has come for the USS *Armageddon*, its new rudder fitted, to sail off to pay a goodwill visit to Fremantle to monitor the America's Cup. It's a stirring sight as the great ship slips out of Sydney Harbour, its band playing hits from *South Pacific,* the marines spick-and-span in their uniforms, waving goodbye to their girlfriends and boyfriends on the wharf. (laughter) Suddenly, Bill Pritchett, your telephone rings at the Ministry of Defence. It's the American Embassy. "Our cryptographer is missing—Lieutenant Bud Weiser—and so are some of the *Armageddon*'s secret code books. He is top security cleared; he's worked at Pine Gap; he knows more about Pine Gap than your Prime Minister. We have to find him before he defects. Can you help?"

PRITCHETT

I will try.

MODERATOR

How will you try?

PRITCHETT

I will ask the police to help.

MODERATOR

Is this a case for the New South Wales Police Force? (laughter) "We have only one lead," the Americans tell you. "In the last couple of weeks we believe he struck up a relationship with a woman called Joan Dark. Ring any bells?"

PRITCHETT

Not with me. (laughter)

MODERATOR

It is midnight, Pat O'Shane, and it's your bell that is ringing. It

is Joan Dark, Lieutenant Weiser in tow. She says, "He's defected
to the peace movement." (laughter)

O'SHANE

Is this a CIA plot?

MODERATOR

"It is not. He is writing an article for the *National Times* on the
real truth about the American bases. It's going to blow them
sky-high. Can he use your basement for a couple of days? I can't
put him up; ASIO are on to me."

O'SHANE

No, he cannot. I am sorry.

MODERATOR

Why no?

O'SHANE

Because I am not satisfied as to his credentials.

MODERATOR

You know Joan; she's a good friend.

O'SHANE

She's a very good friend, but sometimes she tends to go over the
fence — or rather, through it. He won't get asylum in my
basement.

MODERATOR

New South Wales police are tearing up and down the roads of Balmain
looking for him. Can he use your basement, Deborah Brooks?

BROOKS

I don't have an intimate relationship with the editor of the
National Times.

MODERATOR

I don't think anyone does. Not one they would admit to, at any
rate. (laughter)

BROOKS

Am I to assume this story has a guaranteed sale? The editor is
going to publish this story?

MODERATOR

If he is still editor, yes.

BROOKS

He may, after I hear his story, be able to stay in my basement overnight.

MODERATOR

With some reluctance and some concern, you put Lieutenant Bud Weiser up in your basement. But the government has other problems. Two weeks ago there was a coup in Malaria—a military coup led by Colonel Jekel and his junior officers backed by the Malarian Liberation Front which is communist inspired. Fifty innocent American tourists have been arrested in Nirvana, the capital, by Jekel's forces. The new regime talks of trying them as spies. It's re-established relations with Cuba, and invited Vietnamese officers to help with re-education programs. The situation is serious. Bill Hartley has sent a fraternal greetings telegram, so it really is serious. (laughter) But we are getting particularly good information because Colonel Jekel, as he rides around the country in his bulletproof limousine barking orders through the car telephone, is having his conversations intercepted by a satellite twenty-three thousand miles up and flashed back to Pine Gap. We are getting printouts of Jekel's conversations, monitored electronically by our ally's spy in the sky. That's the sort of intelligence you desire from those bases, isn't it, Kim Beazley?

BEAZLEY

Yes.

MODERATOR

We left Bud Weiser in Deborah Brooks' basement tapping out his article—"Spies in the Skies"—for the *National Times*. Unfortunately, the *National Times* has lost so much circulation by publishing articles of that sort that it's been turned into a magazine for yuppies, and so his article hits your desk, Peter Bowers, at the *Sydney Morning Bugle*. It is sensational with a capital "S". It suggests that Aussat is part of the Star Wars program; that the base at North West Cape has a special code that will be sent to Trident submarines to trigger rocket attacks in time of war; and it says that Pine Gap is listening to Colonel Jekel's car telephone. Do you publish it?

BOWERS

. . . Yes, provided you establish that everything he says is true as far as you can establish it.

MODERATOR

What about the "D" notice prohibiting publication of information about our allies' monitoring activities?

BOWERS

It's a voluntary code, and it is not worth the paper it is written on.

PRITCHETT

That is true; it is not worth the paper it is written on.

MODERATOR

Major General Murray, would you mind taking off your uniform and putting on your wig and gown? You are now Kevin Murray Q.C., legal adviser to the government. They have learned through ASIO that Bowers of the *Bugle* is about to publish this terribly damaging article. If Malaria learns that we are helping America to spy on it, our relations with the new regime will be damaged. Is there any way we can stop him publishing?

MURRAY

The truth is that, as the "D" notices have been exposed as having no legal sanction, there is not a terribly clear position under the Commonwealth Crimes Act to cover such a situation. There was a case a few years ago where George Munster and Richard Walsh wanted to publish material that Bill Pritchett thought would damage Australian security. It was to be serialised by the predecessor of the *Sydney Morning Bugle*.

BOWERS

I was news editor that night, and we published.

MURRAY

You bought the material in order to publish it.

BOWERS

The security angle was nonsense. The public had every right to know about it, and the Commonwealth government had no right to suppress it.

MODERATOR

On that occasion, Kim Beazley, the government preferred to take civil action for breach of copyright. But Bowers is going to publish tomorrow. Are you going to prosecute him? There is provision in the Crimes Act, based on the British Official Secrets Act, which has never been used; but it's there. You can have him gaoled for endangering Australian security. Would you ever prosecute a leading journalist?

BEAZLEY

I would say this is not resolvable by legal means. If I knew that Bowers had this material, I do not think I would be worrying too much about talking to Bowers. I would be straight to his principals.

MODERATOR

His proprietor, Sir Rupert Fairpacker, is overseas at the moment, taking out his American citizenship, (laughter) and you talk to Bowers or no-one. A group of *Women's Weekly* World Discovery Tourists were also in the Nirvana Hilton in Malaria at the time of the coup. They haven't been arrested, but they haven't got out yet. We don't want to sour relations with Malaria while they are still there. And we will sour relations if Malaria learns we are spying on them through Pine Gap.

BEAZLEY

Peter, how about a deal?

BOWERS

What's the deal?

BEAZLEY

There is an operation going on in which a rescue might have to be effected for a number of people whose lives are at stake. This has always been the type of situation in which we envisaged a "D" notice would be most applicable. We have potential loss of life on our hands. It is possible that by the publication of this material our ability to secure those lives is going to be seriously compromised. In return for our making absolutely certain that you get, exclusive, our government comments on the situation, would you be prepared to suppress the story—at least for the time being?

BOWERS

I will delete any reference which might endanger the Australian tourists, for twenty-four hours. You had better demonstrate to me by midday tomorrow that it is absolutely imperative to suppress it, because we will publish the next day if you don't.

MODERATOR

It is midday tomorrow. What are you going to do?

BEAZLEY

In that twenty-four hours I would have rung up people who might have attempted to effect a rescue of these tourists and started to get some sort of impression of the time scale. I would ring Mr Bowers and say, "How about another twenty-four hours while I try to work out what is happening and we get some possibility of a rescue in place?"

BOWERS

That is not good enough.

MODERATOR

Do you really publish when you know it's going to damage America's intelligence network? It's going to stop the flow of secret information we get from intercepting Jekel's car telephone conversations.

BOWERS

That is a problem. But if we don't publish, somebody else will. It's a big story. It is most certainly the biggest story we have probably had in Australia. If somebody is going to publish, we have to publish. We have given them forty-eight hours to get off their bums and they have done nothing.

MODERATOR

Your mother-in-law is on the *Women's Weekly* World Discovery Tour.

BOWERS

No deal! (laughter)

MODERATOR

Your proprietor's mother, Lady Fairpacker, is on the *Women's Weekly* World Discovery Tour. Does that make a difference?

BOWERS

No.

MODERATOR

You get a call from New York. It's Sir Rupert: "Don't publish!"

BOWERS

Get yourself another editor.

MODERATOR

Bowers of the *Bugle* will resign if ordered by his proprietor not
to publish this story?

BOWERS

Not only will I resign, I will go to the opposition and make
sure the story is published.

MODERATOR

Would you go to John Pilger to publish it?

BOWERS

I would go to the devil.

MODERATOR

The President of Niger is already there. (laughter)

MODERATOR

There have been some more peaceful political changes in
Australia. A much-loved Prime Minister was accidentally run
down by the peace bus, there's been an election, and a new
government is in power. Michael MacKellar, you have just been
sworn in as Foreign Affairs Minister by the Governor-General,
Lord Fraser of Soweto. (laughter) The first problem on your
desk is Malaria. We have intelligence that Malaria has done a
deal with the North Koreans to take the uranium we sold them
and to enrich it to weapons grade. Jekel wants a bomb. He says,
"A Malarian bomb will bring stability to our region"—a phrase
that he seems to have picked up when he was in Duntroon.
(laughter) What do you do?

MACKELLAR

Who is my permanent head at this stage? (laughter) David, this
is a terrible thing, what are our alternatives?

SADLEIR

Minister, we could allow him to do this, but that has been
inconsistent with government policy, as long as there have been
nuclear weapons, as long as we have had uranium being sold, as
long as we have been exporting uranium. Moreover, it's
something which would discredit that policy completely. Any
proliferation leads to further instabilities and Malaria's neighbour,
Insomnia, will want to develop a bomb and perhaps that will
lead to a nuclear arms race between those two countries. My

advice to you would be immediately to take action.

MODERATOR

To take action of course one would normally sue on the contract in the Malarian High Court. Unfortunately the Malarian High Court has just become the People's Court of Revolutionary Justice presided over by Colonel Jekel's cousin, so we don't stand a chance in the Malarian courts.

SADLEIR

We could take action in the World Court.

MODERATOR

Would that do us much good, Richard Butler?

BUTLER

We have got to take several steps. First of all, to ask Malaria to give us back our uranium. They would presumably say no. The next step would be to take it to our allies in the Nuclear Non-Proliferation Treaty.

MODERATOR

Malaria has just filed a notice at the United Nations withdrawing from the Nuclear Non-Proliferation Treaty.

BUTLER

That is provided for in the treaty, but they have to give three months' notice of withdrawal, giving us time to put pressure on them.

MODERATOR

You go through those stages, but it's a bit difficult because by now we have moved on in time and the old nuclear club of five — America, Russia, Britain, China, France — has expanded a lot. The nuclear club has quite a few new and rather seedy members. South Africa has the bomb; Israel and Pakistan, North and South Korea have the bomb; Malaria is about to get the bomb; Brazil and Argentina have the bomb. There is a lot of worried talk down in the Drover's Dingo. People are saying, "All these other countries now have the bomb; ought we not, if we can't lick 'em, join 'em?" Ought Australia to start thinking seriously about acquiring the bomb?

KEYS

The only condition where I think Australia should possibly

acquire nuclear weapons is on the basis of nations within its region of interest also having nuclear arms. If that is the case, then Australia must think very seriously about the nuclear option. I would ask Professor Titterton's advice.

TITTERTON

History is quite clear on the point. Every single weapon which has been invented has proliferated world wide, from bows and arrows through to guns, through to Exocet weapons and so on and so forth. Nuclear weapons have already proliferated. Indeed, nations representing fifty per cent of the world's total population already have nuclear weapons. Nuclear power is the only option.

HAYDEN

Proliferation is chilling, and if we join it we will accelerate it. We might have to consider that one day, just as a matter of self-preservation. If we get to that situation, we are almost on the brink of the ultimate. Before we get there we have to try and head this off. Malaria has a bomb. I would think we should be trying to mobilise whatever international forces we can against Malaria. Malaria is an underdeveloped country, critically dependent upon markets. I think there is an opportunity to put pressure on there. She is critically dependent on Western financial institutions for support. I think there is an opportunity to put pressure on there. The last thing we should ever do is acquire nuclear capability ourselves. We may be forced to do it one day. I would try everything first before I went down that track.

MODERATOR

You shouldn't have retired.

HAYDEN

It seemed to be a popular decision. (laughter)

MODERATOR

Michael MacKellar, as Foreign Minister, the decision is yours. Do you want your finger on the nuclear trigger?

MACKELLAR

No, I think we should do all that we can to prevent that necessity occurring.

MODERATOR

On one of your frequent visits to Washington you are

summoned to see the new American president, President
Stallone. (laughter) He says, "Mike, we will do you a deal. We
would like Australia, our great ally, to have some sort of nuclear
capacity. You know all those Hornet fighters you bought a few
years back? We will fit a nice little nuclear warhead into their
harpoon missiles. We will do it for free, so Australia can have a
nuclear capacity."

MACKELLAR

I don't see, and neither does my government, any necessity to
withdraw from the Nuclear Non-Proliferation Treaty in order to
accept that American offer.

MODERATOR

Despite optimism in the early days of 1986, the International
Year of Peace, it looks as though 1987 may be the international
year of war. Australia, its attention riveted upon the America's
Cup superpower duels off Fremantle, hardly notices the Soviet
invasion of Iran, the American intervention in Libya or the trial
of the hostages in Malaria. Nonetheless, we are closer to war
than at any time since the Cuban missile crisis. Kim Beazley,
you are in charge of civil defence; how will we know if a war is
started? Will there be sirens, or alarm bells?

BEAZLEY

I think before that occurred you would have seen the rapidly
deteriorating situation very well reported, and you would have
seen numerous parliamentary statements from the Minister for
Defence and the Minister for Foreign Affairs.

MODERATOR

So I just keep watching television. I am watching the America's
Cup at the moment on commercial television; they will never
interrupt that, will they? (laughter) Suppose Colonel Jekel shoots
a bomb in our direction. Where is my nearest nuclear fallout
shelter?

BEAZLEY

The bombs that would be flying in general war would be
between the United States and the Soviet Union. They would
not be aimed at the Australian population.

MODERATOR

That's reassuring. But suppose the mad colonel—"Flaky"

Jekel—targets a bomb here. Where is my nearest fallout shelter?

BEAZLEY

I think if you are in an advantageous situation like Australia, given that we have a relatively limited number of nuclear targets, given that we have very substantial wide open spaces, you would not be silly enough to contemplate a program of nuclear shelters, which are simply coffins. You would be looking at evacuation of your major cities.

MODERATOR

Isn't there even a Bicentennial project nuclear fallout shelter? (laughter)

BEAZLEY

Not unless we have all gone completely Bicentenially mad. There would be a policy of evacuation in Australia. That would clearly be the most sensible thing to do.

MODERATOR

Civil defence in Australia does not really exist, does it?

MURRAY

I could get a headline in the *Bugle* by saying we had our trousers down, but that is just not true. We would have some sort of plan and we are thinking about it now.

MODERATOR

He has offered you a headline, Mr Bowers; "Trousers down on civil defence". I've been reading the *Sydney Morning Bugle* these last few weeks. I know where to go to find a prostitute in Sydney. I do not know where to find a nuclear fallout shelter. (laughter)

BOWERS

There isn't one. Unless we go to Town Hall Station and go down two or three platforms.

MODERATOR

John Pilger, is there some sort of strange machismo at work here? The peace movement alerts us to the horrors of the bomb, and yet we have no plans to protect the population against it.

PILGER

Probably this is the only area of agreement between the

government and the peace movement. The idea of civil defence is perhaps absurd. All the facilities that have been outlined, really do not exist. It is interesting that Kim Beazley said people would be evacuated from the cities. That's a disastrous plan. In Britain, they are now saying you stay where you are when the bomb drops.

MODERATOR

Would you agree, Professor Titterton, that we do not need any precautions against the bomb, even when a lot of countries acquire it?

TITTERTON

I absolutely agree we need no precautions, and the reasons are quite simple. No precautions will protect you at ground zero. Every home in Australia is a fallout shelter. It will protect you from radioactive fallout, keep it at a distance, so it doesn't get on your food.

MODERATOR

But you have to go out to buy that food.

TITTERTON

You have to go out at some stage; but if you are given a warning, you will be storing your carrots in the cellar.

MODERATOR

That is an enormous relief. I have a cellar full of carrots. (laughter)

TITTERTON

And drinking water.

MODERATOR

I hate carrots. (laughter)

TITTERTON

Most people eat carrots.

MODERATOR

At least I could see in the dark.

TITTERTON

That would be useful. There will be no lights.

MODERATOR

If I am at ground zero, how long will I . . .

TITTERTON

You do not need to worry if you are at ground zero. You do not last very long. You disappear into the atmosphere and drift around the world.

MODERATOR

In that case, I hope I'm not at ground zero.

TITTERTON

Oh, it might be the best place to be. If you want to be an absolute pessimist it might be better not to be there after one millionth of a *second*.

MODERATOR

It might not be much fun to survive?

TITTERTON

There is nothing in Australia that needs to be attacked. If there was a global nuclear war, Australia would be sitting like a ripe plum, waiting to be plucked.

MODERATOR

If there is a nuclear war in Europe, won't there be a nuclear winter effect?

TITTERTON

That is very arguable indeed. We are in a different hemisphere, and the whole of the nuclear winter argument is on a knife edge: it depends on how many nuclear weapons are used.

MODERATOR

And if a lot are used, Andrew Mack?

MACK

The explosion of nuclear weapons injects dust and soot into the atmosphere and up into the stratosphere, where it stays for a very long time. Sunlight that would normally shine on the earth is blocked, and the earth becomes chilled. The superpowers are adding nuclear weapons at such a rate that the probability of a nuclear winter effect in the southern hemisphere is going up all the time.

MODERATOR

We will all go together when we go. Well, not quite all. Mr MacKellar, have you seen the plans for the new Parliament

House, with its Crisis Command Centre, which was approved by your government, beneath the ground under the new Parliament House?

MACKELLAR

I haven't scurried around looking for it.

MODERATOR

Well, Minister, let me take you and show you. Here is your personal electronic key. We take this lift, down into the bowels of the new Parliament House, down into the red Canberra soil. Behold: the "John Grey Gorton Memorial Bunker". This is where you will command the nation in time of war. Over there you see the computer which prints out the intelligence analysis from Pine Gap, here's our map of the world with red lights flashing on trouble spots. We've installed a hot line telephone which goes straight to the White House. It rings in President Stallone's gymnasium, which is where he spends most of his time. (laughter) We have food and drink for two hundred people—which reminds me, Minister, we need your help with the guest list. Obviously we take yourself, all members of cabinet, General Murray, all heads of department. I suppose we should invite the leader of the opposition, but we have not made any provision for the parliamentary press gallery.

BOWERS

We burn in hell.

MODERATOR

Should we take an Australian Democrat, Minister, or would that rather lower the tone?

MACKELLAR

I think it is a nonsense to suggest that you could realistically contemplate taking a small group of people into an underground bunker for a year.

MODERATOR

But in fact, the Crisis Command Centre really is being built under the earth; in Canberra; now.

MACKELLAR

But it is not suggested that it is going to be the home of a small number of people who are going to be progenitors of a new Australian nation emerging from their cocoon after a certain period of time.

MODERATOR
It might become a nuclear Noah's Ark. (laughter)

MACKELLAR
As I understand the concept, it is a secure place.

MODERATOR
Secure from what?

MACKELLAR
I imagine from armed attack.

MODERATOR
That is why it was built two floors down in the earth?

MACKELLAR
Similar to the cabinet room in London which operated during the war.

BEAZLEY
The idea is that the Crisis Command Centre might well be where the government conducts its business in time of war. As for the opposition — and all the other people you mention, who are not essential to the proceedings — I would be on the phone to them saying, "My suggestion to you is you head into the countryside while this crisis occurs. There you will be perfectly safe." I am confronting the problem because I am governing the country, and so I will be down here along with . . .

BOWERS
How are you going to feed two million people evacuated from Sydney? Where are they going to be evacuated to?

PILGER
I was wondering how you get eight million people out to the countryside through the arteries of Sydney and Melbourne. How is this going to be achieved? We presume transport is going to be seconded, and the major arteries of the country are going to be clogged. Where are people going to go?

BEAZLEY
I would have to make an assessment of what is targetable. Sydney is not targetable. The naval base is in Jervis Bay and not

in Sydney. The question of evacuation of Sydney is not going to apply.

MODERATOR

Under pressure of the escalating crisis, the nations of the world, with the exception of Malaria, at last sign a comprehensive nuclear test-ban treaty. Some see this as a ray of hope in the gathering darkness, others recall Chamberlain after Munich waving his little scrap of paper. Historians tell us that World War I was triggered by the death of a Duke in Sarajevo, but future historians, if future historians there be, may record that World War III was triggered by the execution for spying of fifty innocent American tourists at the hands of the Malarian Court of Revolutionary Justice. We see America, crazed with grief and righteous anger, threatening to invade Malaria—the President is coming under a lot of pressure from his congress and his people; we see Russia, guaranteeing Malaria's security; and we see Bill Hayden, brought back from his pub like Coriolanus from his farm, to lead a government of national unity in this crisis. Richard Butler, bring him up to date on the seriousness of the situation.

BUTLER

A full-scale nuclear war would destory this earth. As Professor Titterton said in another context, there would be no light. There is no question of so-called escalation control. There is no question that a nuclear war could be limited. Reagan and Gorbachev were right when they said in 1985 that a nuclear war could not be won and must never be fought. So my advice to you is to accept that the full-scale horror of nuclear war is the destruction of this earth and we have to work as quickly as we can to ensure that this threatening situation does not proceed any further.

MODERATOR

Colonel Jekel is undeterred. Our intelligence assessments say he's planning a secret nuclear test. For America, this is the last straw. The President says, "It's time to stand tall against terrorism. We are going to enforce the test-ban treaty ourselves. If we discover that Malaria has tested its nuclear weapon, that will be the signal for us to invade." The Russians say that if America invades Malaria, they will respond "with all appropriate force". In this situation of bluff and counter bluff, what are you doing as Prime Minister of Australia?

HAYDEN

If the situation has reached this stage, it is almost on the edge of international madness because rapid escalation of global nuclear war is the likely consequence. If we got to the point where nuclear weapons were going to be used, there would be massive retaliation from both sides which would destroy the globe. Very few forms of life would survive and very few human beings. Therefore I would have nothing else available to me except appeals — trying to appeal to rational response and restraint — recognising how dangerous the situation is because we are on the edge of madness.

MODERATOR

Dr Denham is beside his seismic array, SPASM, in Alice Springs monitoring Malaria to see whether it secretly lets off a nuclear weapon. If it does, Australia, because of its geography and because of SPASM, will be the first nation to know. Indeed, if the test is of a nuclear weapon under ten kilotons, Australia will be the only country to know that the secret test has taken place. It's ten o'clock in the evening at Alice Springs, SPASM is monitoring the heartbeats of the earth in Malaria. Suddenly, the needle jumps. SPASM says it is a small nuclear explosion in Malaria — three or four kilotons. That news reaches you, Bill Hayden, in the Crisis Command Centre. You and Dr Denham are the only people who know that a secret test has taken place. Should you tell the President?

HAYDEN

No, because the threatened response is out of proportion to the nature of the problem, and there are opportunities for many initiatives to be taken which may head it off.

MODERATOR

You will not tell the President because it will be a signal for him to attack Malaria. You would rather wait weeks — or months — until tempers have cooled and diplomacy has been given a chance to work.

HAYDEN

I don't think it is worth destroying mankind, the civilisation which has been built up over the millennia, or life as we know it. In the meantime I would cling to the slim optimism that one may be able to head this development off by cooling the superpowers.

MODERATOR

The treaty that you signed, that Australia has promoted for years, requires any country to notify the United Nations immediately it learns that another country has set off a nuclear explosion.

HAYDEN

There is a higher morality and that is the preservation of mankind. That is at risk, and it therefore subvenes all of these other undertakings. I would have no compunction at all about not telling.

MODERATOR

The telephone rings. It is the President of the United States. He says, "Mr Hayden, we have received some intelligence that there might have been a nuclear test in Malaria. We cannot verify it. You people are the only ones who can." What do you say?

HAYDEN

If I had to, I would tell a lie.

MODERATOR

You would lie to the President of the United States?

HAYDEN

I would lie to save mankind.

MODERATOR

Is he right, Mr MacKellar, to lie to the President of the United States?

MACKELLAR

It depends on what he actually says, whether he is actually lying. (laughter)

HAYDEN

Let me tell you, I would not bugger around. I would lie.

MACKELLAR

Yes, I think in these circumstances he is right to conceal the fact that this information has come to hand.

MODERATOR

You would lie?

MACKELLAR

Yes. Under those circumstances, yes.

MODERATOR

The President tells you he has the 13th fleet on red alert. You have saved the situation for the next few minutes. You are not sure you can save it much longer. Would you think that in this situation—whatever you tell the President—you should tell the Australian people that the crisis has almost reached breaking point?

HAYDEN

I would do that as quickly as possible and put in place whatever measures seem appropriate—medical measures at the few specific points of evacuation, and so on.

MODERATOR

You would make a broadcast telling the Australian people that the Bicentennial may have to be cancelled. (laughter) Ladies and gentlemen, the Prime Minister made that broadcast, telling us that we had perhaps an hour to go before the world went to nuclear war. Some of us began to pray; others made love or optimistically made wills; some of us started to smoke again; others just stayed glued to the America's Cup replays on commercial television. But SPASM, untried and untested, had got it wrong. It *was* just a small earthquake in Malaria. Not many dead, but they included Colonel Jekel and his military advisers. Those who live by the sword often perish by it; today, alas, they may take the rest of the world with them.

TILL DIVORCE US DO PART

Almost half of Australian marriages are destined to end in divorce. This examination of loving, leaving and litigating looks at the controversial Family Court, established in 1975 in an effort to take the acrimony out of matrimonial disputes. Does the system provide a fair way of deciding questions of custody, property and maintenance? How does the court deal with cases of child abuse and abduction, and how do its lawyers balance their duty of secrecy with their duty to society?

Meet the nuclear family next door: Adam Smith, his wife Eve, their children Matthew and Mary, and their dog Judas. Adam is thirty-eight, and in banking; Eve is thirty-three and in pieces. As their divorce proceedings become increasingly acrimonious, who's to blame—the law, the lawyers or the litigants? Follow the battle over the custody of their children—not to mention their dog—as lawyers seek to outwit each other with the help of police and private eyes and paternity tests, and struggle to keep their clients' all-too-embarrassing confidences.

TILL DIVORCE US DO PART
Participants

BETTINA ARNDT
  Clinical Psychologist

NEIL BROWN Q.C.
  Shadow Attorney-General

VICKI BROWN
  Sergeant, Victoria Police

DIANA BRYANT
  Solicitor and President, Family Law Practitioners, Western
  Australia

JILL BURRETT
  Family Court Counsellor

JOHN FOGARTY
  Judge, Family Court of Australia

JOE GOLDSTEIN
  Solicitor

IAN KENNEDY
  President, Family Lawyers' Association, Victoria

DAVID LENTIN
  Private Investigator

JOHN MARSDEN
  Solicitor and President, New South Wales Council for Civil
  Liberties

KENNETH PAWLEY
  Former Judge of Family Court of Australia

PETER ROSE
  Barrister, Family Court of Australia

DR MALCOLM SIMONS
  Medical Scientist

JULIE STEWART
  Adviser, Women's Legal Resources Centre, Sydney

PATRICK TENNISON
  Journalist and Author

PHILIP TWIGG Q.C.
  Member, Law Council of Australia

Recorded at the Seymour Centre,
Sydney,
April 1986.

TILL DIVORCE US DO PART

MODERATOR

In the olden days, ladies and gentleman, when divorce was difficult without evidence of stains on the sheets or the blonde in Surfers Paradise or illicit passion on the back seat of the FJ Holden—in those *bad* old days, divorce barristers had a favourite question. They'd fix the nervous witness with a glare that would stun a rabbit and they'd ask, "Have you ever done anything of which you are now thoroughly ashamed?" Have *you*, Tina Arndt?

BETTINA ARNDT

Of course.

MODERATOR

If she'd said "no", Judge Pawley, she'd obviously have been lying.

KENNETH PAWLEY

Probably.

MODERATOR

And if she'd said "yes", she's been set up to make a confession—to some matrimonial crime, some misconduct that would, in the bad old days, have disentitled her to custody of the children?

PAWLEY

That's what her husband's counsel would hope.

MODERATOR

But of course it doesn't matter these days. We don't have matrimonial crimes any longer. It doesn't matter how appalling is the conduct she confesses to—a secret lust for Phillip Adams; a tendency to pick her nose in public when having dinner with her husband's boss; an insatiable appetite for group sex with visiting cricket teams. That doesn't matter now?

PAWLEY

No, not for the divorce itself.

MODERATOR
Not even New Zealand cricket teams? (laughter)

PAWLEY
No.

MODERATOR
It's all part of the rich tapestry of married life. As far as the
Family Court is concerned, Judge Fogarty, you're part
psychologist, part social worker, part fortune-teller I guess,
trying to work out what's the best for the children?

JOHN FOGARTY
Part fortune-telling, in the sense that you're predicting future
behaviour. You make a decision on the evidence, but it involves
some predictions for the future.

MODERATOR
You want to be a compassionate court?

FOGARTY
I think what parties want is justice in accordance with the law
in the country at the time. You have to decide their case. The
parties come along to you, unable to agree. They don't want
your compassion, they want a genuine decision on the law as it
is in Australia at the present time.

MODERATOR
So the Family Court tries to give them justice according to the
law as it exists. Does it always do that in your experience,
Patrick Tennison?

PATRICK TENNISON
I don't believe so; no. It takes a special art to be a fortune-teller.

MODERATOR
It's difficult to foresee what's going to happen to kids, ten years
down the track?

TENNISON
Right. And difficult also, particularly when there's so much
animosity very often between the parties, to get at what is the
truth right there in the middle.

MODERATOR
So the problem isn't the court itself, it's the people in it?

TENNISON
Both.

MODERATOR
Both, Julie Stewart? Do you agree?

JULIE STEWART
I think the court works very well for a large number of people who have to go through it, but there are issues that I don't think this court manages well at all and I don't think justice is done. It lacks skills in dealing with those highly emotional issues.

MODERATOR
You mean lawyers lack skills at dealing with highly emotional issues?

STEWART
Certainly.

MODERATOR
A great court; pity about the lawyers? (Laughter)

STEWART
Yes.

MODERATOR
Lawyers who flock like vultures to feed off the carcasses of dead marriages. Well, let's see what lawyers really do. I want you to meet, ladies and gentlemen, the nuclear family next door. Adam Smith, his wife Eve, their children Matthew and Mary, and their dog Judas. Adam is thirty-eight and in banking; Eve is thirty-three and in pieces. After eight years of marriage she's silently suffocating. She has no love for Adam, no faith in herself, no hope for her future as Mrs Smith. She's deeply upset; so deeply that one day she walks into your office, Joe Goldstein. "I want a divorce. We don't communicate. The only meaningful conversations we have is when I remind him to put out the garbage. He's utterly boring and predictable. He's an accountant. You know what they're like."

JOE GOLDSTEIN
Divorce him straight away. Leave, Madam, you cannot stay. Look, you're a big girl now. You're here; if you've gone this far, you've obviously talked to your mother, you've talked to

the girls in the hairdressers, you've talked to the lady next door who recently had a divorce. You're free, white and over twenty-one. Go away and get separated.

MODERATOR

"For how long?"

GOLDSTEIN

Twelve months.

MODERATOR

"Twelve months! Why can't I just go to the court and say, 'I no longer want to be Mrs Smith, I no longer love my husband, please cancel my marriage certificate'?"

GOLDSTEIN

You have to be separated for twelve months because the Family Law Act says you have to be . . .

MODERATOR

"The law says that I've got to be separated from my husband for twelve months before I get a divorce! I'll still be married to him?"

GOLDSTEIN

During that time, yes.

MODERATOR

"Will I have to have sex with him? I don't like having sex with him."

GOLDSTEIN

That's a matter for you, Madam. That's a matter of preference.

MODERATOR

"There's no obligation on a wife to have sex with her husband?"

GOLDSTEIN

On the contrary.

MODERATOR

"I wish I'd known that before. What about the David Jones charge account? There's a new Carla Zampatti line of dresses for deserting wives; can I buy a few of those this afternoon, and will he have to pay for them?"

GOLDSTEIN

Buy a few but don't go mad or someone will kick you to death in cross-examination, and some judge will hate you because his wife will have a David Jones charge plate and he'll hate you for doing that.

MODERATOR

"I'll clear out to my mum's. Can I take the car and the video with me?"

GOLDSTEIN

Oh yes.

MODERATOR

"I can take the lot?"

GOLDSTEIN

No, no, not the lot. You can take the car and the video; not the lot.

MODERATOR

"I see — leave the barbecue and the boat?"

GOLDSTEIN

Please.

MODERATOR

"I distinctly remember, when we were married, he promised, 'With all my worldly wealth I thee endow.' Isn't that binding?"

GOLDSTEIN

That was then. No, it's not binding.

MODERATOR

"The marriage service is a bit of a confidence trick?"

GOLDSTEIN

Well, it has so turned out for you — and for many women.

MODERATOR

Why do women bother still to get married, Jill Burrett? Almost half the marriages in Australia are going to end in divorce. There are fifty thousand kids each year that are victims of broken homes. Why do people still bother?

JILL BURRETT

Because society reinforces it. Magazines are full of glorious wedding dresses, and we all need a mate and a companion.

MODERATOR
But isn't marriage just about the most dangerous and divisive institution in Australian society at present?

BURRETT
I think it can be for some people.

MODERATOR
Tina Arndt, you're getting married next month. You're taking the extraordinary step of marrying a lawyer. (laughter) Why bother?

ARNDT
I think it's worth committing yourself to someone else. I think there are very good reasons to make a public commitment and to acknowledge that publicly — which is what the legal commitment is really all about.

MODERATOR
You're a soppy old romantic at heart. I suppose you'll wear white?

ARNDT
Off-white.

MODERATOR
White, with just a dash of crimson. Very fetching. (laughter) Tell us; Eve has, on legal advice, decided to live separately from Adam. She is going to clear out and go to her mum's. If Adam is a typical Australian man, what's his reaction going to be?

ARNDT
I think he's going to be devastated. Because he would never have assumed this was going to happen to him. I mean he won't have listened to Eve when she said, "Things are going wrong for me." And he would have assumed that life was going to go on . . .

MODERATOR
His little dream of eternal domestic bliss is shattered. He's going to rant and rage and scream and cry?

ARNDT
And behave abominably.

MODERATOR

Eve has one final question. "My mother has a small flat; too small to take the kids. I've lived with them now for seven years, nurtured them since I first felt them kick. I need time and space to grow a little as a person, but in a year, when the divorce is through, of course I'll want custody of them. They're young; I love them; I'll get custody, won't I?"

GOLDSTEIN

Yes. In view of the age of these two children, yes, she'd get custody.

MODERATOR

Do you agree with that advice, Ian Kennedy?

IAN KENNEDY

No, I don't entirely. I think that she runs a significant risk that by leaving the children in the care of her husband for a lengthy period of time, it may ultimately be decided that the best interests of the children are not being served by bringing about yet another change in their custodial situation. In contested custody cases that actually go for determination by a judge, the husband has almost an equal chance of success.

MODERATOR

It may depend on what judge we get?

KENNEDY

Yes.

MODERATOR

But what does the law say? What is the law on this? Doesn't the law say that mothers who love their young children ought, all things being equal, to get custody?

KENNEDY

No, on the contrary, the law says that in determining who gets custody, the court has to take as the most prominent aspect to be considered, what is in the best interests of those children. And while there may be two equally talented and loving parents, you run into a dilemma and a Solomon-type situation.

MODERATOR

"But look, I've brought these kids up—Matthew for seven years, Mary for four. They are so close to me. Adam's never taken a blind bit of notice of them. He's ambitious for them, sure; wants them to grow up to be stockbrokers; tells them stories occasionally—'Bib and Bub Take Over BHP', 'Biggles and the Corporate Raider'. (laughter) But by and large he's too busy making money. Surely the court will give me custody?"

KENNEDY
It certainly improves your situation, Eve, if that is the case, but it would be very interesting to hear Adam's side of the story as well.

MODERATOR
Adam's side of the story is going to be heard by Diana Bryant. "I've got a house that's worth a hundred thousand dollars and I've got a boat and a car that're worth fifty thousand. How much can she take me for?"

DIANA BRYANT
Well, the law's very complex, in relation to property settlement. The law will have to look mainly at contributions that each party's made . . .

MODERATOR
"Oh that's great. I've contributed everything."

BRYANT
But you've only contributed money?

MODERATOR
"Yes, everything." (laughter)

BRYANT
The Family Law Act also takes into account non-financial contributions, and in particular contributions that a wife makes as a parent and a home-maker.

MODERATOR
Ah. How can you value that?

BRYANT
Well, it's not easy to value but the courts have been putting a very high value on it.

MODERATOR
Have you, Judge Fogarty?

FOGARTY
Certainly. Although the High Court has tended to disagree with

me from time to time. (laughter) The Family Court has tried to
develop a concept that marriage is a partnership in which each
side puts in their own particular efforts; maybe financial on one
side, home-making on the other. In a long marriage, and
putting aside extraneous factors, at the end, property which
they've acquired during that marriage ought to be divided
equally.

MODERATOR
But what is the court likely to do in this case, where the assets
are the family home of a hundred thousand dollars and material
goods of fifty thousand?

FOGARTY
As a starting point I suppose the court would try to maintain
the home for the children in their younger years.

MODERATOR
So the court might end up awarding the family home to Eve if
it awards custody to her?

FOGARTY
Or it might allow her to remain living in the house for a period
of time—until the children are older—and then divide it equally
between them when the two parents' economic positions are
more equivalent.

MODERATOR
"There's something, Diana Bryant, that I'm sure she can't get
her hands on. I've been playing the stock market at work. Eve
hates all forms of gambling, so I haven't even told her, but I've
made about thirty thousand dollars on my share dealings. She
can't get hold of that, can she?"

BRYANT
She certainly can.

MODERATOR
"Really?"

BRYANT
Really.

MODERATOR
"But I haven't even told her that I've got this money."

BRYANT
If there are proceedings instituted, you've got an obligation to disclose all your assets.

MODERATOR
"Even though she hasn't contributed a thing to those assets? Even though she loathes the idea of gambling on the stock market, she's still entitled to half of it?"

BRYANT
Yes, I think that's highly likely.

MODERATOR
"I gather she's got a solicitor called Joe Goldstein. Do you know anything about him? Is he a fighter or a settler?"

BRYANT
He's certainly a fighter.

MODERATOR
"Well, I want to fight too. I want to fight for custody of my children. I suppose it would be very helpful to keep an eye on Eve now she's left me—to see if she has a different man every night, or meets drug dealers?"

BRYANT
Yes, that may have a bearing on her capacity to care for the children.

MODERATOR
David Lentin, can I hire you to do that sort of thing?

DAVID LENTIN
Yes, you can, as long as you pay me twenty dollars an hour.

MODERATOR
"Round-the-clock wife watch; twenty dollars an hour." You're hired. Eve is living with her mother in a block of flats.

LENTIN
Well, surveillance would be commenced on her on a daily basis. We'd have a chat to the neighbours.

MODERATOR
Go through the garbage?

LENTIN

No, we wouldn't go through the garbage.

MODERATOR

You only do that when you're looking for Liberal Party policy documents? (laughter) You're sitting outside in the car night after night. Her mother is a member of the Neighbourhood Watch, and calls up Vicki Brown. "There's a suspicious man been outside in a car for the last week. I think he's casing my flat for a robbery."

VICKI BROWN

What are you doing outside this house?

LENTIN

I . . . I'm watching a workers' compensation case down the street. (laughter) I have my licence with me.

VICKI BROWN

Oh? And your occupation?

LENTIN

I'm a private detective.

MODERATOR

So you'll ring up Eve's mum and say, "Oh it's only a private detective, don't worry." (laughter)

VICKI BROWN

No, I'd just say that there was no substance to her belief.

MODERATOR

Mr Lentin, you keep an eye on Eve, and you discover that she's sleeping with Bruce, who is Adam's best friend. Bruce tells his wife that he's consoling Eve over the break-up of her marriage, but the consolation is taking place in a Kings Cross motel that rents rooms by the hour. So you've got to break to Adam the fact that his best friend is having an affair with his wife.

LENTIN

It's not going to be easy. But what I might do is I might pass the buck to Diana and let her tell him.

MODERATOR

Are you going to accept that buck?

BRYANT

Oh yes, I'd tell him. (laughter) I'd break it to him as compassionately as I could.

MODERATOR

With photographs? (laughter)

BRYANT

Not immediately, but I'd tell him I had the photographs.

MODERATOR

"Not Bruce! Not my mate Bruce . . .!"

BRYANT

Yes, I'd tell him who it was.

MODERATOR

After a couple of months, Mr Lentin's high-powered binoculars pick out the fact that Eve is pregnant. Sure enough, Joe Goldstein, she's back in your office.

GOLDSTEIN

"Hello, stupid," would be the welcome, I think.

MODERATOR

That's not very compassionate. Diana Bryant broke it to Adam far more compassionately.

GOLDSTEIN

Adam didn't get pregnant. (laughter)

MODERATOR

"I was really in a mess. I didn't take precautions, and it could be Adam's, or it could be Bruce's. I had some real teeth-grinding sex with Adam the night before I left him, and I started with Bruce the next week. I really don't know who's the father."

GOLDSTEIN

Could be either? Off to the doctor, I suppose?

MODERATOR

"No, I'm not going to do that. Ian Kennedy, I want maintenance. Can I get it from Adam?"

KENNEDY

You may do. Your conduct is not necessarily going to be held against you if you have a situation where you are by yourself, unable to support yourself and a new child . . .

MODERATOR
"And the law will assume that the child is Adam's?"

KENNEDY
Adam has the ability to help you out financially and he's likely to be required to do so.

MODERATOR
The child is born, the divorce petition is filed, Adam's back with you, Diana Bryant. "That child isn't mine; I'm not going to pay for it. I don't have to, do I?"

BRYANT
Not if the child's not yours.

MODERATOR
"I'm sure it's not. I mean it looks like Bruce. It's incredibly ugly." (laughter)

BRYANT
Well, that's not sufficient. There is a legal presumption of legitimacy—that it's yours because you were married at the time.

MODERATOR
"If the law presumes that, the law is an ass. Can't I prove that I'm not the father?"

BRYANT
Well you can certainly try and do that, and the best way of doing that's to get some blood tests done.

MODERATOR
Dr Simons, you do blood tests. I suppose they would be more accurate if Bruce submitted to a blood test as well?

MALCOLM SIMONS
That's true. Since only one man can be the father.

MODERATOR
Would the court order Bruce to submit to a blood test?

FOGARTY
Yes.

MODERATOR

You make the order that Bruce submits to the blood test. Bruce rushes into your office, John Marsden. "The courts are ordering me to submit to a blood test. Do I have to obey?"

JOHN MARSDEN

I'd tell him he shouldn't obey it, and I'd tell him . . .

MODERATOR

Shouldn't?

MARSDEN

Yes, I'd say that you don't have to take a blood test. It's an invasion of your privacy.

MODERATOR

"But isn't there a danger that if I don't take it they might draw some inference of guilt—If I don't take it and Adam does?"

MARSDEN

That danger exists, but let's wait and see how the blood test on Adam comes out first. Let's get that information first before we take the risk.

MODERATOR

The blood test on Adam shows that he's unlikely to be the father. He's about as unlikely to be the father as on the present opinion polls John Howard is likely to be Prime Minister. (laughter)

PAWLEY

That's about fourteen per cent; yes. On those figures, I'm sufficiently satisfied that Adam is not the father, and to urge Eve to look to Bruce to support her child.

MODERATOR

Suppose the Family Court had jurisdiction to make third parties pay for maintenance?

FOGARTY

If Bruce continued to refuse to take the blood test which might exculpate him, I'd be inclined, given the other evidence that David Lentin will provide me with, to conclude that the father was clearly Bruce and he ought to support the child rather than the taxpayers.

MODERATOR

"This is where your advice gets me, John Marsden. (laughter)
I've now got an order to pay fifteen dollars a week for the next
eighteen years for this child."

MARSDEN

I think the judge is wrong. It's fairly typical of judges these
days that they make mistakes. Let's take him on. Let's take him
up to the Appeal Court. Let's get some reasonable judges who
know what they're about.

MODERATOR

Let's get a reasonable counsel's opinion. Philip Twigg, is the
judge wrong?

PHILIP TWIGG

I'm sorry to disagree with someone who might brief me in the
future, but I'm afraid both the judges are right. They are
looking at the facts and making a judgement, not beyond
reasonable doubt, but on the balance of probabilities. On the
evidence before them, the decisions are correct.

MARSDEN

Then I would have to advise my client that maybe we should
take the blood test and keep our fingers crossed.

ARNDT

I've been sitting here getting hopping mad at all this talk of how
men can avoid responsibility for children; how they can minimise
the amount they have to pay. I mean, it's revolting, this attitude.
You should be concerned about the welfare of the children.

MODERATOR

If the client has that attitude, then his lawyer has to represent it.

ARNDT

But it's the attitude that's also coming through from all the
lawyers—"How can we avoid responsibility?"

MODERATOR

Do you blame them for following their clients' instructions? Ought
they to be their clients' judges, rather than their clients' lawyers?

ARNDT

The male who is angry about the fact that his wife has walked

out on him has to be helped not to think in terms of
punishment; not to think of hitting out at someone. He has to
be helped to think about what would he have wanted for his
children when he was still married to that woman. Why should
that change just because the situation's changed?

MODERATOR
Do you agree, Patrick Tennison, that the lawyers are stoking up
the fight?

TENNISON
Well, you asked earlier was the problem the people or the
system, and I said both. We're seeing it with the system. This
is a system which was supposed to take deceit and untruthfulness
and chicanery out of divorce. It hasn't. We've had the same
tactics as in the old court. In fact these tactics are as devious, or
even more devious, than they were under the old divorce law.

MODERATOR
How do you answer this criticism, Joe Goldstein? That you're
still up to your old tricks; that the 1975 Family Law Act wasn't
a watershed?

GOLDSTEIN
I think that really there's been no difference in human nature
between things as they were before 1975 and now. There seems
to be some sort of pious hope—indeed I think the Family Court
was set up with the pious hope—that all of a sudden the world
was going to turn into a beautiful place because we've got a
new piece of legislation. People won't lie, people won't have
defended divorce cases, we don't need to have wigs and gowns,
we don't need to have courts. We'll just have coloured chairs
and counsellors and tea and biscuits and, whoopee, everybody's
going to be lovely and tell the truth. People haven't changed at
all. This legislative stroke of the pen has made no difference to
people as such.

MODERATOR
At present, blood tests are not definitive. But they soon will be.
What does genetic technology have in store?

SIMONS
The answer to that is the new DNA genetic technology, which
is going to enable each of us to be essentially "fingerprinted" to

the point where the only individuals we'll fail to distinguish are identical twins.

MODERATOR

So by unravelling the twists and turns of the DNA in our body, you're going to be able to take genetic fingerprints to prove beyond any doubt that a particular child is fathered by a particular man?

SIMONS

To a 99.99999 per cent certainty.

MODERATOR

When is this genetic fingerprinting going to be available?

SIMONS

It's already being introduced in England and the United States, and Australia is going to get it in the next few months.

MODERATOR

And in a year or so, when you have developed this technique a little further, it's going to be available quite cheaply, I suppose?

SIMONS

Yes. We envisage that we will soon have test results available in twenty-four or forty-eight hours, costing a few tens of dollars.

MODERATOR

So, in a year's time perhaps, for fifty dollars, we can have our genetic fingerprints taken to tell whether our children are really ours?

SIMONS

Yes, I think that's likely to be the case by 1987.

MODERATOR

It could be available in local chemists? In a do-it-yourself kit?

SIMONS

Yes, that's not difficult to imagine. Certainly the reagents that are required for this DNA genetic testing are now being put in cardboard boxes and sold to pathologists for other reasons, so it's envisagable that individuals could acquire access to those.

MODERATOR

So that next year, all those jealous husbands in Australia are going to be able to take their children down to the local medical centre, pay fifty dollars and find out whether they are really their own. Does that worry you, Neil Brown? You're the Attorney-General. Do you think it's in the public interest that these tests should be available at chemists, and at medical centres?

NEIL BROWN

I'd need a lot of persuading about that. Frankly what I would do at the very beginning would be to refer that issue to the Law Reform Commission. After all, that's why the Law Reform Commission was set up.

MODERATOR

But that will take years, now that Michael Kirby's gone. (laughter)

BROWN

Now that I'm Attorney- General, I assure you they'll investigate these matters promptly and we'll get a report within six months.

MODERATOR

Jill Burrett, you are asked to advise the Law Reform Commission on the wisdom of allowing genetic fingerprinting kits in chemists.

BURRETT

I would be very very wary as to their widespread availability without a proper, very carefully monitored referral system for use in specific cases.

MODERATOR

You really worry that jealous husbands around Australia will take their children into the local chemist and for fifty dollars find out whether they're really theirs?

BURRETT

Yes, I would, because I would think that we should have a responsibility to ensure that before somebody goes and does that, the real underlying issues are looked at with a counsellor.

MODERATOR

John Marsden, you are asked to give evidence on behalf of Civil Liberties. How does the widespread availability of genetic fingerprinting appear to you?

MARSDEN

We would oppose the idea of it being available on a widespread basis. The taking of kids into chemist shops by jealous husbands is an horrific idea and Civil Liberties would totally oppose that.

MODERATOR

The father doesn't have the right to know whether the child is really his?

MARSDEN

I would rather it was the right of the child. I don't think the father should be running around checking out his wife because she happened to go out with someone else or something like that.

PAWLEY

But surely the man is entitled to know whether a particular child is his or not?

MODERATOR

There was a survey done in England a couple of months ago on this very question and it found that twenty-five per cent — one in four — of children born in ostensibly happy marriages were in fact not fathered by the husband. There's going to be an awful lot of shocked husbands when this kit gets into the chemist shop.

PAWLEY

Only the jealous ones, and perhaps they deserve a shock.

MODERATOR

You've had those opinions, Mr Attorney-General. How does it come down for you?

BROWN

The first thing I would decide to do would be to allow this genetic engineering test to be done under judicial supervision in cases where it was made out.

MODERATOR

So genetic testing is fine in court proceedings.

BROWN

With judicial approval.

MODERATOR

Forcing people to give their genetic fingerprints?

BROWN

We're forced to do a lot of things we don't like doing. If there's a case made out to satisfy a judge then I think the judge should be given power to make such an order.

MODERATOR

And what about public availability in chemist shops?

BROWN

I would not on present evidence allow that.

MODERATOR

You might in the future?

BROWN

Things change; social standards and attitudes change. These things should be taken step by step.

MODERATOR

Let's go back to Adam and Eve. The divorce petition has been filed, and they're due to go for counselling. What are you looking for when you're counselling couples enmeshed in a raging custody battle?

BURRETT

I would first of all want to acquaint myself by ringing up a solicitor on both sides.

MODERATOR

Ring one up now.

BURRETT

I'm ringing you up Joe, on behalf of Eve who's waiting outside to see me, and I'm going to ring Adam's solicitor too in a minute to ask the same questions. Where, in your view, have the custody proceedings got to?

GOLDSTEIN

Jill, these kids have been with their father for about the last twelve months. The mother left very distraught. It's one of those cases where the mother had to leave the house, and so she can't be penalised for leaving the children. True, she's let it go a little longer than one might otherwise expect, but as you will realise when you see her, she's had a bit of an accident in the meantime and she just hasn't been in the position either emotionally or financially to take the children back. They're very little. She's the one that relates better to them; I think that's what you'll find . . .

MODERATOR

He's arguing a case for you?

BURRETT

That's fine. I am about to ring Diana Bryant, too. Diana, what's the state of play with the custody proceedings?

BRYANT

Well, my client's sincere in his wish to have custody of the children. He was devastated when his wife left, quite unexpectedly. She left him with the children. He had to totally rearrange his life to look after them. He's arranged a housekeeper and now leaves for work later and comes home earlier. He's really readjusted his life and he's been doing a very good job. In the meantime his wife has had an affair and is now pregnant by his best friend. He's concerned very much about her capacity to care for the children and he thinks she's quite irresponsible.

MODERATOR

In fact, that morning Eve went to her solicitor. She says, "I've got to go to counselling this afternoon. I've got to see Jill Burrett. How should I impress her? Should I carry the *Women's Weekly* under my arm and come across as all knitting patterns and recipes? Or should I have the *National Times* and pretend that I'm a trendy nurturer?"

GOLDSTEIN

Look, don't go in there plucking threads out of your cardie; just go in there and tell this lady the truth. She's a nice sympathetic lady; just tell her the truth. Tell her how you feel about the children.

MODERATOR

Just tell her the truth? Diana Bryant, Adam comes to you and he's terrified. He says, "I've got to go and see Jill Burrett this afternoon. I mean, she'll be against me, won't she? She'll hold it against me that I never wiped the babies' bottoms or bathed them or did anything like that."

BRYANT

No, she won't. She won't hold it against you.

MODERATOR

"I've got to go in there with Eve. I really hate that bitch for what she's done to me, and for the business with Bruce. But if I let that show, then Burrett's going to put the thumbs down on me, isn't she?"

BRYANT

I would counsel you to be polite and to be natural but . . .

MODERATOR

"More in sorrow than anger?"

BRYANT

Yes.

MODERATOR

"So I should hide my real feelings about Eve?"

BRYANT

I would certainly counsel you not to be angry and to not be too aggressive.

MODERATOR

"Well, I'll go and take some acting lessons and see what I can do." Jill Burrett, you've got two nervous people, both advised by their lawyers on how to get round you. How do you get through their defences? What sort of things are they going to do to try to get round you?

BURRETT

They're going to tell me passionately how committed they are to the welfare of their children. With equal passion.

MODERATOR

Eve's little baby died a cot death a few weeks ago, so she's even more desperate to have those two children.

BURRETT

Right. I would explain to them that my task was to pass to the court information that it can't otherwise get about relationships in the family. In the final analysis, I'm looking at which parent is best able to meet the children's emotional needs.

MODERATOR

Adam comes back to you, Diana Bryant, and says, "Look, that counselling session went really badly. I think she's on Eve's side, and I'm going to get a bad report. The judge is going to follow her recommendation, and what worries me is that the court will never hear my kids say to me, 'Daddy, I love you. I want to stay with you always.' How can I get that sort of evidence before the court? Perhaps I could get Mr Lentin to wire me up for sound. I could tape-record my children when they say that sort of thing?"

BRYANT

Well, you could do that.

MODERATOR

(to Lentin) "Would you do that for me?"

LENTIN

Yes, I'd do that.

MODERATOR

Would you accept that evidence, Judge Fogarty—the tape-recording of little children?

FOGARTY

With the greatest of reluctance. In most cases it would reflect against the person who was doing that. I would say it demonstrates excessiveness and manipulativeness. If you're looking for a good custodian, you would tend to avoid those qualities if you could.

MODERATOR

The custody battle is coming up. I want the best counsel. How much is he going to cost?

GOLDSTEIN

Ah well, that's a great deal of money. About thirty thousand dollars all up.

MODERATOR

How much a day for a good Q.C.?

GOLDSTEIN

Three thousand dollars.

MODERATOR

Three thousand dollars a day, and a Q.C. needs a junior, so we'll have to get Peter Rose in.

GOLDSTEIN

Oh well, that's much more money.

MODERATOR

That's another two thousand; and you're a thousand a day, I guess?

GOLDSTEIN

Round about.

MODERATOR

So six thousand dollars a day. Do you really need a junior, Philip Twigg?

TWIGG

Two minds are better than one in most cases, but you're quite right, there are cases where you don't need assistance by way of junior. But you're emphasising the cost, and I agree with you that the adversary system we have, whilst it is the best system, is getting too expensive.

MODERATOR

Judge Pawley, do you find that barristers in your court make a great difference—that they affect the outcome?

PAWLEY

One likes to think they don't affect the outcome, but yes, they make a difference and in a sense of course, do affect the outcome. In the ordinary run of cases a competent junior is all that is required. Somebody competent who will present the facts, because there are some people who aren't.

MODERATOR

Are there many incompetent lawyers in your court?

PAWLEY

Yes, yes.

MODERATOR

What are their names? (laughter)

PAWLEY

I can't remember.

MODERATOR

But you must talk about them with your brother judges?

PAWLEY

I don't know that judges ever talk together these days.

MODERATOR

They certainly don't talk to magistrates. (laughter) Neil Brown, judges are suggesting a system of accreditation of counsel. The Family Court's good housekeeping seal of approval on certain lawyers.

BROWN

I would oppose that as Attorney-General. I would not take a single step towards implementing that system.

MODERATOR

But there are some lawyers who've never studied family law and yet they're practising in the Family Court.

BROWN

That's right, and most lawyers would have the commonsense to refer a client to an expert in family law if that were needed.

FOGARTY

Neil, they haven't got the commonsense to do so and that's why there are incompetent lawyers in this field. Litigants in this field need informed access to competent advice.

MODERATOR

So you'd be in favour of a list of approved lawyers?

FOGARTY

Yes.

MARSDEN

There are incompetent judges, too. Once they become judges, they join this little club. Now they've come from right wing society, they've all lived on the north shore, kids went to private school . . .

MODERATOR

Let's see what judicial prejudices have in store for the custody battle. A lot of water's flowed under the Harbour Bridge since Eve left Adam. She lived with her mother for a few months, but one day she hailed a taxi and fell in love with the driver. Wayne is a happy-go-lucky taxi driver. He's so laid back he's constantly in danger of falling over. (laughter) They settle down to a stable relationship in a rented house in West Balmain. David Lentin has been snooping under the verandah late at night, and every Saturday night after the kids are in bed, the distinctive aroma of an exotic but illegal substance wafts on the breeze.

LENTIN

I certainly will have to report that to the solicitor.

BRYANT

I'd discuss his report with my client.

MODERATOR

He says, "The kids will be brought up as potheads. Use it"

BRYANT

I think it's quite reasonable to use it. In the end it's a matter for the judge to decide whether or not it's pertinent.

MODERATOR

Is it pertinent, Judge Pawley?

PAWLEY

I think it could be relevant.

MODERATOR

Wayne has admitted to Jill Burrett that he hopes in a couple of years to be able to take the kids off to a commune at Nimbin. Is that relevant, Judge Fogarty?

FOGARTY

Any proposal for the future of the children would be important.

MODERATOR

And the fact that in a couple of years' time they're going to be taken to a commune is going to count against Wayne and Eve, isn't it?

FOGARTY

I wouldn't think that it was any advantage to the case, yes. (laughter)

MODERATOR

Let's be frank; they're going to lose custody. You've said in your judgements, time and time again, that you're not going to put kids in an unorthodox hippie lifestyle when there is the orthodox alternative.

FOGARTY

In a close-run affair, a trend towards a conservative response rather than a non-conservative response is extremely difficult to avoid.

MODERATOR

You were right, John Marsden.

MARSDEN

They've forgotten to take into account that Adam has whisky every night, with two beers and port, and everything else that goes with it.

MODERATOR

But Judge Fogarty, this is really stabbing in the dark. If you give custody of these kids to Eve and Wayne to bring up in a commune, you could be depriving us of Matthew Smith Q.C. If you give custody to Adam, you could be depriving us of Matt Smith, the world's greatest bass guitarist. It's a stab in the dark, isn't it?

FOGARTY

Of course it is. Any predictions about the future have all sorts of hazards. You have to throw your mind forward as to what is more likely to happen to those two families in the future. A most unenviable task, but it has to be done.

MODERATOR

It looks as though Wayne and Eve are going to lose custody. However, let's take a look at Adam. He was distraught at the break-up, but whereas most men seek solace in drink or other women, Adam seeks it in religion. He joins a strict religious sect — the Exclusive Church of Jehovah's Brethren. It teaches that only cult members will gain salvation — all outsiders are evil. Children of cult members can't eat with other children, can't be taken to the beach, can't watch television. Is that a relevant factor, Judge Pawley?

PAWLEY

Yes, I think is it. It doesn't give them the opportunity for ordinary social intercourse, which they should have.

MODERATOR

But is it altogether bad for children not to be allowed to watch television? Given the state of Australian television, that can only be good for them, can't it? (laughter)

PAWLEY

Oh, I think they should be allowed to see these terrible things.

MODERATOR

Make them believe that life is like *Perfect Match*, or that the Logie Awards are fair? (laughter)

PAWLEY

They ought to be allowed to see dreadful television so they know the horrors of the world.

MODERATOR

Do you agree, Judge Fogarty, that a strict, eccentric religious upbringing is not for the welfare of the children, and the partner who offers it will not get custody?

FOGARTY

That's the view of our society and I think I'd reflect that in my judgement.

MODERATOR

So it looks like Adam may lose. But you get a call from him, Vicki Brown, a week before the custody battle goes to court. He tells you that his mother was putting little Mary to bed last night, just after she'd got back from an access weekend with Wayne and Eve. The child cried and said to her grandmother, "I love Daddy. Daddy doesn't do things to my bottom and hurt me like Wayne does." He believes that his child is being sexually molested by his ex-wife's lover.

VICKI BROWN

Well presumably he wishes me to make an investigation.

MODERATOR

As urgently as possible. It's obviously happened this weekend.

VICKI BROWN

The first thing I would want to do is to have the child medically examined.

MODERATOR

You get a medical report. The doctor says, "Well, actually there is some old bruising on the vagina. It could have happened in a number of ways. The child could have been molested, but certainly not last weekend." Can you take it any further? Eve knows nothing. She's amazed at the allegation.

VICKI BROWN

I'd have to look for corroboration. It's very difficult without convincing evidence.

MODERATOR

It's very difficult, but the custody hearing is next week. Adam says, "I want it raised. I want my counsel, Mr Twigg, to destroy Wayne in cross-examination. I want him to get the confirmation that the police can't get."

TWIGG

We are short of evidence and I'm merely to go in blind with the bald allegation? That's not the way of the prosecutor. I don't want to ask such a blind question. It's not good enough just to cross-examine Wayne and suggest to him that he's guilty of this offence. I'd make a fool of myself and my client.

MODERATOR

Would you go in hard, John Marsden, if the client wanted you to?

MARSDEN

It's a difficult question because you're looking at the interests of the child. I suppose, unfortunately, that a lawyer is a hired gun and has a duty to his client as well as to the court and as well as to the child. If the client wanted me to I suppose I would go in hard and go for the big kill.

MODERATOR

You go in hard, you go for the big kill. Wayne is utterly convincing in denying your allegations and the medical evidence is shot to pieces. There could have been a dozen ways those old bruises occurred. Judge Fogarty, you have a feeling that the grandmother, in her desire that Adam should get custody, probably schooled the child—put the child up to making the allegations—and Adam probably knew about it. How is that going to affect your decision on the custody issue?

FOGARTY

These are very difficult areas. I regard it as a very worrying matter. These are the cases which are the most difficult in Australia to deal with. Here, Adam has put forward an allegation without proof, which is unlikely to be true, and he runs a risk of being seen as making a last desperate lunge to victory.

PAWLEY

They are terribly difficult cases. One has to bear in mind the paramount welfare of the child. If the child is being interfered with in that way, of course it's a terrible danger. But on the other hand there's the danger that if such a story is accepted too readily the child may be deprived of having the companionship of a very proper, loving parent.

MODERATOR

So the rule in your court is: don't make these serious allegations unless you can prove them.

PAWLEY

Unless you've got a pretty good basis.

MODERATOR

Is that good enough, Vicki Brown, with the growing problem of child abuse?

VICKI BROWN

It's very difficult to get sufficient evidence. The laws are such that with a child of that age corroboration is necessary, but I believe that children rarely lie when they make these allegations.

MODERATOR

Children rarely lie, Joe Goldstein?

GOLDSTEIN

No, I don't agree with that. But this is the one allegation that rings all the alarm bells. This is the one where I think lawyers stop playing adversary law. You say, wait a minute, there's something horrendous potentially happening here. You don't say "it has happened", you don't prejudge that, but if there's a suspicion, I think I'd be asking Eve a few questions, I'd be asking Wayne a few questions, and I'd be on the phone to Jill Burrett, saying, "What the hell should I ask? This is out of my field."

MODERATOR

Judge Fogarty reserves his judgement on the difficult case of Adam versus Eve.

MODERATOR

The next action is called on. It involves that larger-than-life public figure, Senator Bill Gladhand—president of the Society for the Preservation of Marriage. He's an outspoken conservative on moral issues; he described the Family Law Act as a "Casanova's Charter" when it was enacted in 1975. He's being divorced from his wife of fifteen years and six children, having left them to have an affair with a seventeen-year-old secretary in the Attorney-General's Department. (laughter) Patrick Tennison, you're the court correspondent for the *Antipodean*. Are you going to report this case?

TENNISON

I'd like to, but I can't name the senator or any of the parties. I can't say anything that will identify him.

MODERATOR

But Senator Gladhand's *marriage* was in all the newspapers. He's exploited it relentlessly in his political propaganda—big picture of his wife and six children—"Vote Gladhand for faith in the family". You can't even report the fact that Senator Gladhand has been divorced?

TENNISON

No.

MODERATOR

During the custody hearing there are some interesting things to come out. His wife gives evidence that he used to come home after late night sittings in the House and beat her up. Can you report that?

TENNISON

No.

MODERATOR

Under cross-examination from Philip Twigg, he admits to involvement in a bottom of the harbour tax scheme. Can you report that?

TENNISON

Not a word.

MODERATOR

So in Australia, the Prime Minister could be divorced in proceedings where he admits even to criminal conduct, and the press couldn't report it?

FOGARTY

This question of publicity is a very unsatisfactory one, because it's the court that gets the criticism. It's suggested that the court is enforcing secrecy, whereas the responsibility for this unsatisfactory situation belongs to parliament, which makes these laws.

MODERATOR

Mr Brown, I can understand why politicians want to be divorced in secret, but isn't this ridiculous?

BROWN

No, it's not ridiculous. You have to strike a balance, and it might be interesting to get these facts about Senator Gladhand published, it might satisfy some people's curiosity, but there's a greater public interest, I would have thought, in protecting the names of thousands of others who could be exposed to the sort of muck-raking that the *Truth* newspaper used to report in divorce cases.

MODERATOR

But what about justice? Surely justice has to be seen to be done?

BORWN

Of course it does, but the right course, if a crime is revealed, is to refer the papers to the Attorney-General.

MODERATOR

So you'd like to know. You'd be the only person who does know.

BROWN

Well, what side is he on? (laughter)

MODERATOR

We'll have to rely on Mr Tuckey to rake the muck. (laughter)

ARNDT

But what about justice for Mrs Gladhand and all the little Gladhands? That's the issue, in terms of privacy. However ridiculously this man has behaved, surely his family have a right for it not to be publicly displayed.

TENNISON

We can't have secret births, secret marriages or secret deaths—all these must be matters of public record. It's not that people will take a prurient interest, but people should be able to know whether, quite simply, a particular couple have been divorced.

MODERATOR

Judge Pawley, you've been pondering your decision on the custody battle, and your decision, after weighing all the pros and cons, is that custody of the children should go to Eve, with fortnightly access to Adam. Adam is too bitter, too religiously eccentric, and too willing to make fabricated allegations. That's your decision. There's only one problem—who gets the dog. Can you give custody of a dog?

PAWLEY

Yes, I once had a case about a cat named Smoochy—he was the only thing the couple were fighting about. Smoochy blew through just before the case. (laughter)

MODERATOR

Judas is sticking around. Jill Burrett reports that it's very valuable for the children's sense of continuity to keep the dog.

PAWLEY

I have no hesitation in giving custody of Judas to Eve.

MODERATOR

But Adam feeds it better, Adam throws sticks for it, while Wayne kicks it occasionally. What's the test—the welfare of the dog, or the welfare of the kids?

PAWLEY

The welfare of the kids.

MODERATOR

Judge Fogarty, suppose you have to deliver that judgement, taking the kids away from Adam. Will you deliver it in court with Adam a few feet away from you?

FOGARTY

Yes, that's the way it's done.

MODERATOR

Adam is going to hear you read out his imperfections, he'll feel that you're killing his children in front of his eyes.

FOGARTY

That's possible.

MODERATOR

How do you feel in the middle of a judgement when you hear the party who's just realised they're going to lose sobbing in the back of the court, and running screaming out into the corridor? Isn't that a pretty brutal way to break it, in the Family Court—the court that cares?

FOGARTY

It's a problem in any court.

MODERATOR

Why don't you send the judgement to Diana Bryant? Let her break it to Adam.

FOGARTY

Yes, that's a possible way of doing it, but I think the community expectation of justice is that the judge should come in and attempt to explain why the case has gone one way or the other. If you think you're going to satisfy them both and they are going to applaud you when you're finished, then of course you're mistaken, but that is your duty and your life.

GOLDSTEIN

I think this is the area where the Family Court is probably more difficult for judges than any other court, because the informality of the court makes it very hard to hand down a judgement. In the old days the courts were a conventional kind—barristers in robes, judges in robes, benches were up high, courts were fairly big places, there were no coloured chairs. When the judgement was given, it was given by the system—all judges looked alike, nobody could recognise them. These days the angry husband, Adam, is sitting in a small court, close to the judge, who's wearing a suit much the same as his, and he's an identifiable person. I think that that's one of the things I like the least about the Family Court.

MODERATOR

Diana Bryant, Adam is stunned. He breaks down sobbing. You get him back to your office, but he's still slightly hysterical. He grabs a Bible from his pocket, holds it up and says, "I'll kill that judge, I swear it, I'll get even." What do you do about that threat?

BRYANT

I make some personal assessment of whether he's serious or not.

MODERATOR

The Jehovah's Brethren don't take oaths lightly. You've noticed a glint of fanaticism in his eyes.

BRYANT

Nevertheless, that's still a very emotional area, and a lot of clients make those threats. If I am really concerned, then I would notify the judge or the court.

MODERATOR

Would you do that, John Marsden?

MARSDEN

I don't think I would, because at that stage the emotion would be taking hold of the individual.

MODERATOR

Even in these days, when you can buy the ingredients of a car bomb from Woolworths?

MARSDEN

No, I wouldn't notify the authorities.

MODERATOR

Three days later you read in the paper that a bomb has been found under Judge Fogarty's car . . .

MARSDEN

That's bloody hard, isn't it. (laughter) I think that I would really, at that stage, have to look at my duty to the court, and I would probably ring the Family Law Court and seek to have a discussion in chambers with the judge. Ask his advice as to whether he wanted me to speak to the police.

MODERATOR

You'd dob your client in.

MARSDEN

No, I would be putting the court on notice. If the judge hands down judgements as he seems to be handing down today, there would probably be a lot of other solicitors also ringing up saying that their client had threatened the judge.

MODERATOR

So the switchboard is jammed with solicitors dobbing their clients in. (laughter)

MARSDEN

You've got to work out the situation at the time. I don't think there's any Family Law Court matter that I've dealt with when the losing party hasn't made some sort of threat, either to the solicitor on the other side, or the judge.

MODERATOR

While Marsden is agonising, Joe Goldstein, you're having a wonderful time. Eve and Wayne are over the moon at getting custody. They've taken you to a champagne lunch to thank you for winning their case. Eve goes off early to collect the kids, and Wayne says to you over coffee, "Joe, I need your advice. We're going to have Mary around the house a lot now. I play with her sometimes when Eve's out, and she's a real little flirt. She pulls her dress up and stuff like that—you know. And, well, I know I denied it in court and all that, but sometimes I just can't help myself. I get this terrible urge to touch her. Do you know a doctor, a shrink perhaps, who might help me?"

GOLDSTEIN

I agonise with that information, but I think I'd probably break a lot of rules and finish up shelfing Wayne.

MODERATOR

But Wayne has just confessed to you that he has committed a perjury. As a result of that perjury, the judge awarded custody to Eve. Eve is your client, her child will probably continue to be sexually abused. You're a solicitor, and he's given you this information in confidence.

GOLDSTEIN

Well I think I may be about to break the confidence this time.

MODERATOR

Who do you ring? Do you ring the police and say, "Arrest Wayne"? Do you ring the judge and say, "Reconsider your judgement"?

GOLDSTEIN

I think I'd probably ring the Law Society and say look, you'd better come and get me because I'm going to do something awful. (laughter)

MODERATOR

Marsden is acting president of the Law Society.

GOLDSTEIN

John, I've just won a great custody case and it turns out that contrary to the evidence that came out in court, contrary to the boyfriend's adamant protestations, he has been doing something frightful to this five-year-old girl, and I'm going to ring the coppers. What should I do, what do you think?

MARSDEN

Joe, please, if you breach a confidence, there'll be another complaint on your complaint file and it's really getting very big. (laughter) You should think about this. You do have an obligation to keep that confidence. There is a special legal privilege, and I think that you should probably discuss it with your partners and sit on it for a day or so, and then make your decision. There's got to be other ways of handling this matter. Maybe the mother didn't know. The mother was your client, and maybe by telling the mother you may be able to overcome the problem.

MODERATOR

Is that what you'd do, Ian Kennedy?

KENNEDY

Yes, I'd tell Eve.

MODERATOR

You tell Eve. She says "Yes, I know. I've been begging him to get some help."

KENNEDY

My overriding duty is to the child. If that child is at risk, I ought to tell the police.

MODERATOR

But if lawyers dob their clients in, people aren't going to come to lawyers for advice. Or they are not going to be honest with their lawyers when seeking that advice.

KENNEDY

It's a risk that I'm fully prepared to take in these particular circumstances. There has to be a balance of duty—it's an impossible dilemma to resolve. It has to be resolved in favour of the welfare of the child.

MODERATOR

Neil Brown, as Attorney-General, head of the legal profession, shouldn't these questions be resolved on the principle that anyone, a murderer or a child molester, should be able to come to a lawyer and obtain advice in confidence?

BROWN

That's a sound principle. But I think there's a higher principle and a higher duty. I think the matter should be reported to the police, no question about it. There's a crime being committed, there's an innocent victim, and there's an obligation towards that innocent victim. I think it's the solicitor's responsibility to report it to the police.

MODERATOR

So all you people out there who thought that your lawyers never broke a confidence, who thought that what you said to your lawyers within the four walls of his office would never go any further, you were wrong.

BROWN

That, frankly, is so hypothetical I don't think it need be a practical consideration. Life will go on. Confidences will continue to be shared with doctors and lawyers. Those confidences will, in virtually all cases, not be broken, but if such a case as this arises, I think there is a higher duty.

MODERATOR

John Marsden, they're all going to go to the police. Are they right?

MARSDEN

I still think they've got a primary obligation to their client. One matter they haven't considered—if they do report it to the police and the child has to go through the trauma of a court case, is that in the best interest of the child?

MODERATOR

The child could be happier being abused?

MARSDEN

No, wait a minute. Is it in the best interest of the child to go through that trauma? Is it not handled in a much more efficient way by medical advice? Now, if it comes to the ultimate, where Wayne refused to do anything about it, where Wayne continues this type of activity and you know it, then the individual judgement would have to lie with the individual solicitor handling the matter. I think the Law Society would respect that individual judgement.

MODERATOR

It would respect the lawyer who dobbed his client in for child molesting. It doesn't respect lawyers who dob their clients in for other crimes. Child molesting is so uniquely heinous that it justifies breaking all understanding about lawyers' confidences?

MARSDEN

I don't know what the Law Society would do. There're twenty people on the Law Society . . .

MODERATOR

Twenty different opinions?

MARSDEN

Yes, twenty different opinions. Most of them rather conservative, like judges, so I don't really know what they'd do.

MODERATOR

In fact, Wayne solves the problem himself by clearing off to Nimbin, leaving Eve in the rented house at West Balmain with two children and a hungry dog. The house costs eighty dollars to rent. Adam earns three hundred dollars a week. What sort of maintenance, Ian Kennedy, will Adam be obliged to pay?

KENNEDY

What the court will have to do is to try to work out what is reasonably needed to maintain children in the proper lifestyle, and what money Adam has to assist the family.

MODERATOR

So you can't predict?

KENNEDY

It's unpredictable. It's a difficult equation, but the range may be anywhere between twenty-five dollars for each of the children a week, up to fifty dollars, depending on his take-home income.

MODERATOR

Adam says, "What's the law on maintenance? How much does the *law* say I have to pay?"

KENNEDY

The law doesn't talk in dollar terms; what it says is that both parents have a duty to help maintain the children, according to their respective means and ability. Your means are much greater than Eve's; therefore you are required to contribute more.

MODERATOR

You are Adam's constituency MP, Neil Brown. He writes to you complaining, "I can't get a sensible answer out of my lawyer."

BROWN

There should be some clearer guidelines laid down. The whole thing seems to be like so many aspects of this field, at large, and we should at least make an attempt to lay down some guidelines, so that people know where they stand.

MODERATOR

Would it be better to have the system in some American states, where you know that you're going to have to pay seventeen per cent of your gross salary for one child; twenty-five per cent for two; twenty-nine per cent for three—that sort of thing?

BROWN

There may be something to be said for that. I think the very least we should do is try to lay down some guidelines.

MODERATOR

Judge Fogarty, you order Adam to pay thirty dollars a week for each child, plus fifty dollars towards the rent. He pays for a few months, then he says, "I've been talking to some of my mates. They've told me of all these great maintenance lurks. They say, 'Don't pay till the summons arrives, then go and tell the judge you can't afford it.' They all say nothing will happen to you if you don't pay maintenance." Is that good legal advice from his mates?

FOGARTY

The advice he got from his friends is very right, because less than forty per cent of maintenance orders are complied with.

MODERATOR

So Australia is becoming a nation of maintenance defaulters. Sixty per cent of men who are ordered to pay maintenance fall behind in the first three years, and forty per cent of them don't pay a penny. Why don't you gaol them? Why don't you send out a message on the bush telegraph to all the pubs and clubs where divorced men gather, telling them, "The Family Court is toughening up. We're gaoling maintenance defaulters."

FOGARTY

I think that other things that could be done short of gaoling them would get better results. We should look very seriously at some form of collection agency.

MODERATOR

Like the New Zealand system, where maintenance is automatically deducted from men's wages, like tax, collected by a central organisation which sends it on to the wife?

BROWN

I am opposed generally to setting up more bureaucracies, but frankly this particular area is becoming such a scandal, and members of parliament are flooded with constituents who have problems of this sort. It's getting to scandalous proportions. The advice from his mates was undoubtedly correct factual advice. There are a number of things that can be done, one of which is to set up a government agency to collect the maintenance; secondly, to give the court the power to imprison in appropriate cases; and I think, thirdly, to give those who are responsible for collecting it now a bit of a rev, because there's a bit of slackness in enforcing the order as it is.

MODERATOR

It's eleven o'clock on Sunday evening, and Eve is a worried woman. It's Adam's access weekend and he should have had the kids back by six. He's never been this late before. She just knows, with a mother's instinct, that something is wrong. She wants to call Joe Goldstein, but he's ex-directory, so she calls you, Philip Twigg.

TWIGG

I'd call Judge Pawley.

MODERATOR

It's eleven-thirty on Sunday night. He's asleep.

TWIGG

I'll get him out of bed . . . Judge, I've got a very urgent

situation. I'm sorry to disturb you, but these are the facts, and I ask you for an order directed against this man with warrant attached to give us power immediately to go into his house and investigate if the children are there and take possession of them.

PAWLEY

Is there any suggestion that the children are being hurt or physically attacked in any way?

TWIGG

My client instructs me that the husband has said that if he ever gets the chance, he'll take them overseas. And also, he has, we have found out since the case, some history of violence.

PAWLEY

And is this the first time that he's been this late with the children?

TWIGG

It's the first time he's been this late, but he has been late before.

PAWLEY

Has your client attempted to get in touch with him by telephone?

TWIGG

We've attempted to telephone, with no success.

PAWLEY

Yes, very well. I'll make an order that he hand the children over.

MODERATOR

You can make an order over the telephone?

PAWLEY

Yes you can. To all police officers.

MODERATOR

The police have no luck, so Eve hires you, David Lentin.

LENTIN

The first thing I would ask is that the Family Law Court allow publicity. The moment we have an order for publicity we would launch a massive publicity campaign.

MODERATOR

You've got a story about missing children, a tearful mother, a

pining dog—it's a must for *Willesee*. (laughter)
Would you give a publicity order, Judge Pawley?

PAWLEY

Well, I don't think immediately. One would have to allow
some time. There would be an order out preventing aircraft and
ships from carrying the children. I'd order publicity if they
weren't found within a few days.

MODERATOR

Despite all the publicity, there's still no sign of Adam and the
children. Not a word from them for six months. Then, Diana
Bryant, you get a telephone call. "Hi, it's Adam Smith. We're
up in crocodile country in northern Queensland. We're having a
wonderful time although we do miss the dog. Listen—you've
still got my power of attorney, and there are ten BHP shares
left in my portfolio after paying your fees. There's this fellow in
Perth who wants to buy them—he's tracked me down where
no-one else can. (laughter) I want you to arrange the transfer.
Will you do that for me?"

BRYANT

Yes. But I would also tell him that I had an obligation to
inform . . .

MODERATOR

"I don't want you to tell anyone that this conversation has
occurred."

BRYANT

But I have an overriding obligation to the court because of the
welfare of the children.

MODERATOR

"Ah. So you're going to rat on me again?" (laughter)

BRYANT

Yes. Because the welfare of the children is the most important thing.

MODERATOR

"But they're having a wonderful time."

BRYANT

No, the High Court says that lawyers have to inform when
children are involved.

MODERATOR

So, if he's on the run with his kids, he can't get any legal assistance? That's the brute truth.

MARSDEN

He's safe with me.

MODERATOR

Ah. Safe with Marsden. (laughter)

MARSDEN

No worries, no worries. I haven't read the High Court decision, and it's wrong anyway. I'll sell his shares.

MODERATOR

Six months have passed, Ian Kennedy. Eve is pestering you every week. Isn't it about time you gave Marsden a call, see if he's heard from his client?

KENNEDY

John, have you heard from your client recently?

MARSDEN

Oh no mate, and he even owes me money, you know. (laughter)

MODERATOR

Who should burst into our office the next day, but Eve. She says, "Mr Marsden, you're a father, you must know how I feel. I'm in pieces over this, can't you just tell me: are my kids safe, are they all right?"

MARSDEN

I'd tell her that she had to go back to her own solicitor and that I couldn't help her.

MODERATOR

You are actually going to keep from a grieving mother, who doesn't know whether her children are alive or dead, that her children are in fact happy and well?

MARSDEN

No, she can go and see Joe and I'd probably call Joe and say look, we've been mates for a long time, and I think you can tell your client the kids are okay, but I don't know where he is, and I don't know much about him, but between you and I you can tell her that the kids are okay.

MODERATOR

But he said, "Keep this call absolutely confidential."

MARSDEN

Well . . . that's *pretty* confidential. (laughter)

MODERATOR

Everything comes out in the wash, because it's obvious from what he's told you—without breaking his client's confidence, but just wearing it a little thin at the edges—that he's in touch with his client.

GOLDSTEIN

I'd probably bring an application to the court for the return of the children. I'd subpoena John and stick him in the witness box and say, "Now tell us, Anzac, where are the kids?" (laughter)

MODERATOR

Philip Twigg, you're acting for Eve, you've got Marsden in the witness box. You, John Marsden, have not only had the telephone call, but Adam has left you a contact number, the telephone number of a friend of his up in Port Douglas.

TWIGG

Mr Marsden, have you spoken to your client in the last twelve months?

MARSDEN

I refuse to answer that.

TWIGG

Why?

MARSDEN

On the grounds of legal professional privilege.

PAWLEY

I'm sorry, Mr Marsden, but you must answer the question.

MARSDEN

I refuse.

TWIGG

I've got an application to make, Your Honour.

PAWLEY

Yes, yes, what's your application?

TWIGG
> I would ask that Mr Marsden be committed for contempt, in the
> face of the court, and I would ask to present particulars of that
> straightaway to you so that it can be dealt with by you now.

PAWLEY
> Yes, and I would deal with Mr Marsden for contempt.

MODERATOR
> How would you deal with him for contempt?

PAWLEY
> Oh well, I'd have to hear him on that.

MODERATOR
> Ah, your opportunity to be your own counsel.

MARSDEN
> No, I'd select a solicitor. I'd select Ian Kennedy.

KENNEDY
> What's your story, mate?

MARSDEN
> Oh well, the story, mate, is that I'm not prepared to divulge
> that confidence and I'm quite prepared to go to gaol. I think,
> you know, quite frankly, that it would be good for my practice,
> the publicity of a solicitor going to gaol to protect his client.

MODERATOR
> Depends on how long you go to gaol for.

MARSDEN
> Oh yes. I forgot about that. (laughter)

MODERATOR
> What do you do, Judge? How long does Marsden get?

PAWLEY
> If he continues to refuse to answer, I wouldn't hesitate to give
> him, say, three months.

TWIGG
> I have an application to make, Your Honour.

PAWLEY
> Yes, Mr Twigg . . .

TWIGG

And it's not just for costs . . . (laughter) In respect of Mr Marsden's file, I would ask you to make an order directing all constables to have the authority to enter Mr Marsden's premises, and take the file that he has in relation to this matter.

PAWLEY

Have I got the power to do that, Mr Twigg?

TWIGG

Yes, Your Honour has. Your Honour has power under Section 114 to make an order with the suitable attachment for a warrant.

PAWLEY

Yes, I make that order.

MODERATOR

So Vicki Brown can go and raid John Marsden's office?

PAWLEY

Yes.

MODERATOR

You're going to lose a lot by your defiance of the court, John Marsden.

MARSDEN

I'm prepared to take that in the interests of the confidentiality of my client, and they won't find anything in the file. No way.

MODERATOR

You will have removed that before you go to the court?

MARSDEN

No, I wouldn't have put it in the file in the first place, anyway. (laughter)

MODERATOR

Where *do* you put your confidential documents?

MARSDEN

Oh . . .

TWIGG

He refuses to answer on the grounds that it may incriminate him. (laughter)

MODERATOR

Time passes, ladies and gentlemen, as time is wont to do.
Halley's Comet comes and goes, so does the Royal marriage, the
Bicentennial, Mr John Howard, the Royal divorce. (laughter) Six
years have passed since Adam stole his children—long and bitter
years for Eve. David Lentin, you're reading the newspaper one
morning, and in the "Deaths" section you notice "Mavis Smith,
dearly beloved mother of Adam, grandmother of Matthew and
Mary. Funeral tomorrow." Think you might pop along?

LENTIN

Yes, I would attend.

MODERATOR

Six years is a long time, Adam's probably changed beyond
recognition; you only have some old photographs and he'd be
disguised anyway. Eve says, "Take Judas, he'll remember."
(laughter) So off you go to the Gethsemane Garden of Rest with
Judas the dog. Sure enough, Judas barks with joy and runs
toward the man with the suntan and the heavy beard, licks him
all over the face. It's obviously Adam. Do you arrest him?

LENTIN

I can't arrest him. I have not got the power to arrest him.

MODERATOR

Vicki Brown is directing funeral procession traffic around the
corner.

LENTIN

Vicki, I've sighted our wanted fellow, would you come around
and help us arrest him?

VICKI BROWN

Right. Whereabouts is the warrant being held?

LENTIN

That's the problem. (laughter) We can never find these warrants
when we want them.

MODERATOR

Where is the warrant?

LENTIN

The federal police have it in Queensland.

MODERATOR

So the funeral will be well and truly over by the time you get it down. Don't you have the power of citizen's arrest?

LENTIN

No. Every time that this has occurred, we've had to wait for the federal police to come.

MODERATOR

Well, this time you're lucky. There's an airline strike and Adam has the misfortune of travelling Ansett and you capture him in the terminal lounge. Vicki Brown escorts him to gaol. You go and see him in the cells, Diana Bryant, and you make a few inquiries about him. Six years have changed Adam Smith beyond recognition. He's now a happy-go-lucky taxi driver; loves his kids. Matthew and Mary are getting on really well at school in Port Douglas. Matthew's fourteen, Mary's ten. All the neighbours and the school headmistress say that Adam's a really terrific parent.

BRYANT

Well, I'd advise him that he should come clean about the whereabouts of the children, and he should make an application to the court for custody.

MODERATOR

Make an application for custody? But he stole them six years ago!

BRYANT

But the court has to look at what's in the best interests of the children, and it may well be, despite what he did then, that it is in their best interest to be with him now.

MODERATOR

And if it *is* in their best interest, Judge Fogarty, the child stealer retains the children?

FOGARTY

If you ultimately came to that conclusion, yes.

MODERATOR

Consider what's happened to Eve. She became slightly unhinged when she thought her children had gone for good. She drifted into hard drugs, and into part-time prostitution to pay for the hard drugs. She has a squalid flat at Kings Cross, but she still wants custody of the children. No doubt, is there, where their best interest lies?

FOGARTY
If that's the case, well then it answers itself, doesn't it.

MODERATOR
What's the answer?

FOGARTY
The answer is that the children go where their best interests lie.

MODERATOR
The children go to Adam, the man who stole them?

FOGARTY
In that case, yes.

MODERATOR
Judge Pawley?

PAWLEY
Yes.

MODERATOR
The children go to the man who abducted them.

PAWLEY
Yes, but that's taken into account, and if it's still in their best interest that they be with him, they're with him.

MODERATOR
So that if a man steals his children, drives his ex-wife mad with grief, and then stays with the kids long enough to bond with them, he can keep them.

PAWLEY
If it's in their best interests . . .

MODERATOR
If it's in their best interests . . . What about the best interests of justice, Neil Brown? Justice for the community, on a man who broke the law. Justice for Eve, who was driven mad with grief.

BROWN
There obviously must be justice for the community, but the

question is what is in the best interest of the children at the time the question comes up for resolution.

MODERATOR

It's being resolved now in Adam's favour because he broke the law and took the children, and because he drove Eve to desperation and drugs.

BROWN

The court is not a morals court, or a moral censor.

MODERATOR

And in this case, Judge Fogarty, the court is going to reward the guilty person and punish the innocent.

FOGARTY

No, it would conclude that the children would not be best served living with a heroin addict.

MODERATOR

But she is only a heroin addict because of what Adam did to her six years ago.

FOGARTY

Yes.

MODERATOR

Jill Burrett, have you decided that in this situation the welfare of the children undoubtedly lies in keeping them with Adam?

BURRETT

Yes.

MODERATOR

Yes, Patrick Tennison? The innocent punished, the guilty rewarded?

TENNISON

Yes, you could say that.

MODERATOR

Adam is overjoyed. He takes the next flight to Port Douglas, singing the praises of the Family Court. He's the happiest father in the land. One day, as the Smith family is passing the local chemist, Matthew says, "Hey Dad, let's go and have our genetic fingerprints taken. All the other kids are having theirs done."

Laughing confidently, the indulgent parent takes them for the test. Alas, his genes match neither child. As Eve says, smiling slyly as she remembers the days she spent as a volunteer in Senator Gladhand's electoral office, "It's a wise father that doesn't seek to know his own child."